THE
LATE-MING
POET
CH'EN
TZU-LUNG

KANG-I SUN CHANG

The Late-Ming Poet Ch'en Tzu-lung

CRISES OF LOVE AND LOYALISM

Yale University Press
New Haven & London

Grateful acknowledgment is made to the following for permission to reprint copyrighted material: Columbia University Press for two lines of poetry from *The Columbia Book of Later Chinese Poetry*, trans. Jonathan Chaves, copyright © 1986 by Columbia University Press. Used by permission. Columbia University Press for five lines of poetry from *Chinese Rhyme-Prose*, trans. Burton Watson, copyright © 1971 by Columbia University Press. Used by permission. Hua-tung Normal University Press, Shanghai, for a figure from *Ch'en Tzu-lung wen-chi*, 1988. *Ku-chi ch'u-pan-she*, Shanghai, for two figures from Ch'en Yin-k'o, *Liu Ju-shih pieh-chuan*, 1980. Dr. Howard S. Levy, English Department, Odawara Women's Junior College, Odawara, Japan, for an excerpt from his *A Feast of Mist and Flowers* (Yokohama: Privately printed, 1966). Ōtsuka Kogeisha, Tokyo, for a figure from *Sō Gen Min Shin meiga taikan*, ed. Nikka Kokon Kaiga Tenrankai (1931). Penguin Books for eight lines of poetry from *Poems of the Late T'ang*, trans. A. C. Graham (Penguin Classics, 1965), copyright © A. C. Graham, 1965. Princeton University Press for eight lines of poetry from *Major Lyricists of the Northern Sung: A.D. 960–1126*, by James J. Y. Liu, copyright © 1974 by Princeton University Press.

Designed by Nancy Ovedovitz. Set in Sabon type by Tseng Information Systems, Durham, North Carolina. Printed in the United States of America by Book Crafters, Inc., Chelsea, Michigan.

Library of Congress Cataloging-in-Publication Data

Chang, Kang-i Sun, 1944-
The late-Ming poet Ch'en Tzu-lung : crises of love and loyalism / Kang-i Sun Chang.
    p.   cm.
Includes bibliographical references (p.   ) and index.
ISBN 0-300-04872-6
1. Ch'en, Tzu-lung, 1608–1647—Criticism and interpretation.
I. Title.
PL2698.C4556Z6   1990
895.1′146–dc20   90-12485
                                                                                              CIP

10   9   8   7   6   5   4   3   2   1

In fond memory of

Tao-cheng Jacob Chang (1948–1986)

and the artistic spirit

he stood for

CONTENTS

ILLUSTRATIONS

PREFACE

The subject of this book, the meaning of love and loyalism in the poetry of Ch'en Tzu-lung (1608–47), has occupied me for a long time. My original starting point was a general study of seventeenth-century Chinese poetry. But as I studied various methods of interpreting the poetic and cultural trends of that period, I found my interest becoming more and more focused on Ch'en Tzu-lung. Ch'en lived through troubled times and reacted to them intensely. His writing gives imaginative expression to his day-to-day experience while forming a significant part of seventeenth-century Chinese culture. Moreover, he is regarded by many as one of the best poets of his time.

Ch'en Tzu-lung is generally remembered as a Ming loyalist who died for his sovereign. This has no doubt helped secure Ch'en's position in history, but it has also led scholars to see him exclusively as a patriotic poet. I contend that Ch'en's contribution to literature has never been fairly judged as a whole—or as *literature*. One crucial concern in his poetry, largely neglected by scholars and readers, is the subject of romantic love, more specifically his intense involvement with the poet and courtesan Liu Shih. Perhaps in an attempt to protect Ch'en's reputation as a Confucian hero, traditional biographers have often withheld the truth about the romance. (One such distortion can be found in *Mu-chai i-shih*, as cited in *LJS*, 1:88–89.) Not until very recently, with the appearance of Ch'en Yin-ko's biography of Liu Shih, were we able to gain insight into Ch'en Tzu-lung's emotional experience.

The belief that emotional purity sustains and redeems the full meaning of life was at the center of the concept of romantic love in the late Ming. Such love was distinguished by being of such constancy that it was considered an inner loyalty. For the concept of *chung* (loyalty), an ancient virtue governing an official relationship, was here being given a new content. To a large extent, the late-Ming woman was viewed by Ch'en and his circle as a mediator between love and loyalism. An ideal woman was the principal inspiration for those who felt the power both of romantic passion and of patriotism. And such a role was appropriate to the ambience of the late Ming, when images of courageous and talented women were most treasured. This goes a long way toward explaining why the late-Ming intellectuals found little conflict between love for a woman and love for the nation. In an age much given to these two concerns, it is natural that literature from Ming to Ch'ing exhibits a particular blend of attributes concerning love and loyalism. In particular, the dynastic transition and its accompanying upheavals brought many of these ideals and attitudes to a state of crisis.

Ch'en Tzu-lung's poetry has much to tell us about these topics. First, his love relationship with Liu Shih engendered a whole new interest in love poetry, responsible for the revival of the *tz'u* (song lyric) genre in the late Ming. Second, the later poetry of Ch'en Tzu-lung, especially his *shih* poetry on patriotism, reveals the Chinese conception of the tragic vision— that man must accept his imperfect destiny with heroic equanimity. In both love and loyalism, the poet faced some painfully dialectical "last alternative." Third, it is interesting to see how the feeling of love expressed in Ch'en's early *tz'u*, far from impeding, gave rise to the powerful expression of patriotism in his later songs. In particular, I have tried to identify some of the ways in which the *tz'u* songs of loyalism unify themselves around Ch'en Tzu-lung's metaphorical and symbolic tendencies, how the poetics of his early love songs is adapted for his later songs of loyalism, and how patriotism in the end is most effectively expressed through the semblance of romantic love in the *tz'u* genre. I have also explained the manner in which Ch'en Tzu-lung the *tz'u* poet consistently sees his lover Liu Shih as a symbol of the passing dynasty and how he reinforces the rhetoric of loyalism by elaborating, dwelling on the symbolic power of human passion.

While exploring the various meanings of love in Ch'en Tzu-lung's poetry, I have inevitably become concerned with late-Ming images of women—especially their function in contemporary society, art, and literature. As my table of contents indicates, I felt I had to familiarize the reader with Liu Shih's life and art, if only to explain Ch'en Tzu-lung's poetry more fully. In many ways, Liu Shih seems to provide a paradigm of concerns and abilities for the numerous courtesan-artists of her time.

In the process of researching my book, I paid close attention to Liu Shih's poetry and was especially taken by the many *tz'u* poems she wrote for Ch'en Tzu-lung. For her, as well as for Ch'en, poetry became an active part of an endless search to communicate life's meaning and experiences. Most important, her poetry poses the problem of gender roles in a wholly new way. Thus, whenever relevant, I have included observations on Liu Shih's life and poetry, focusing on her relationship with Ch'en Tzu-lung and her qualities of astonishing erudition and creative imagination.

At the center of my book lies one other persistent concern, the problem of genres. During a period when the literati exhibited enormous concern for past literary models, generic discrimination seemed to have become the poets' most powerful strategy for creating their individual voices. Generic solutions, then, not only represent the poet's responses to conventional requirements, but they also reflect the poet's private aesthetic values. One of the purposes of this book is to demonstrate how both of two genres of writing (*tz'u* and *shih*) in Ch'en have a dual focus on personal love and loyalist emotion, and how the poet used these two genres to express *different* aspects of love and loyalism. In particular, I have been interested to see how certain differences of meaning accompany the shift of genre— whereas Ch'en's *tz'u* poetry tends to dwell on mourning for loss, his *shih* poetry is often characterized by a transcendence of loss. I believe that such a generic study is vital to an understanding of Ch'en's literary contribution, and it also has broader implications concerning the nature of Chinese poetry.

To date, no studies of Ch'en Tzu-lung's poetry have been made in English, and few in Chinese. Poetry of the Ming and Ch'ing has been generally ignored by modern scholarship partly owing to an inappropriate notion of generic evolution prevailing among Chinese scholars—namely, that the T'ang dynasty (618–907) was the golden age of *shih*, the Sung dynasty (960–1279) of *tz'u*, the Yüan (1234–1368) of *ch'ü* and drama, and the Ming (1368–1644) and Ch'ing (1644–1911) of vernacular fiction. Such a view seriously distorts the real nature of generic development in traditional China. For, in fact, genres such as *shih* and *tz'u*, once created, rarely became obsolete; they continued to be used and to develop. Thus, one of the objectives of this book is to fill this serious gap in the study of Chinese poetry. Moreover, there was a renaissance of classical poetry in seventeenth-century China that lasted until the beginning of this century. Especially in the area of *tz'u* poetry, I shall argue, the renaissance was due largely to the efforts of Ch'en Tzu-lung, who organized the Yün-chien School of *Tz'u* to redeem Ming *tz'u* from its decadence—decadence, as

Ch'en saw it, by comparison with the golden age of *tz'u* in the Southern T'ang (937–75).

The transition from Ming to Ch'ing continues to be thought of in Chinese minds as the end of a certain kind of world (comparable to 1914 in the memories of many elderly people in the West). It was a drama of which K'ung Shang-jen's play *The Peach Blossom Fan* (translated by Shih-hsiang Chen et al.) is one act, and Ch'en Tzu-lung's career another. As Jonathan Spence and John Wills put it, "The rebellions and the Ch'ing conquest gave new and tragic scope to the ideal of the exemplar of moral purity, pursued with such intensity in the late Ming. In certain dramatically conspicuous areas of China, much of the flower of a generation sacrificed itself in futile resistance, often when there was a chance of withdrawing to fight another day, or refused to serve the rebels or the Ch'ing and went defiantly to execution."[1] This book attempts to show what was at stake for one talented late-Ming poet in such sacrifice.

Exceptional yet representative—this is the light I try to show Ch'en Tzu-lung in. It is for the reader to decide whether Ch'en succeeded in his poetic enterprises—the interweaving of the disparate themes of love and loyalism and the creative adaptation of inherited styles and genres to express this new content—and whether the poetic renewal he called for actually came to pass.

I hope the reader will enjoy the large selection of translations of the poetry of both Ch'en Tzu-lung and Liu Shih. All translations of poems and prose passages are mine, unless otherwise noted.

ACKNOWLEDGMENTS

I take great pleasure in acknowledging the many people who have offered me help. I am deeply grateful to Yu-kung Kao, who generously shared his ideas with me and gave much shrewd advice about the revision of my manuscript; to Edwin McClellan, who showed enthusiasm for my project from its early stages, lightened my discouragement, and kept me from delaying the completion of the book; to Haun Saussy, who carefully went over all the chapters in their various versions and never failed to catch me up when my critical thinking and writing were fuzzy; to Shih Chih-ts'un (Shi Zhi Cun) of Shanghai, who provided me with important Chinese materials and information otherwise unavailable to me; to Jonathan Spence, who inspired me with his views about the crucial connection between literature and history and kindly read this book before publication; and to Yü Ying-shih, who repeatedly enlightened me with his vast knowledge and literary resources. I also wish to express my appreciation to F. W. Mote and Andrew Plaks, who first taught me Ming–Ch'ing history and literature and have continued to give me guidance and advice. Ch'ung-ho Chang and Hans Frankel have for many years become my "teachers" in Chinese poetry, and my debt to them is too many-faceted to sum up in a few words. I am also grateful to my colleague Edward Kamens, who offered valuable comments on a draft of my manuscript, and to others who have read and commented on portions of the book: Marston Anderson, William Atwell, Jonathan Chaves, and Yeh Chia-ying. Many of my students (their names too numerous to mention) helped by procuring rare materials or checking parts of my work— among them Mary Kivlen, Charles Kwong, Hui-shu Lee, Nanxiu Qian, Ruth Rogaski, and Stephen Shutt. I am especially indebted to Ay-ling

Wang, my research assistant, for providing valuable assistance during the final preparation of the manuscript.

The conception of my book owes a great deal to those persons who listened to my lectures at the Annual Convention of the Association for Asian Studies and at Rutgers University. I thank Ronald Egan, Ching-i Tu, and Chun-fang Yu for inviting me to lecture and those people whose questions and suggestions made me rethink my argument. I also want to express my gratitude to Pauline Yu and Stephen Owen for organizing a *tz'u* conference and for asking me to write a paper that helped sharpen my main theories for this book. In addition, my thanks to Alex Preminger, T. V. F. Brogan, and Earl Miner for inviting me to become involved in the *Princeton Encyclopedia of Poetry and Poetics* (3d edition) project; writing the article "Classical Chinese Poetry" helped me gain a broader perspective on Ming and Ch'ing poetics.

Much of the exhilaration of researching this book has come from the assistance of scholars in China who were involved in the recent renovation of Ch'en Tzu-lung's tomb in Sung-Chiang, China. First, Hsü Shuo-fang of Hangchow University informed me of the tomb renovation project. Then, Ku T'ing-lung of the Shanghai Library, head of the project, gave me valuable rubbings of the tomb tablets with inscriptions ingeniously done by him. My friend Diane Perushek deserves special credit for organizing on my behalf a "tomb exploration crew" and expedition to Sung-Chiang during her trip to China in May 1989. The car and driver were generously provided by Ku T'ing-lung. Accompanying the crew were Wang Shou-ming of Hua-tung Normal University, who copied the entire inscription of the Ch'ien-lung stele at the tomb; and Richard Bodman, who took numerous photographs for me there. I was also fortunate to have help from Sun Yong of Nanking, who made available to me photos of the newly renovated Ch'in-huai riverbanks. My thanks also to Joseph Szaszfai and Richard Caspole of Yale University, who provided me with excellent photographic services.

Throughout the years of this book's making, I have benefited immensely from the staff of Yale University Library—in particular Hsiao-ch'iang Ch'en (my former teacher) and Boksoon Hahn, whose expert advice and gracious assistance have been invaluable. Other scholars, librarians, and friends who offered similar help include Susan Cherniack, Stephen Little, Anthony Marr, Weilin Tang, Melissa Thompson, C. K. Wang, and Yü Sung-ch'ing. In this connection, I want to thank Henry Schwab for always getting books promptly for me. My debts to many literary critics and historians are acknowledged in my notes and bibliography, but I would like to mention a few Ming–Ch'ing specialists whose works I have frequently consulted: Pei-kai Cheng, Patrick Hanan, Joanna Handlin, Robert Hegel, C. T. Hsia, Paul Ropp, Richard Strassberg, Lynn Struve, Frederic Wakeman, James Watt, Ellen Widmer, and Anthony Yu. Over the years, several friends have provided intellectual and moral support, and I thank them: Richard Barnhart, Shan Chou, Grace Fong, Charles Hartman, Dore Levy, Shuen-fu Lin, Victor Mair, Frances LaFleur Mochida, Bill Nienhauser, Judith Rabinovitch, Hugh Stimson, C. H. Wang, Lucie and Stanley Weinstein, Carolyn Wheelwright, Tim Wixted, Monica Yu, and Longxi Zhang. To Bill Carney, whose friendship was often expressed in generous terms, I owe a special debt of gratitude. My father, Professor Paul Sun, not only prepared Chinese calligraphy for my manuscript copy, but also, along with my mother, aided me in many other significant ways.

I am grateful for the financial support of a Morse Fellowship (1985–86), Yale's Griswold Research Fund (1986), and a fellowship from the Joint Committee on Chinese Studies of the American Council of Learned Societies and the Social Sciences Research Council (1989) that gave me the time to complete this book. I wish to express my special appreciation to Ellen Graham of Yale University Press, who supported my work with enthusiasm and perceptiveness and saw the book through to final publication; and to Lawrence Kenney, who edited the manuscript with superb skill and thoughtfulness. I am also grateful to an anonymous reader who reviewed this book for the press and offered helpful suggestions.

Finally, I want most of all to acknowledge the help of my husband, Chézy: without the pleasure of his company and the benefit of his constant inspiration, this book could not have been completed so smoothly. I also owe a great debt to my daughter Edith, who has demonstrated the good virtue of cooperation since her birth four years ago, which coincided with the beginning of my writing of this book. The untimely death of my cousin Tao-cheng Jacob Chang has left me greatly saddened; but his artistic spirit will be a permanent resource for me, and thus to him this book is dedicated.

CHRONOLOGY

1608   Ch'en Tzu-lung born in Sung-Chiang. He was named Tzu-lung (Child-Dragon) because his mother dreamed about a dragon glowing on the bedroom wall the night before his birth.

1612   Ch'en Tzu-lung's mother dies. He is left in the care of his paternal grandmother, Kao T'ai-an-jen, for the next several years.

1613   Ch'en Tzu-lung begins formal studies in Chinese classics.

1615   Ch'en Tzu-lung begins to learn the technique of parallelism in poetry.

1618   Liu Shih born.

1619   Ch'en Tzu-lung engaged to the eldest daughter of a renowned scholar-official, Chang Fang-t'ung.

1626   Ch'en Tzu-lung's father dies in December; Tzu-lung becomes head of the household.

1628   Ch'en Tzu-lung marries Miss Chang after completing the mourning period for his father.

1629   Ch'en Tzu-lung joins the Fu-she (Restoration Society), led by Chang P'u.

1630   Ch'en Tzu-lung passes the provincial examination held in Nanking and becomes a *chü-jen* (Provincial Graduate).

1631   Ch'en Tzu-lung fails the imperial examination in Peking.

1632   Ch'en Tzu-lung meets Liu Shih.

1634   Ch'en Tzu-lung fails the imperial examination a second time.

1635   Spring and summer: Ch'en Tzu-lung lives with Liu Shih in the Southern Villa.
       Autumn: Liu Shih leaves Ch'en Tzu-lung. She later returns to the Courtesans' Quarter in Sheng-tse.

1637   Ch'en Tzu-lung passes the imperial examination and becomes a *Chin-shih* (Metropolitan Graduate). The death of his stepmother prevents him from serving immediately in the government.

1638   Ch'en Tzu-lung writes the preface to *Wu-yin ts'ao*, a collection of poems by Liu Shih.

1640   Ch'en Tzu-lung begins to serve in the government.

1641   Liu Shih marries Ch'ien Ch'ien-i.

1644   Peking falls to the Manchus. Liu Shih inscribes a painting with Ch'en Tzu-lung's verses to her.

1645   Nanking falls to the Manchus. Liu Shih tries to commit suicide by jumping into a pond but is rescued.

1646   Ch'en Tzu-lung's grandmother dies. Soon afterward he joins the loyalist army led by Wu I.

1647   Ch'en Tzu-lung is involved in the Wu Sheng-chao Resistance Movement. He dies a martyr in the fifth month.

1648   Liu Shih is involved in the Huang Yü-ch'i Resistance Movement.

1649   Liu Shih completes the section on women poets for Ch'ien Ch'ien-i's *Lieh-ch'ao shih-chi*.

1654   Liu Shih assists Koxinga's invasion of the Yangtze River region.

1659   Liu Shih helps in persuading other loyalists to join the Koxinga army in Nanking.

1664   Liu Shih commits suicide after the death of Ch'ien Ch'ien-i, as a protest against the unreasonable demands of Ch'ien's relatives.

ABBREVIATIONS

AYTK   Ch'en Tzu-lung, *An-ya-t'ang kao*. Reprinted in 3 vols. Taipei: Wei-wen Books and Publishing, 1977.

CST   Tang Kuei-chang, ed. *Chüan Sung-tz'u*. 5 vols. Peking: Chung-hua shu-chü, 1965.

CTLS   Ch'en Tzu-lung. *Ch'en Tzu-lung shih-chi*. Edited by Shih Chih-ts'un and Ma Tsu-hsi. 2 vols. Shanghai: Ku-chi ch'u-pan-she, 1983.

CTS   P'eng Ting-ch'iu (1645–1719) et al., eds. *Ch'üan T'ang-shih*. Punctuated edition in 12 vols. Peking: Chung-hua shu-chü, 1960.

CTWT   Lin Ta-ch'un, ed. *T'ang Wu-tai tz'u*. 1956. Reprinted as *Ch'üan T'ang Wu-tai tz'u hui-pien*. 2 vols. Taipei: Shih-chieh shu-chü, 1967.

HCHW   Lu Ch'in-li, ed. *Hsien Ch'in Han Wei Chin Nan-pei-ch'ao shih*. 3 vols. Peking: Chung-hua shu-chü, 1983.

IC   Nienhauser, William H., Jr., ed. and comp. *The Indiana Companion to Traditional Chinese Literature*. Bloomington: Indiana Univ. Press, 1986.

LJS   Ch'en Yin-k'o. *Liu Ju-Shih pieh-chuan*. 3 vols. Shanghai: Ku-chi ch'u-pan-she, 1980.

THTP   T'ang Kuei-chang, ed. *Tz'u-hua ts'ung-pien*. 5 vols. Rev. ed. Peking: Chung-hua shu-chü, 1986.

PART 1

Loyalism and
Changing Ideals
of Romantic Love

ONE

The Loyalist Tradition

To outsiders, the seemingly endless succession of dynasties in traditional China may seem like a natural phenomenon of flux and temporality. But to the Chinese themselves, the collapse of a dynasty is surely the most symbolic of the dynamics of human tragedy. And especially to those loyalists who refuse to accept the death of the old order, the dynastic transition is the very definition of the tragic moment in history, a period when man finds himself facing the hard choice of dying or not dying, or the decision of when to die. Ch'en Tzu-lung was one of the many Ming loyalists who witnessed the fall of their country, and whose poetry reflected the national tragedy from this perspective. Ch'en therefore belongs to a special class of poets, and the vision of life and death embodied in Chinese culture is often revealed with particular depth and poignancy in his poetry.

As a loyalist, Ch'en Tzu-lung participated in various resistance movements after the fall of the Ming. In 1645 he was involved in a heroic though losing battle against the Manchu troops in his hometown, Sung-chiang, and managed to escape to a Buddhist monastery soon after the fall of the city. In the guise of a Buddhist monk, he changed his name to Hsin-chung (Faithful and Sincere). Soon afterward, he began to plot an attempt to restore the Ming dynasty. But in the fifth month of 1647, his plans for an uprising leaked out, and he was arrested by Manchu officials. On the way to Nanking for further questioning, in order to avoid personal humiliation at the hands of the enemy, he committed suicide by jumping into the river. He was only thirty-nine. According to some sources, his final dialogue on

3

earth ran as follows: "The Ch'ing official asked: 'Why haven't you cut your hair [in compliance with Ch'ing regulations]?' Ch'en answered: 'I am keeping my hair in order to see my emperor [with dignity] in the world below.'"[1]

It was the cause for which he chose to die that eventually won Ch'en Tzu-lung the immortality of a hero's position in history.[2] At the same time, his poetic work records what he saw and felt during the fugitive years leading up to his martyrdom in 1647. His contemporaries lauded him as a first-rate poet distinguished by heroic vision and poetic elegance.[3] Even today he has been honored by the Chinese as an exemplar of moral courage and literary accomplishment, and a large-scale renovation of his tomb has recently been completed in China.[4] Indeed, Thomas Carlyle would have found in Ch'en Tzu-lung an excellent subject for his chapter "The Poet as Hero."[5]

But Ch'en Tzu-lung and his poetry largely escaped attention for more than a century after his death. A telling case is that none of his poems were included in Cho Erh-k'an's (fl. ca. 1675) prestigious collection "Poems of Ming Loyalists"—the earliest known anthology on that subject.[6] The problem is that Ch'en Tzu-lung's political position had caused his works to be banned by the Ch'ing government until 1776, when Emperor Ch'ien-lung finally rehabilitated him and honored him as a hero. Emperor Ch'ien-lung somehow felt it his duty to establish the poet-hero's place in history, and he sincerely admired Ch'en's "upright spirit." He canonized Ch'en posthumously as Chung-yü (Loyal and Noble).[7] Following this rehabilitation, people were allowed to read Ch'en Tzu-lung's poetry again, but by then only a fraction of his works could be found. Under the auspices of Emperor Ch'ien-lung, scholars actively began to search for his lost writings, but the task of locating and editing the works proceeded slowly because many of them were in private collections. In 1803 Wang Ch'ang (1725–1807) managed to finish his official *Complete Works of Ch'en Tzu-lung*,[8] but the edition was far from perfect—it was heavily censored in order to make its content acceptable to the Ch'ing court. In fact, not until 1983 was a satisfactory annotated edition of Ch'en's poetry published by the mainland scholars Shih Chih-ts'un and Ma Tsu-hsi, thereby restoring Ch'en's reputation as one of the great poets of traditional China.[9]

In many respects the fate of Ch'en Tzu-lung recalls that of Wen T'ien-hsiang (1236–83), the famous Sung patriot who died as a result of his steadfast loyalty to his country.[10] Following his martyrdom in 1283 Wen's literary works were not in the public eye for several decades. And not until forty years after his death did people dare to offer sacrifice openly on his behalf.[11] Although he was executed by the Mongols, he was highly respected by the Mongolian leaders, especially Qubilai Qayan.[12] As William Brown has observed, however, it was only after "the overthrow of the alien Yüan dynasty and the re-establishment of a Chinese hegemony under the Ming" that Wen T'ien-hsiang emerged as a hero, "a symbol of undying loyalty to China."[13]

There is no doubt that Ming loyalists and resisters such as Ch'en Tzu-lung and his many friends looked up to Wen T'ien-hsiang as a model. In particular, Wen's famous poem "Crossing the Ling-ting Sea"[14]—written as a final reply to his enemy's repeated attempts to make him surrender during his trip north—had become for Ming loyalists the best perpetuation of heroic values:

> I've endured great hardships since I began my career,[15]
> Swords and shields have been with me for four years.
> Mountains and rivers were overturned, catkins swept by the wind,
> I live a wandering life, a duckweed pelted by rain.   4
> On the Huang-k'ung Beach I cry out my alarm,
> On the Ling-ting Sea I lament my loneliness.[16]
> In all the ages past, has anyone failed to die?
> Let's leave our loyal hearts to shine upon history.   8

Thus, as the modern historian Yü Ying-shih has said, the Huang-k'ung Beach Wen T'ien-hsiang mentioned in his poem (line 5) eventually became a kind of Mecca for Ming loyalists.[17] And it is no accident that the famous scholar Fang I-chih (1611–71), after being indicted by the Ch'ing for his involvement in a resistance movement, resolutely drowned himself near the Huang-k'ung Beach as an expression of his identification with the Sung patriot.[18] Perhaps the most poignant of all the allusions to Wen is that Fang Chung-lü, the son of Fang I-chih, entitled the collection of his own writings "Collected Works on Huang-k'ung Beach,"[19] obviously in remembrance of his father's martyrdom. All of these references serve to demonstrate that Wen T'ien-hsiang's example was responsible for a new notion of heroism: the sacrifice of one's life for one's country became the highest form of taking action, transcending personal suffering, and achieving the ultimate morality of *jen* (humanity) and *i* (righteousness). In his poetic testament, entitled *I-tai tsan* (An elegy sewn between my sash and garment), Wen T'ien-hsiang wrote:

> Confucius said, "Preserve humanity."
> Mencius said, "Embrace righteousness."
> Only when righteousness is exhausted,
> Is humanity complete.[20]

Following Wen T'ien-hsiang's example, many Ming loyalists composed their own elegies before meeting their deaths in an act of moral commitment.[21] It was not a coincidence that in 1774, only two years before the rehabilitation of Ch'en Tzu-lung, Emperor Ch'ien-lung inscribed words of praise on the back of Wen T'ien-hsiang's inkslab.[22] Indeed, the image of Wen T'ien-hsiang had become so central to the concept of heroism from the late Ming on that even the famous lore about Ch'ü Yüan underwent a dramatic change—the ancient poet of *Li-sao* was now seen primarily as a hero of political resistance, despite earlier writers' emphasis on his relations with his king and court rivals.[23]

A factor integral to the formation of patriotic heroism in the late Ming has to do with the pervasive influence of the Fu-she (Restoration Society). One need only look at the large numbers of Fu-she members who participated in the Chiang-nan resistance movements to perceive the close link between Fu-she and loyalism.[24] First of all, as William Atwell has observed, the Fu-she was "probably the largest and most sophisticated political organization in the history of traditional China," and "many of the best minds of the late Ming period" belonged to it.[25] Unlike previous literary clubs in China, which had been "organized as a diversion from, or an alternative to, official life,"[26] the Fu-she strove to involve its members in political activity. For the first time in Chinese history young scholars were determined to dominate the political scene through collective strength.

In many ways Ch'en Tzu-lung was a spokesman for his fu-she friends: especially notable was his interest in propagating "the question of reform in a scholarly manner."[27] He was constantly in search of practical solutions to pressing contemporary problems, as may be demonstrated by his monumental effort to edit the *Huang Ming ching-shih wen-pien* (Ming writings on practical statesmanship) in more than five hundred *chüan*.[28] He was one of the founders of the Chi-she, a local branch of the Fu-she, in Sung-chiang. Along with Chang P'u (1602–41) and other friends, such as Hsia Yün-i (1596–1645), Ch'en Tzu-lung advocated a philosophy of striving, willing, and fervor. Like other leaders of the Fu-she, Ch'en accepted large numbers of students and frequently organized public lectures to advocate high moral standards.[29] Thus, it was only natural that numerous Fu-she members remained Ming loyalists after the collapse of the dynasty. The numbers of martyrs were indeed unprecedented in Chinese history. As Emperor Ch'ien-lung later commented in his "Records of Ming Martyrs," "My purpose has been to make this information available to later students of history, especially because so many Ming officials died as martyrs. It was something unheard-of in the Han, T'ang, and Sung dynasties."[30]

This is, of course, not to say that all the loyalists died during the resistance movements. For one dies only when honor demands it. There were committed loyalists such as the poet Wang Fu-chih (1619–92), who took an active part in the resistance, eventually escaped death, and became a private scholar, refusing to compromise with the Manchus. Others, like Chang Tai (ca. 1597–after 1671), were never involved in a resistance movement but acknowledged that suicide was, as Stephen Owen puts it, "the next inevitable stage"; these loyalists simply turned into "men of the wilderness" and were "compelled to live on in degradation" so they could complete their literary and historical works, apparently following Ssu-ma Ch'ien's example.[31] Such scholars, conscious of their ambiguous position and their alienation from contemporary society, were trying to give new meaning to their cultural mission in history. They were anticipating how future generations would see them and were trying to mold that vision. The discovery in 1638 of an important Sung manuscript, Hsin-shih (The history of my heart and soul), written by the Sung loyalist poet-painter Cheng Ssu-hsiao (1241–1318), also gave them new inspiration.[32] As the modern historian F. W. Mote said, "It appeared at a time when its racist resentments and its appeal to loyalty were of potential use in stiffening resistance to the Manchu threat."[33] If Cheng Ssu-hsiao's works, preserved in an iron case at the bottom of a well in Soochow, were able to survive for well over three hundred years and still, being found one day, provide new hope and meaning to others, certainly the Ming loyalists could do the same by leaving "writings stored in a stone casket."[34] In many ways, these surviving loyalists have become the archetypal symbol of suffering and of the redeeming power of literature. For gradually, as political action was denied them, the emphasis was shifted from the outer expressions of politics to inner feelings. Yet it is in their works, especially their poems, that we read about such an attitude toward life, the attitude which eventually delivers them from the torment of despair and personal tragedy. To a large extent, the expression of feelings in poetry has become, for the loyalists, a way of taking action.

It is in this sense that Ch'en Tzu-lung's life and poetry provide a strikingly significant perspective on the loyalist's personal values and artistic perceptions. Like Wen T'ien-hsiang, he died a martyr after having experienced real suffering in the real world, as opposed to some abstract notion of suffering. Like Wen T'ien-hsiang, he had created poetry that

would make his moral character shine throughout history. But unlike Wen
T'ien-hsiang, who was captured by the enemy shortly before the fall of
his country,[35] Ch'en was able to escape and went into hiding until his
martyrdom in 1647. He could have remained a surviving loyalist until old
age, like Chang Tai, had his plot to restore the Ming not been uncov-
ered by the Ch'ing authorities. Ch'en lived for only three years after the
Ming fall, but they were crucial years of dynastic transition. In the period
between the dynasty's fall and his death, he was able to record his experience as a wandering loyalist, as a poet who was openly concerned with
the tragic reality and the dialectical nature of life and death. On the other
hand, his poetry often conveys what Murray Krieger calls the "soothing
grace," a vision possessed by "the tragic hero" through a final uniting of
the ethical and the aesthetic principles.[36] In other words, Ch'en's works,
especially those written after the fall of the Ming, enable us to see a new
role of poetry in fashioning tragic understanding into a moral and lyrical
totality—a totality characterized by the coexistence of loyalism and loss.

TWO

The Concept of *Ch'ing*
and Late-Ming
Images of Women

If Ch'en Tzu-lung's later poetry on
loyalism is distinguished by an intensity of feeling, his earlier poetry on
romantic love is equally so marked. In reading Ch'en's poetry, one is struck
by the kinship between these two kinds of human feeling and by the force-
fulness of the emotions expressed. A revealing comment by a traditional
Chinese scholar, Ch'ai Hu-ch'en, reads,

> The tragic grief at Hua-t'ing,
> The romantic rapture of Sung Yü,
> Only Wo-tzu [Ch'en Tzu-lung] succeeds in combining these two.[1]

But Ch'en Tzu-lung was only one of the many late-Ming literati who believed that romantic love, far from detracting from the character of the
great man, was an essential part of it. Such an idea was possible because
of a changing attitude toward women on the part of seventeenth-century
literati—a woman was no longer seen as a femme fatale whom a moral
man should avoid. In his "Ying-hsiung ch'i-tuan shuo" (which Lin Yutang
translated as "On Heroes and Women"), the late-Ming scholar Chou
Ch'üan explicitly dwells on this new notion of love:

> It is often said that "the great heroes of history met their match in woman."
> By this people mean that the love of a woman is a dangerous thing and that

such episodes somehow take away from our idea of a "hero." One must keep away from the snares and temptations of women. And so forth. I beg to differ. I think that what makes heroes heroes is that they love in greater measure than others. . . . Only those who can make great sacrifices can love truly.[2]

In fact, Chou Ch'üan was merely articulating a concept central to late-Ming culture—the concept of *ch'ing*, which sees love "as the psychological stimulus necessary for virtuous action."[3] In his *Ch'ing-shih lei-lüeh* (Anatomy of love), the famous short story writer Feng Meng-lung (1574–1646) provides moving accounts of numerous men and women, both historical and fictional, whose actions of love and courage demonstrated the highest ideal of Confucian morality.[4] Indeed, as Patrick Hanan says, the whole book focuses "on the point at which the heroic and the romantic meet."[5]

At the center of the *ch'ing* concept lies the idea that love, or more specifically romantic love, transcends death. What C. T. Hsia says about the "timeless dimension" of *ch'ing* as revealed in T'ang Hsien-tsu's (1550–1616) famous play *Mu-tan t'ing* (*The Peony Pavilion*)[6] is itself the shared belief of late-Ming literati. According to this cult of love, *ch'ing* not only supplies the supreme experience of life but also gives one the courage to redefine traditional concepts of life and death. T'ang Hsien-tsu's famous preface to his *Mu-tan t'ing* is a good summary of this late-Ming ideal of *ch'ing*:

> Of all the girls of this world, who is ever so committed to love (*yu-ch'ing*) as Tu Li-niang? Once she dreams of her lover, she falls ill and her illness worsens until with her own hand she transmits to the world a portrait of her features and then dies. After being dead for three years, she can still in her limbo-like existence seek the object of her love and regain her life. Verily Li-niang can be called a person committed to love (*yu-ch'ing jen*). She doesn't know how she has fallen in love, but once in love, she is totally committed to it. . . . To stay alive without the courage to die, and to die without the volition to regain life—such is not the condition of one supremely committed to love.[7]

The theme of the dedicated lover is thus central to late-Ming drama and fiction. Aside from T'ang Hsien-tsu's romantic plays, notably *Mu-tan t'ing* and *Tzu-ch'ai chi*,[8] numerous short stories and novels produced during this period dwell upon this very theme, leading us to believe that such description of the sheer intensity of *ch'ing* reflects a new emotional and moral consciousness. We see in Feng Meng-lung's collection of the *San-yen* stories such dedicated lovers as the Ch'en couple who are bound in life and death, and the humble oil peddler who courts the courtesan Mei-niang with a devotion almost unprecedented in the history of Chinese romance.[9] Moreover, the overwhelming popularity of *ts'ai-tzu chia-jen* (talented man and beautiful woman) fiction certainly reflects a widespread belief in the primacy of romantic love—according to which, as Richard Hessney has observed, a talented man and a beautiful woman are destined to marry, and "their life together should constitute an exemplary 'wonderful tale that will last for a thousand autumns.' "[10] Some decades later the dramatist Hung Sheng (1645–1704), in his famous play *Ch'ang-sheng tien* (Palace of immortality), rephrased the same notion by revising the traditional image of Yang Kuei-fei: "I only borrow the story of T'ai-chen [Yang Kuei-fei] to write a new song-drama, in order to illustrate the meaning of *ch'ing*."[11]

It might be argued that such emphasis on *ch'ing*, largely revealed in fiction and drama, reflected nothing more than fantastic imaginings and idealism on the part of late-Ming literati authors—a kind of wishful thinking, quite contrary to our notion of "realism or the traditional Chinese emphasis on duty to family and sovereign."[12] However, as Oscar Wilde puts it, oftentimes "life imitates art far more than art imitates life," and when "a great artist invents a type," "life tries to copy it."[13] I believe this is precisely what happened to late-Ming men and women. In other words, the blossoming of the cult of *ch'ing* in the late Ming took place largely through readers' imitation of the role types created in contemporary fiction and drama, role types that focused on the idea of love and encouraged a cultural reevaluation of human feeling. In fact, the impact of typical role types was so great that as early as the sixteenth century some conservative scholars feared "the pernicious influence on female readers of vernacular fiction."[14]

Another side of the story—one frequently neglected—is that the typical role type of the devoted lover in fiction and drama was often based on the real lives of contemporary courtesans. Fiction and life interpenetrated in ways both mundane and sublime. This is especially interesting when we realize that authors like Feng Meng-lung befriended courtesans and regularly supplied works for them to read.[15] Indeed, in reading late-Ming stories and plays, one is struck by the central place courtesans have there, particularly those who lived in the Ch'in-huai quarters of Nanking, the Southern Capital. The courtesan's life itself became a kind of fiction that played a crucial part in the formation of the *ch'ing* concept. On the one hand, we see a new fictional and dramatic image of the courtesan Yü-t'ang-ch'un,[16] serving as an exemplar of the ideal lover. On the other hand, we read about Mao Hsiang's (1611–93) biographical account of the famed courtesan Tung Pai, which emphasizes that patience and self-sacrifice had become the hallmark of a new love ethic current among the courtesans and their circle.[17] Of course, the image of the courtesan as a dedicated lover had already existed in the T'ang *ch'uan-ch'i* tales, for example, the stories of the fictional Li Wa and Huo Hsiao-yü. And long before the late Ming there were real courtesans like Wu-ling-ch'un (Ch'i Hui-chen), a woman whose devotion to her lover until death was celebrated in Hsü Lin's (1462–1538) inscription on a portrait of her.[18] But it was not until the beginning of the seventeenth century that the "courtesan type" became the metaphorical equivalent of the *ch'ing* idea. Indeed, one can say that the cult of love was largely a product of the courtesan culture.

The role of the courtesan in transforming the *ch'ing* concept into a cult is exemplified in K'ung Shang-jen's (1648–1718) masterpiece, *T'ao-hua shan* (*Peach Blossom Fan*), a historical play completed in 1699 and based on real events of the late Ming. In the play the courtesan Li Hsiang-chün's devotion to her lover Hou Fang-yü is symbolized by a fan stained with her own blood. (In resisting the prime minister's order to marry Master Ts'ao, Li Hsiang-chün knocks her head against the ground and bleeds so profusely that she stains her fan.) The bloodstained fan, later converted by the artist Yang Wen-ts'ung into a fine painting of peach blossoms, is a microcosm of late-Ming idealism—an idealism based on the integrity of genuine love. Thus, the world of the Peach Blossom Spring, traditional symbol of an earthly utopia, is here given an entirely new content.[19] The fan has become so powerful a symbol of idealism that the musician Su K'un-sheng, a mutual friend of Li Hsiang-chün and Hou Fang-ü, risks his life to keep the fan from falling into the water:

> The river rose up to my shoulders,
> But I held the fan over my head
> To save the precious message.[20]

Some modern historians, notably Willard Peterson, have warned of "a tendency in many writings" to "romanticize the liaisons" between courtesans and literati.[21] While it is true that some writers used the idea of *ch'ing* in different ways and for different purposes—and that even within the Ch'in-huai quarter itself there was a vital difference between *chiu-yüan* courtesans, who tended to maintain their chastity until meeting their soul mates, and *nan-shih* girls, who were mere "prostitutes"[22]—there is no denying that romantic idealization of love was precisely what *ch'ing* meant to late-Ming literati and courtesans. The main point is that a talented literatus remains unfulfilled until there is a gifted woman to match him. The late Ming, of course, did not invent romantic passion, but it made the concept fashionable so that it became a cult dominant in the culture. And this cult in turn gave direction to the literary trends of the period. Unlike the traditional hero in earlier fiction and drama, who delays his wedding until the day he becomes a successful examination candidate, Hou Fang-yü in the *Peach Blossom Fan* marries the courtesan Li Hsiang-chün right after he fails the examination. He even prides himself on being able to value love over worldly success: "Though I did not pass the examination / I have now become the sweetheart of the Moon Goddess."[23] This romantic idealization of love is embedded in the idea of "lovers coming in pairs," a notion strongly reflected in *ts'ai-tzu chia-jen* (talented man and beautiful woman) drama and fiction.[24] But in real life, the most enduring images of love were drawn from matching literatus–courtesan couples such as Hou Fang-yü (1618–55) and Li Hsiang-chün, Mao Hsiang (1611–93) and Tung Pai, Wu Wei-yeh (1609–71) and Pien Sai, Kung Ting-tzu (1611–73) and Ku Mei,[25] Yang Wen-ts'ung (1596–1646)[26] and Ma Chiao, Ch'en Tzu-lung and Liu Shih.

In this sense, the romantic love expressed by Ch'en Tzu-lung and Liu Shih in their poetry was a direct reflection of the literati and courtesan culture of their times. As I shall note later, Liu Shih was one of those famous courtesans who lent color to the period and considerable stature to women. She enjoyed a reputation for being a courtesan of superb literary and artistic accomplishments.[27] She published her first collection of poems at the age of twenty and became a distinguished poet in her day. And her love relationship with Ch'en Tzu-lung engendered a new style of love poetry, effecting an important revival of the *tz'u* genre. Years later, in 1649, she completed an anthology of women poets, ultimately to be included in Ch'ien Ch'ien-i's (1582–1664) *Lieh-ch'ao shih-chi*. Like numerous other courtesans of her time, she became a respectable "woman of learning" by entering the cultural elite of the Chiang-nan cities. As Yü Huai (1717–?) describes in his *Pan-ch'iao tsa-chi*, many of Liu's contemporaries—courtesans who specialized in poetry, calligraphy, painting, and dramatic arts—were known as female artists, and they mingled freely with male poets and scholar-officials.[28] Howard Levy, in the preface to his English translation of *Pan-ch'iao tsa-chi*, sums up this point:

[The courtesan] dabbled in calligraphy, collected books, studied painting, and decorated her rooms with taste and simplicity. . . . She played melodies unforgettably on the lute, sang and recited poems with distinction, and performed plays in either male or female roles with such finesse as to render her audience spellbound. It is evident, then, that the courtesan who enthralled members of high society did so primarily through artistic attainment rather than physical appeal.[29]

Rather than being confined to the entertainment quarters like the courtesans of earlier times, these late-Ming female artists were regular guests at the residences of literati[30]—among these was the famous house owned by Wen Chen-heng (1585–1645), the great-grandson of Wen Cheng-ming (1470–1559), which Liu Shih seems to have frequented. The acceptance of courtesans at the literary gatherings held in these elegant residences, as James Watt has noted, "sometimes resulted in romantic marriages and was another noteworthy aspect of the openness of late Ming society."[31]

The new status of the late-Ming courtesans, somewhat similar to that of cultured courtesans in sixteenth-century Venice,[32] undoubtedly encouraged the exploration of new aspects of the male–female relationship. First, Liu Shih's poetic achievements suggest not a reactionary effort on the part of the courtesan to claim some separate status for the feminine, but rather a capacity to erase traditional boundaries between male and female roles. Her example further suggests that courtesans were no longer just "conversationalists and *artistes*"—conventional images existing since T'ang times[33]—but had in fact become published authors and *artists,* sharing one and the same literary tradition and context with men. As a result, they also gained the respect and support of the cultural elites of the Chiang-nan cities. Whereas the increasingly popular image of the talented woman (*ts'ai-nü*) as portrayed in contemporary fiction and drama represents perhaps no more than "a projection of the wishes of the female audience,"[34] courtesans like Liu Shih had themselves become such talented women. In fiction, we are reminded of the famous story of the talented Su Hsiao-mei (sister of the Sung poet Su Shih), made popular by Feng Meng-lung's *San-yen* collection. The story celebrates Su Hsiao-mei's superb poetic skill and tells of her testing of her poet "husband" Ch'in Kuan on their wedding night. But the story was of course completely fictional.[35] For the historical Su Hsiao-mei could not have met the Sung poet Ch'in Kuan: she died long before Ch'in Kuan became an adult and came to study with Su Shih. Moreover, the wife of the historical Ch'in Kuan was surnamed Hsü rather than Su.[36] Obviously the anonymous author of the story purposefully distorted the historical facts in order to create an image of a talented woman whose poetic skills surpass those of her husband, an image apparently appealing to late-Ming readers.

Similarly, in his "Ssu ch'an-chüan" (Four lovely women), the early Ch'ing dramatist Hung Sheng celebrates the literary and artistic accomplishments of four female talents—Hsieh Tao-yün in *shih* poetry, Wei Lu in calligraphy, Li Ch'ing-chao in *tz'u* poetry, Kuan Tao-sheng in painting—though his play is obviously a recreation of historical accounts of these women. In any case, such fictional creation and historical drama testify that the prior concept of "talented man and beautiful woman" (*ts'ai-tzu chia-jen*) had gradually been transformed into that of the "talented man and gifted woman," focusing not on the woman's beauty but on the equality and compatibility of the hero and the heroine.

Even more interesting, the dramatist Hsü Wei (1522–94) exaggerated this notion of sexual equality in his short play *Nü chuang-yüan* (The female *chuang-yüan*), which tells of a young woman who wins first place in the imperial examination by dressing as a man. (Women were simply not allowed to take such examinations.)[37] She eventually marries the prime minister's son, who has also won first place in a later examination. The dramatist then sums up his message in a couplet toward the end of the play: "The female *chuang-yüan* and the male *chuang-yüan* / Are destined to marry in the residence of the prime minister."[38] There is every reason to believe that, being avid readers of stories and plays, courtesans like Liu Shih would have been familiar with this new fictional image of the talented woman.[39] Whereas male authors created the stories of the gifted Su Hsiao-mei and of a female *chuang-yüan* in the disguise of a man, Liu Shih had become a real-life Su Hsiao-mei and a woman scholar-poet who frequently adopted men's attire. Thus, in 1641 when Liu traveled by herself to visit Ch'ien Ch'ien-i at his Pan-yeh-t'ang residence, Ch'ien could not at first see through her male disguise and was extremely impressed with the exceptional talents of the "young man" who had come to visit. Like Portia in Shakespeare's *Merchant of Venice*,[40] Liu Shih adopted male attire to gain a new freedom and position for herself. Moreover, Liu often signed her letters "your younger brother" (*ti*) when writing to her male friends (*LJS*, 2:387). Such attempts at erasing the female–male boundary go a long way toward explaining why late-Ming courtesans were very different from earlier palace women and singing girls, whose lives and roles were, as Anne Birrel says, "radically different from men's."[41]

In response to this altered image of courtesans and of women in general,[42] Ming literati naturally developed relationships with women that reflected, if not true equality, at least compatibility and mutual respect. Literati and courtesans exchanged poems, traveled together, shared political and moral commitments, and formed true friendships. Thus, although the courtesans often ended up becoming merely the concubines of the literati, their function and position resembled those of the modern wife, as may be demonstrated by Liu Shih's legendary marriage to Ch'ien Ch'ien-i years after her separation from Ch'en Tzu-lung. Such relationships evolved because the scholars' legal wives, acquired through arranged marriages, usually had limited access to the emotional and intellectual lives of their husbands, thus preventing men of that age from associating romantic love with their formal wives. At the same time, love and friendship under the influence of the cult of *ch'ing* gradually brought a literatus and his courtesan-lover together to a socially acceptable position.[43] Indeed, what Anthony Yu says of the "extraordinary" nature of "love that flourishes between the two cousins" in the eighteenth-century novel *The Story of the Stone*[44] can be traced back to this late-Ming model of the talented man and gifted courtesan relationship.

A factor integral to the development of the reciprocal literatus–courtesan relationship has to do with the new trends of thought promoted by literary societies like Fu-she and Chi-she. Earlier I noted the crucial links between literary societies and Ming loyalism, for almost all Ming loyalists were members of the Fu-she. In fact, many distinguished courtesans—for example, Liu Shih, Pien Sai, and Li Hsiang-chün—were unofficial members of the Fu-she or Chi-she and thus shared the literary and political concerns of their male friends. Later, after the fall of the Ming, many of them (like Ko Nen, the concubine of Sun K'o-hsien) sacrificed their lives for their country. And some others (chief among them Liu Shih)[45] participated in various resistance movements in a manner quite similar to male loyalists like Ch'en Tzu-lung and Wang Fu-chih. There is no question that the Fu-she's emphasis on political and moral commitment strongly urged among its members a new synthesis of love and loyalism and consequently provided them with a direct correlation between these two kinds of human passion. Indeed, it is no coincidence that many renowned lovers, men and women alike, turned out to be strong patriots as well.

As a matter of fact, in the Ming–Ch'ing texts the courtesan often serves as the essential link between love and political commitment. As mentioned above, K'ung Shang-jen's *Peach Blossom Fan* portrays a vivid image of the courageous courtesan Li Hsiang-chün, who has consistently resisted the political pressures exerted on her and her lover Hou Fang-yü. It is Li Hsiang-chün who persuades Hou Fang-yü to reject the patronage of the notoriously corrupt official Juan Ta-ch'eng. Moreover, she strongly believes in the moral cause of the Fu-she, defends it, and would die for it if necessary. On the wall of her Ch'in-huai quarters, she has inscribed patriotic poems by Chang P'u and Hsia Yün-i, both leading figures of the Fu-she.[46] And finally it is the constancy of her love that leads Hou Fang-yü to heroic action. In his biography of the historical Li Hsiang-chün, Hou Fang-yü also praised the courtesan as an "upright and intelligent" (*hsia erh hui*) woman.[47]

Similarly, Liu Shih was known for her courage and chivalry—she often compared herself to Liang Hung-yü, a courtesan and later wife of the Sung general Han Shih-chung, who helped her husband win a battle against Jurchen troops (*LJS*, 1:166). Indeed, in Liu Shih and Li Hsiang-chün we see most vividly the image of the brave and righteous courtesan that offers the greatest possible contrast to the traditional stereotype of the femme fatale, who ruins men. The fact that all of the "four aristocratic youths" (*ssu kung-tzu*) who were known for their personal involvements with courtesans—Hou Fang-yü, Mao Hsiang, Ch'en Chen-hui (1605–56), and Fang I-chih—remained steadfast resisters after the Ming fall also proves that romantic liaisons with such women did not interfere with, but indeed helped cultivate, their dedication to patriotism. In any case, the late-Ming courtesans' political commitment—and hence their ability to combine sensual experience with moral action—perhaps marks the greatest difference between them and the singing girls of earlier times.

Most important, after the fall of the Ming, the courtesan became a metaphor for the loyalist poets' vision of themselves. The development is easy to understand, for both the loyalist and the courtesan experienced similar dramatic reversals after the dynastic fall and had to make similar decisions regarding their public and private roles. Some of them, like Ch'en Tzu-lung and Liu Shih, assumed the role of persistent resisters by participating in various restoration schemes. Others, like Hou Fang-yü and Pien Sai, simply chose the option of seclusion and became eremites and Taoists. But all of them shared the sense of loss and loneliness resulting from the national tragedy, as Wu Wei-yeh has vividly described in his "A Song on Hearing the Taoist Priestess Pien Yü-ching Play the Zither."[48] In many ways, the hardships borne by the courtesans during the dynastic transition paralleled the sufferings of the loyalists:

> The moon is bright, but strings are cold and silent,
> Shan-t'ang is desolate, suffering from the ravages of war.
> Of my ten-years' companions, only two or three are left.
> The rouged faces of Sha and Tung have turned to dust.
> Women of royal chambers have become dust on the road,
> We who wander about are not worth mentioning.[49]

Thus, the loyalists who suffered and survived the terrible tragedy of dynastic collapse often viewed the courtesans' fate as a reminder of their own helpless situation, and even as an extension of their own fate. Perhaps it was this inspiration that led the poet Wu Wei-yeh in the 1650s to produce a flood of new poems centering on the changing lives of courtesans, most

notably "The Song of an Old Courtesan from Lin-huai" (1655). In this
work a revealing statement on the woman reflects the poet's view of himself in old age: "This year every strand of the old lady's hair has turned
gray, / All alone, anguished, she witnesses each rise and fall of human
events."[50]

That the Ming loyalists could see their fates reflected in a courtesan's is
one evidence of respect; even more revealing is the fact that the precari-
ousness of the courtesan's fate could become for them a general metaphor
for dynastic rise and fall itself.[51] Yü Huai begins his *Pan-ch'iao tsa-chi*
with an analogy between his story of the Ch'in-huai courtesans and that
of "the rise and fall" of the Ming.[52] Wang Shih-chen (1634–1711) in his
"Miscellaneous Poems on the Ch'in-huai" laments the sad experiences of
the courtesans as an expression of his longing for the lost country.[53] In his
poem addressed to a certain courtesan, the young poet-hero Hsia Wan-
ch'un (1631–47) elaborates on the striking contrast between the glorious
past and the desolate present, focusing on the tragic passing of the courtesan culture.[54] K'ung Shang-jen in his *Peach Blossom Fan* announces in
the prologue that the purpose of his play is to depict "the rise and fall
of the dynasty" (*hsing-wang*) through a story of "union and separation"
(*li-ho*).[55] And as we shall see in a later chapter of this book, in his *tz'u*
poetry Ch'en Tzu-lung turns his lover Liu Shih into a symbol of the Ming.
If we pursue all the metaphorical implications of the courtesan in the Ming
loyalists' works, what appears to be a mere literary device is seen in fact
to be based on a real-life conviction: the courtesan has become a mediator
between love and loyalism.

THREE

Ch'en Tzu-lung
and the Woman Poet
Liu Shih

Literature produced by Ch'en Tzu-lung's circle of friends in Sung-chiang vindicates our belief that accomplished courtesans in the seventeenth century had much more freedom and higher status than women of earlier times. Liu Shih began her own rise as a young female artist and courtesan in Sung-chiang around 1632. Ch'en Tzu-lung and other literati there—chief among them Sung Cheng-yü, Li Ts'un-wo, and Li Wen—admired her literary learning as well as her fine poetry and calligraphy and apparently came to look upon her as a peer and political ally. The fact that several portraits of her were made by Ming–Ch'ing literati painters is proof of her standing among her male contemporaries.[1] In any case, as Ch'en Yin-k'o has meticulously documented in his three-volume biography of Liu Shih, no one who came in touch with her seemed to escape being captivated by her.

Liu Shih's beginnings are obscure. The problem is compounded by the fact that she changed names several times before her marriage to Ch'ien Ch'ien-i in 1641, around which time she began to assume the name Shih, with a style name Ju-shih (*LJS*, 1:17–37). During her years in Sung-chiang, she had apparently used several different names—for example, Ying-lien (Pitying My Reflected Image), Yün-chüan (Cloud-Beauty), Ch'an-chüan

(Loveliness), Liu Yin (Liu the Hermit). Her childhood in particular was cloaked in mystery, and today no one seems to know much about her early life. According to Ch'en Yin-k'o, Liu Shih was first a maidservant (under the name Yang Ai) working in a courtesans' quarter, Kuei-chia-yüan, in Sheng-tse. Then, during her early teens she became a concubine of the retired prime minister Chou Tao-teng in Wu-chiang. A favorite with Chou, Liu Shih eventually incurred the jealousy of other concubines in the same household, who maliciously implicated her in a sex scandal. As a result, the fifteen-year-old Liu Shih was banished from the Chou family (LJS, 1:39–53).

That same year, 1632, Liu Shih settled in Sung-chiang, Ch'en Tzu-lung's hometown. The Sung-chiang prefecture was a center of cultural activity in the late Ming; it "shared with Soochow an economic prosperity" based mainly on silk and cotton textile industries.[2] Sung-chiang was also called Yün-chien. In literature, it was known for its Yün-chien School of Poetry, comparable to the Sung-chiang School of Painting in art. Indeed, few places could boast so many famous scholars, poets, painters, and calligraphers.[3] Thus, on arriving in Sung-chiang, Liu Shih was surrounded by the most enlightened and brilliant minds of her time. Although she knew the humiliation of poverty, she also had had the privilege of being thoroughly trained in poetry and the arts under Prime Minister Chou, and she possessed the kind of talent one needed to make one's way into high social and literary spheres. One of Ch'en Tzu-lung's friends, Sung Cheng-pi (1618–67), expressed his admiration for Liu Shih's extraordinary demeanor in a preface to his own poem on the courtesan. His views reflect the Sung-chiang scholars' (especially Ch'en Tzu-lung's) attitude toward Liu Shih:

> Ta-tsun [Ch'en Tzu-lung] and I were out boating in the Ch'iu-t'ang Lake. The boat was our shelter against the storm outside, which reminded us of what Tu Fu said in his "Songs on Mei-p'i."[4] Among us there was the Collator [Courtesan][5] who had just left the former Prime Minister's home in Wu-chiang to begin her wanderings in the world. Whatever she said was distinguished by deep feeling and vigorous conviction, absolutely different from the usual womanly talk. . . . After many drinks, Ch'en Tzu-lung asked me to compose a song right there. [LJS, 1:48]

At this time, Ch'en Tzu-lung, aged twenty-four, was already a renowned poet and leader of the literary society Chi-she in Sung-chiang, which served as a local branch of the famous Fu-she. Like many other intellectuals of the late Ming, Ch'en and his friends sensed that China was in the midst of a crisis which threatened the survival of the reigning dynasty and indeed of Chinese civilization itself. Whether they spoke as poets or social critics, the idea of achieving a true cultural and political restoration was never far from their minds. In fact, the name of their society, Chi (a term taken from the *I-ching*), means "seeds," the seeds of the restoration of classical learning.[6] For these self-conscious scholars and poets, saving civilization was not only a response to political problems, but also a reaction to the degradation of the educational system in the late Ming. In an attempt to restore the ideal civilization of the past, these scholar-poets advocated returning to the ancient spirit of prose and poetry. To them a poet should be not only talented, but also socially and politically oriented, especially when the country's civilization is at stake.[7] Their efforts at integrating literature, culture, and politics are such as to merit the name renaissance, for, as with the postmedieval European Renaissance, a rediscovery and reinterpretation of forgotten antiquity were at the root of it all.[8]

An important aspect of this renaissance was the gradual liberation of women and men's changing attitude toward women, as discussed earlier. Parallels to the English and European Renaissance should not be dismissed as mere coincidence. Many contemporary Western scholars, such as Linda Woodbridge, have attempted to locate the origins of modern feminism in the Renaissance and regard Renaissance works as early landmarks in the literature concerning women authors and readers.[9] In our context, Liu Shih's example should provide an excellent ground for such comparative speculation—especially with regard to such issues as man's relation to woman, the woman poet's view of herself, and the role of literary convention and originality.

Compared to her Western counterparts, Liu Shih was fortunate in one respect: her poetic vocation did not arouse resistance on the part of her male literati friends. According to Sandra Gilbert and Susan Gubar, verse writing in the West was traditionally considered a "holy vocation," and since women could not be priests, they were often denied the opportunity of becoming lyric poets.[10] Similarly, Margaret Homans argues that women are often treated as silent objects rather than creative poets in the English tradition.[11] In fact, some even claimed that *woman poet* is "a contradiction in terms."[12] Therefore, Gilbert and Gubar concluded that in the English-speaking world when people say "women writers" they usually mean "women novelists" like Jane Austen, Charlotte Brontë, George Eliot.[13] Yet, the reverse is true of traditional China—anthologies have recorded the accomplishments of numerous distinguished women poets since the Han dynasty, though there were no notable women novelists until this century. Indeed, beginning with Ts'ai Yen (born ca. 178), Hsüeh T'ao (768–831), Li Ch'ing-chao (1084–ca. 1151), Chu Shu-chen (fl. ca. 1170), and culminating in Liu Shih and other Ming–Ch'ing woman poets, Chinese lyric poetry seems to have been in good part associated with feminine sensibility. This is especially true of the *tz'u* genre, in which the relationship between men and women has always been a central topic. Moreover, the female persona was a device often adopted by male poets to express their deep concern for women's problems and feelings.[14] As I mentioned earlier, from the seventeenth century on, an increasing number of women (especially courtesans) became involved in prolonged poetic exchanges with men. Alternating poems, like those exchanged between Liu Shih and Ch'en Tzu-lung, function much as letters, expressing the reciprocity of private feelings and revealing the particular immediacy of a personal relationship. No doubt this partly explains why traditional Chinese men never considered poetry by women "somehow problematic in its essence," as was apparently the case in the English-speaking world.[15] In fact, men in the Ming and Ch'ing often promoted women poets and were extremely enthusiastic in recognizing female talents. For example, Ch'en Tzu-lung encouraged Liu Shih to publish her collection of poems, *Wu-yin ts'ao* (1638), and it was he who wrote the following complimentary preface to the collection:

> I have studied poetry of the Han and Wei, the Six Dynasties, the Early T'ang, High T'ang, and Late T'ang. The ways of creating landscape poetry and lofty expressions, and the ways of employing beautiful and flowery words, are indeed infinitely varied according to individual talents. . . . Thus, I can see that in the area of description, no one was as great as Pao Chao [ca. 414–66] and Hsieh Ling-yün [385–433]. . . . In feeling, none were as profound as Ts'ao Chih [192–232]. . . . And in literary expression, none were as accomplished as Tu Fu [712–70]. As for poets of later generations, they were either lacking in the ability to create refined expressions of emotions, or unable to write "poems celebrating objects" (*yung-wu*) with profound implications—being largely misled by the principle of descriptive similitude. . . . But now, these poems by Lady Liu: how they are pure, creative, and far-reaching, impressively learned yet subtly uninhibited. . . . Indeed she can rank in the first class of poets. Since my early childhood, I have been fond of writing verse, and have seen numerous changes in the world. I realized that most contemporary works are about trifling experiences, not necessarily containing significant ideas. It was only after [Li Meng-yang, 1473–1529] of Pei-ti established his school of poetry, and after the gentlemen of Chi-nan [16] attained profundity in literary pursuits that the idea of "gentleness and elegance" (*wen-ya*) came to be cultivated and poems of lively imagination began to be composed.

But still there are few works that are genuinely spontaneous and elegantly beautiful. . . . Finally, in my thinly-populated hometown, there emerged several distinguished authors who valued poetry of great eloquence and beauty. Meanwhile Lady Liu came from the inner-chamber (*ch'ing-so*), and by sheer chance, her style of poetry turned out to be quite similar to those of ours. Isn't this rare? Isn't this rare? [*LJS*, 1:111–13]

For all its profound implications, Ch'en Tzu-lung's preface is also a statement of self-definition on behalf of his Yün-chien School of Poetry, a school to which Liu Shih zealously claimed allegiance. Ch'en's statement expresses his personal conviction that true poetry can be reborn only through a return to its origin, though returning to the past does not mean slavish imitation of the past. This conviction grows out of the notion that the past, being the storehouse of so much of the civilization's wisdom, should be regarded as an enduring authority from which individual creativity must necessarily draw inspiration. The members of the Yün-chien school (itself an offshoot of the Chi-she) saw their poetic theory as satisfying a broadly defined moral and intellectual need typical of late-Ming literati—that a return to the ideal model of past literature was the only means of saving the contemporary society from further deterioration. Thus, their goal was not to practice imitation for its own sake, but rather to maintain a balance between individual creativity and tradition. Indeed, what T. S. Eliot said a few decades ago about himself and some like-minded writers is reminiscent of this view: "We do not imitate, we are changed; and our work is the work of the changed man; we have not borrowed, we have been quickened, and we become bearers of a tradition." [17]

To Ch'en Tzu-lung and Liu Shih (and their Sung-chiang friends), who saw themselves as called upon to restore the glories of Chinese civilization, the question was, What literary models from the past should be used in order to renew the vitality of poetry in the present? And in his preface to Liu Shih's collected poems, Ch'en Tzu-lung revealed that he chose his poetic models carefully—that is, Ts'ao Chih for expression of feeling, Pao Chao and Hsieh Ling-yün for description, Tu Fu for literary articulation. However, generic discrimination remains a central concern for Ch'en Tzu-lung. Implied in his preface is the fact that he clearly distinguished the tradition of Ancient Style poetry (*ku-shih*) from that of Regulated verse (*lü-shih*): whereas his model poet for Ancient Style poetry seemed to be the Six Dynasties poet Ts'ao Chih, his model poet in the Regulated verse was the High T'ang poet Tu Fu. And as I explain later in this book, Ch'en had models for his *tz'u* poetry as well. In view of his critical evaluation of various past models in different genres and different ages, it is reasonable for us to conclude that the conventional view of the Yün-chien poets as being primarily in the High T'ang camp is both simplistic and misleading.

Under the influence of Ch'en Tzu-lung (or perhaps as a result of their mutual influence), Liu Shih chose the same poets (all male) as models for her verse writing. In sharp contrast to Western women poets, who were frustrated because of "the lack of a viable female tradition,"[18] Liu Shih would have had no problem finding a long tradition of female poets—she could have easily chosen Hsüeh T'ao and Li Ch'ing-chao as role models. But it was clearly not Liu Shih's goal to celebrate the "feminine" tradition in poetry; she preferred instead to erase the traditional boundaries between male and female poets, between masculine and feminine images. Liu not only had studied a range of male models, but also went so far as to reverse the gender roles on which Chinese love poetry was conventionally based, as in her extraordinary poem "Nan Lo-shen *fu*" (*Fu* on the Male Spirit of the Lo River), written as a love poem for Ch'en Tzu-lung.

From the time of the "Nine Songs" (ca. fourth century B.C.), it had been conventional for a poet to woo a goddess,[19] either as an inheritance from shamanistic ritual or as a political allegory expressing one's loyalty to a king. But the image of the Goddess of the Lo River as an ideal woman was created by the third-century poet Ts'ao Chih, who happened to be the model poet for both Liu Shih and Ch'en Tzu-lung. In his "Lo-shen *fu*" (*Fu* on the Goddess of the Lo), Ts'ao Chih tells the story of his romantic encounter with a beautiful goddess who miraculously emerges from the banks of the Lo River. In his *fu* (a genre traditionally noted for panoramic and dazzling images), the poet gives an elaborate account of the charms of the goddess—her body "soars lightly like a startled swan"; her manner is "quiet" and "wonderfully enchanting"; "gold and kingfisher hairpins" adorn her head; and she is like a "lotus flower topping the green wave."[20] The description of the goddess is so enticing and persuasive that many Chinese critics believe the story was based on some actual love affair of the poet, despite the poet's reassurance in the preface that the poem is about the real goddess of the Lo. Some critics, refusing to accept the story on its own terms, "have attempted to impose an allegorical interpretation on the poem, seeing it as a declaration of loyalty addressed by the poet to his brother the emperor."[21]

What is unique about Liu Shih's "*Fu* on the Male Spirit of the Lo River" is not merely that the traditional gender roles are reversed—for now a woman is courting a male god—but rather that the poet explicitly states in her preface that the poem is about her feeling for a young man whom she loves and respects:

> My friend's sensitive spirit is as broad as the blue sea, and his mind dwells on profound beauty. He is regarded by other intellectuals as extremely eloquent; he is distinguished by marvelous virtue and fine perception. Whatever he does, he will not stop at fulfilling the requirement, and indeed, his mind is concerned about the pursuit of perfection. Occasionally he came to me to have a chat when he appeared a bit gloomy and dismal—as if coming forth out of the water in a most graceful fashion. I am touched by his elegant beauty, and have obtained insight into his wondrous spirit. Then, I realized that the ancients' writings were often inspired by fancy and emptiness, not necessarily like my experience which is genuine and authentic. Therefore, I have recorded this matter, trying not to stray from the truth. Sincerely respecting my friend's request, I have composed this *fu*. [*LJS*, 1:133]

Unlike Ts'ao Chih, who saw the goddess unexpectedly as he chanced to cross the Lo River, Liu Shih sees herself as a questing lover who single-mindedly seeks the river god. In sharp contrast to Ts'ao Chih's goddess, who simply appears in the beginning of the poem, Liu's Male Spirit has to be "wooed" and sought after. Thus, Liu's poem opens with a quest scene in which the poet goes out in a boat in search of the beloved:

> The setting sun sends forth its brilliant light,
> The blustering whirlwind swirls into the distance.
> Then things are concealed by the pouring rain,
> My mind is confused, like ripples running crisscross.
> I gaze upon the beautiful water, glimmering and bright,
> The radiant, inky-blue waves are widely apart.
> Tides rise and fall, twining and curving,
> Then comes a truly tranquil flow, refined and pure.
> I know this must be the dwelling of the pure eminent one:
> Let the exalted guests get across!
> The water is surging and overflowing,
> The boat in the dark, submerged by swelling waves.   [ll. 1–12]

The river god, deeply touched by the sincerity of the poet, slowly appears:

> Startled, I see his beautiful form descending lightly,
> Saddened by the gloomy, dismal river scene,
> Swiftly he turns his eyes all around,
> Then, slowly he approaches me in tiny steps.
> In splendor, he is truly unsurpassed,
> In manner, uniquely enchanting.

> He is enticingly beautiful, yet gracefully gentle,
> His spirited form glowing with radiant light.
> He lifts his body in the midst of the fragrant mist,
> Traversing the cold waves in an exquisite and quiet manner.   [ll. 43–52]

The beauty of this Male Spirit is awesome: he is as splendid as Ts'ao Chih's goddess. In fact, he is almost identical to the Goddess of the Lo River—his movement is just as light and graceful; his manner is quiet, and his pose demure; he walks on the perfumed waves with a similarly radiant warmth shining from his body. However, although firmly grounded in conventional rhetoric, Liu's poem has acquired a new poetic voice through a simple reversal of gender roles. Heretofore male authors celebrated the beautiful eyes, mouth, and smiles of women, but never the other way around. And traditional love poetry by women seemed to be always directed *to* men, rather than being *about* their appearance.[22] Now, Liu Shih has created the image of a male beloved who is distinguished for his physical beauty as well as other, inner qualities. This poetic image of male beauty viewed from the woman's perspective suffices in itself to pose the problem of the male–female relationship in a new way. Moreover, when Liu Shih reveals in her preface that her love poem is not a moral or political allegory—although she is sure that some conservative critics will read it that way—her new rhetoric declares itself to be based on a willing acceptance of love sans allegory, if only to be achieved by a symbolic analogy of the Male Spirit and her beloved.

When we look at Ch'en Tzu-lung's "Ts'ai-lien *fu*" (*Fu* on picking the lotus)—a poem written perhaps some time after Liu Shih's *fu* on the god of the Lo—we find a symbolism of love that likewise discourages a moral or political interpretation. Ch'en has apparently borrowed his poem's title from Wang Po's (ca. 650–76) "Ts'ai-lien *fu*." But unlike Wang Po, who indicates in his preface that his poem is intended as a political allegory (as an expression of his loyalty to his king),[23] Ch'en Tzu-lung explains in his preface that the subject of his *fu* is a female, portrayed figuratively as a lotus, of whom he has become enamored:

> By nature I am quiet and withdrawn, and I long for pristine beauty. From time to time I touched her fragrant heart, and my inspiration suddenly took on myriad forms. At dawn by the lake in Mo-ling [Nanking], and in the evening by the banks of Heng-t'ang, I see her beautiful figure like graceful jade, erect, receiving the fragrant gift of the breeze. Even her loving and gentle manner, and her skills in singing freely and dancing extravagantly, do not suffice to fully capture her noble demeanor or to express her moral chastity. The short pieces by Chiang Yen [444–505] and Hsiao Kang [503–51] origi-

nate in folk songs long ago.[24] Chanting Tzu-an's [Wang Po's] unrestrained verse can hardly give satisfaction to my feelings. Looking into his allegorical meanings—is that not sheer drudgery? Thus, although I do not have much to add by way of expressing profound beauty, I have composed this *fu*.

In the poem proper, Ch'en Tzu-lung plays the part of a persistent seeker of the lotus (Liu Shih), which is on the surface merely in keeping with the traditional image of the male lover. However, under the pretense of composing a conventional *fu* on love (written from the male perspective), Ch'en has in fact devised some important aesthetic strategies that allow him to give the reader access to his secret self. In the poem we have observed a crucial interplay between the traditional rhetoric of love and a new poetics of personal allusion—a combination in keeping with the Ming literati's valuation of intimate personal relations. Ch'en Tzu-lung's "*Fu* on Picking the Lotus," an unusually long poem (166 lines), reveals much that is relevant to the poet's art and life:

What a bright, clear, blazingly hot summer,
Lofty clouds linger in the fair morning.
My mind reaches far to the meandering streams,
I embrace the pure softness of the gentle breeze.   4
Supremely beautiful are the shallow rapids,
The wandering ripples overflow and move toward the flats.
Across the winding river shore,
I gaze tenderly upon the distant, wind-tossed blossoms.   8
The gloomy marsh is surrounded by the limpid cold,
My feeling reaches out to the margin of the green banks.
Vast and expansive are the distant rivers on the plain,
Reeds and rushes, blended with each other, all look alike.   12
Beautifully cloaked in mingled fragrance,
I've been nourished by the sweet angelica.
Standing tall in their midst is this intoxicating plant,
Delighting herself in the enchanting cool mist.   16
Oh! how pure and lovely is its elegant pose,
Standing between the sand and the waves, it radiates beauty.
Stirring dark ripples,
This fragrant jade-plant is so fine and dazzling.   20
This aquatic plant grows at the shore of the Li River,
With admirably chaste countenance, she is gentle and graceful as well.
Fleetingly gleaming into the hazy distance,
Her refined, resplendent lines are unrivaled.   24
I traverse the marsh to pluck this fragrant plant,
But in the distance, I don't know where she is.

What does she look like? Scintillating and bright,
Glimmering and abundantly charming.   28
In gleaming brilliance,
She is splendid and gentle.
Beautiful without gaudiness,
Proud without insolence.   32
Her colorful patterns are wonderful,
Her refined charm is exceptional.
With graceful bearing,
She displays her sublime beauty.   36
First buds appear unfolding their spectacle,
Then in the early breeze, blossoms come into view.
Closely linked together,
These blossoms are most painterly images.   40
Their shadows are reflected on the expansive river,
While they frolic with the water.
A towering array of attractive figures
Appear in morning brilliance, leaving behind them a dark hue.   44
Extensive are the bright, red petals,
Their slender, silken profile recalls the form of a goddess.
These splendid blossoms of silk are grown on wild islets;
I'm distressed to see their crimson visages turn away from me.   48
With their jade stems soaking in the purple ripples,
These enchanting, elegant figures face each other silently.
At times they turn about to display their dazzling beauty,
But I suspect they are trying to entice yet elude me.   52
I receive their fragrant hearts in the distant eve,
Longing for their love, I give them a girdle-jade.
I'm afraid their hidden fragrance will be difficult to woo,
But my thoughts trickle on—they seem forever present.   56
They truly know how to bewitch me.
I'd like to dress myself up, and embark on a long journey.
Thereupon I instruct my people to be calm and gentle;
We preen ourselves in exquisite adornments,   60
Fix the beautifully patterned oars,
And set the painted boat in motion.
Then, with brocade sails,
The boat glides over the clear river.   64
Fragrant flowers are dense and mingled,
Their silk sleeves ripple gracefully.
Gently, gently, glides the boat;
Lightly, lightly, ply the oars.   68
They move back and forth in unison,

Delicately and smoothly,
Amidst rejoicing fish and humming bees—
It's indescribable. 72
Then comes the frightening surge of a whirlwind,
Shattering the jade pool with a swirling force.
The oars move together, emerging and submerging;
Having reaped so many, sometimes I have to give them up. 76
My heart is deeply grieved,
The radiance of the lake vies with the distant sky.
The green boat moves slowly forward,
And lingers by the cluster of flowers. 80
Washed clean and fresh in the clear mist,
The exquisite blossoms flaunt a lingering charm.
I feel the cool breeze along the path,
And pluck these secluded beauties to look them over. 84
I brush the rich red petals, and they shine brightly,
I ponder as I am enchanted by their shimmering loveliness.
Green water rushes on to the serene islet,
Slowly breaking up the purple duckweed. 88
The entwined fibrous stems cling together,
They dip their pale wrists into the water.
The mandarin ducks are frightened by the magnolia oars,
The sleeping egrets rest quietly. 92
They drop their bright earrings into the Hsiao and Hsiang,
And present me with selinia in profusion.
I caress the sparkling dark ripples,
The mingled fragrance entrances me. 96
I touch the jelled pearls of the fragrant plant,
Like the moist dew at Mount Three Hazards.
Gazing at the dimmed shadow of the jade ripples,
I ascend the clear and cold Divine Tortoise. 100
Plucking some stems, I cast a side-glance,
I caress them, as if my own.
Breaking them off is not my intent,
But I fear they may soon grow old and be abandoned. 104
In my heart I understand what they desire,
As I hold these vermillion flowers tenderly in admiration.
The fragile leaves half unfurled,
Their fibrous lines lightly frolicking. 108
I admire these graceful emerald leaves;
Clinging to the fragrant water, they support one another.
Gazing upon their own reflected images, these majestic flowers
Enshroud their companions on the other side. 112

With their enchanting smiles blocked by the other side of the bank,
These blooming flowers are not known to the world.
They conceal fallen pollen in their light sleeves.
I pity them, for their fragrant hearts are disturbed.   116
I cast a sidelong look at their elegant carriage,
Their delicate hearts are shivering with cold.
I pluck them by the bright riverside,
Deep vermillion petals floating on the pool.   120
Layers of fine jade-seeds are enwrapped,
Like a cluster of lovely pearls.
Each pearly seed is individually swathed,
Holding their pure green bodies, I find them more fragrant than the   124
    orchid.
The gleaming seed-cores are fine and smooth,
I peel off their jade-skin, the sap hard to dry.
My teeth are replete with the lovely smell of the sap,
As I look at those fragrant seeds at the evening meal.   128
I think of the misery they went through,
Melancholy and sorrow in the midst of such goodness.
Touched by the emerald hearts of these linked beauties,
I express my hidden feelings to them.   132
I entrust my grief to the lotus seeds,
Swaying with the blossoms dangling in the gusting wind.
Suddenly, their garments are entangled by the spine,
No more red luster on their wet silk coats.   136
Broken white lotus roots are like sliced clouds,
Magnificent is their well-formed beauty.
Wind-tossed filaments are blown afar.
But they are deeply embraced in my heart.   140
They cast a strong fragrance to fill my bosom,
Glad that we may form our nuptial tie in our prime years.
I cut the mermaid's gauge to cloak the lotus seeds,
Harboring lovesickness in great abundance.   144
At dusk, I embark to the northern ford,
I silently depart in the midst of a light song.
My boat splashes their slim reflected images at night,
I long for their slender, elegant beauty.   148
A pure mist is drawn from the great void;
The lotus blossoms emit their lingering charm.
I think of the Goddess of the K'un River,
Passing the heavenly cliff, I repose a while.   152
Indeed I forget my feelings, and my burden dwindles,
All cast off as I face her loveliness.

I gaze upon this lingering beauty,
Enraptured by her serene virtue.   156
I feel sad as I leave off plucking,
In the cutting autumn wind, the blossoms will close for a long while.

Envoi:
I cross the five lakes, azure waves undulating,
I make through the purple ripples, feeling anguished within.   160
The road to the lotus pond is difficult and long,
My longing for the Fair One is immeasurable.
What did I go to pick? The Lotus of the Low Gleams.
On my return, what did I sing? "The Melody Without End."   164
What limit was there to my joy?
But, now, how deep my sorrow is, like the autumn frost.[25]

Like Liu Shih's "*Fu* on the Male Spirit of the Lo River," this poem
by Ch'en Tzu-lung is modeled after Ts'ao Chih's "*Fu* on the Goddess of
the Lo," though with significant modifications. The central symbol of the
poem is of course the lotus, which symbolizes purity and perfection but as
a rhetorical figure is essentially no different from the goddess. For in Ts'ao
Chih's poem the goddess has been compared to the lotus: "She flames
like the lotus flower topping the green waves."[26] And, conversely, Ch'en
Tzu-lung's lotus is referred to as a goddess (line 151) or a mermaid (line
143). Like Ts'ao's goddess, Ch'en's lotus flowers "dip their pale wrists
into the water" (line 90). And again, like Ts'ao's goddess, Ch'en's lotus
willingly drops her earrings into the water as a pledge of her good faith
(line 93) and in direct response to the girdle-jade she has received from
the poet (line 54).[27] Indeed, reading about this deeply impassioned lotus,
one is inevitably reminded of Ts'ao's goddess, who makes the following
moving confession of love:

> No way to express my unworthy love,
> I give you this bright earring from south of the Yangtze.
> Though I dwell in the Great Shadow down under the waters,
> My heart will forever belong to you, my prince![28]

But despite such similarities to Ts'ao Chih's *fu*, Ch'en Tzu-lung's poem
exhibits not only a different mixture of rhetoric and realism, but also
a different predilection for the private symbology of personal allusions,
whereby the notion of a masked autobiography has gained a large place.
In Ch'en's case (as in Liu Shih's *fu*), the rhetorical interplay between the
preface and the poem proper plays a vital role in balancing the referential and the metaphorical elements in poetry—where the preface speaks of

factual data, the poem becomes the best vehicle for revealing emotional truth.[29] In other words, the preface and the poem represent different yet complementary ways of speaking the truth. If Ch'en's *fu* is made meaningful and emotionally effective by the use of symbolic associations, then his preface can be said to serve as a referential nucleus that guides readers to the poem's intended, though largely implicit, meaning.

In his preface, Ch'en Tzu-lung writes about a refined and virtuous beauty whom he has been meeting in Mo-ling and Heng-t'ang, saying that "from time to time" he "touched her fragrant heart," such that his "inspiration . . . took on myriad forms." Although he does not actually spell out Liu Shih's name, the identification of the woman in question with Liu Shih would have been unquestionable for contemporary readers. First, by late Ming times, the place-name Heng-t'ang had become a specific term referring to the courtesans' quarters in the Wu-Yüeh area, as may be seen in the numerous references to it made by the literati (*LJS*, 1:57). Thus, in characteristic late-Ming style, Ch'en Tzu-lung uses "Heng-t'ang" to allude to Liu Shih, a distinguished courtesan coming from the Kuei-chia-yüan quarter in Sheng-tse. Besides, it has become a current practice for seventeenth-century poets to use the lotus-picking theme to refer metaphorically to courtesans—for example, in 1651 Wu Wei-yeh says of the famous courtesan Ch'en Yüan-yüan, "In former life she must have been a lotus-picking girl / Outside her door, an expanse of water—the embankment of Heng T'ang."[30] And in Liu Shih's collected works is a piece entitled "Ts'ai-lien ch'ü" (Song of lotus-picking), which contains many images that are similar to those used in Ch'en's *fu*. This greatly substantiates the assumption that Liu's poem was composed as a poetic answer to Ch'en's *fu* on lotus-picking (*LJS*, 1:299). There can be no doubt that Ch'en Tzu-lung's *fu* was written for Liu Shih.

But the point is that what may be seen as factual and tangibly referential in Ch'en's preface becomes imagistic and symbolic in the poem itself, where meaning is derived from the associative power of the poet's aesthetic imagination and private symbols. The way the poetic images and symbols have acquired meaning will no doubt enrich our understanding of the poet's life, but that does not mean that the symbolic imagery can be completely reduced to literal, fixed, specific meanings. In fact, the richly suggestive power of Ch'en's private symbology, when used to evoke crucial concrete circumstances, only helps to reinforce the basic tenet of the Chinese hermeneutic strategy, namely, that a poem's meaning can never be exhausted in any single reading, for reading is an endless unfolding of the symbolic meaning of the text. The imagistic density of the poem encourages us to constantly unweave its immensely complex textural web.

In my reading of Ch'en's "*Fu* on Picking the Lotus," I have found a particularly effective poetic device—what I call the symbology of names. That is to say, in the context of his poem, Ch'en turns actual personal names and place-names into symbolic images, thus establishing a magical connection between life and art.[31] Of course, this device had already been used in earlier Chinese poetry. But, as Ch'en Yin-k'o has observed, only in the late Ming did it become such a prominent poetics of "secret communication" (*LJS*, 1:17). And Ch'en Tzu-lung's "Ts'ai-lien *fu*" can be said to be an ideal example of this symbology of names—from the very beginning of the *fu*, Liu Shih's name "Yün-chüan" (Cloud-Beauty) is carefully embedded in the text and becomes figurative:

> Lofty clouds [*yün*] linger in the fair morning.
> My mind reaches far to the meandering streams,
> I embrace the pure softness of the gentle breeze.
> Supremely beautiful [*chüan*] are the shallow rapids.   [ll. 2–5]

Indeed, such a dual play of literality and imagination, reality and reverie, clarity and ambiguity runs through the entire poem. On one level, we see the sensual experience of a sexual act narrated figuratively in the poem, with the blossoming lotus serving as a nucleus image of richly erotic significance. The man in a rowboat embarks on a long journey before he finally finds those charming lotus flowers; he plucks the flowers, caresses them, and even peels off "the jade-skin" of their seed-cores to eat them (lines 125–28). The "emerald hearts" of the flowers are "beautiful" (*chüan*), while the "broken lotus roots" are like the sliced "clouds," *yün* (lines 131–38). Just as in Mallarmé's *Le nénuphar blanc* (The white waterlily), the recurrent image of the reflecting pool in Ch'en's poem enhances the centrality of erotic desire.[32] At the very climax of the intimate encounter the lotus flowers are reflected beautifully in the water, as the male boat rower perceives "layers of fine jade-seeds" like "a cluster of lovely pearls" (lines 121–22). It is the reflection of the flowers in the water that recalls the image of the lady: "My boat splashes their slim reflected images at night / I long for their slender, elegant beauty" (lines 147–48). Here again the poet is adopting Liu Shih's name figuratively to create a poetic form of intimacy: to her close friends in Sung-chiang, Liu Shih was known by the name Ying-lien (literally, Pitying My Reflected Image).[33] Thus, Ch'en Tzu-lung's use of the words "ying" (reflected image) and "lien" (pity, love), heightened by the central image of the reflected pool, encourages a reading of the poem that is constantly shifting between reality and fantasy, the tangible and the intangible—a tension that characterizes the erotic experience itself. The elusive (and allusive) powers of such a poetic device go far beyond mere techniques of wordplay.

On another level, the poem can be read as a figurative description of the journey from courtship to marriage, and then from union to separation. The most forceful description of the conjugal bliss occurs halfway through the poem, where the budding love between the man and his beloved is symbolized by pairs of mandarin ducks and sleeping egrets:

> The mandarin ducks are frightened by the magnolia oars,
> The sleeping egrets rest quietly. [ll. 91–92]

The use of conventional love birds as symbols of conjugal love could hardly be said to be original were it not for the fact that the names of these birds are highly personal to the poet himself. For "mandarin ducks" (*Yüan-yang*) and "egrets" (*Chu-yü*) were names of buildings in the Southern Villa (Nan-yüan), where Ch'en Tzu-lung and Liu Shih resided during the peak of their romance in 1635. The Southern Villa, which belonged to Hsü Wu-ching (*LJS*, 1:280), was the site of the Chi-she members' regular literary meetings.

The love relationship between Ch'en and Liu began perhaps as early as 1633, but they did not actually live together until the spring of 1635, at which time the generous Hsü Wu-ching apparently offered them a place called the Southern Chamber (Nan-lou) in the Southern Villa. We may assume that, for various reasons, Ch'en intended to keep the relationship secret from his wife and family. It may be, as the historian Ch'en Yin-k'o has argued, that Ch'en Tzu-lung feared his wife née Chang (being extremely jealous by nature) would object to his taking his real love Liu Shih as a concubine. In fact, earlier in 1633, Ch'en's wife went so far as to obtain for Ch'en Tzu-lung a concubine called Ts'ai, apparently with the purpose of distracting him from Liu. For every action she took, Ch'en's wife seems to have gained the support and permission of Ch'en's grandmother, whom Ch'en Tzu-lung deeply respected.

Whatever the circumstances, the period during which Ch'en and Liu lived together in the Southern Chamber (the spring and summer of 1635) turned out to be the most productive of their literary careers. It is evident that the atmosphere of romantic love was essential to the maturing of these two poetic souls, for during this time they completed their first collections of love poems. Ch'en's was entitled *Chu-yü t'ang chi* (Poems from the Hall of Egrets) and Liu's *Yüan-yang lou tz'u* (Songs from the Chamber of Mandarin Ducks). The titles explain why Ch'en's use of the two love images, the egrets and the mandarin ducks, has acquired a new meaning in poetry, quite different from the conventional stereotyped expression of love. The connotation has moved from "true love" to the "poetry of true love"—the egrets and the mandarin ducks are now the "expression" of the expression of love. But the power of such coded images lies precisely in mingling the conventional meanings with personal secrets, so that they are effective as means of exposure and concealment.

Not only are the place-names endowed with a double (mimetic and symbolic) function, but the apparent inconsistencies of the poem's time frame also bear on these two levels of significance. We are told that the journey begins in the summer, and after it has ended, the man in the boat is afflicted with sorrow, standing "in the harsh autumn wind." If we take the poem to be a figurative description of a sexual act, then it is to be expected that at the end of the "trip" the lover would lament the brevity of his happiness. And, on this level, the poem reflects the functioning rhythm of an erotic experience, which metaphorically starts in a happy summer and ends in a mournful autumn.

When we look into the details of Ch'en's and Liu's lives in 1635, we also gain a realistic perspective for the poem: around autumn of that year Liu Shih left Sung-chiang permanently to return to the courtesans' quarter in Sheng-tse. It seems that some time before that, as was concluded by Ch'en Yin-k'o, Ch'en Tzu-lung's wife actually came to the Southern Villa to force Liu Shih to leave. Unable to resist the pressures, Liu Shih left the Southern Villa and found her own residence somewhere in Sung-chiang before actually leaving the town a few months later. Compared with another renowned courtesan, Tung Pai, Liu Shih obviously did not have fortune on her side, for Tung Pai was well received by Mao Hsiang's wife upon becoming her lover's concubine. Mao Hsiang writes in his *Ying-mei-an i-yü,* "My wife went to bring her back to my house. My mother, on seeing her, took a great fancy to her at once, and so did my wife. Both treated her with special favor."[34]

By way of contrast, Ch'en Tzu-lung's personal circumstances were completely different from Mao Hsiang's. Being poor and as yet undistinguished in his official career (by then he had twice failed the imperial examination), Ch'en had to let Liu Shih go. Conscious of the tragic conditions of his love, Ch'en ends his *fu* with a helpless outburst of anguish:

What limit was there to my joy?
But, now, how deep my sorrow is, like the autumn frost.

After their separation, Liu Shih often made references, implicit and explicit, to Ch'en Tzu-lung's "*Fu* on Picking the Lotus." For example, the following poem referring to Ch'en as the man "in the magnolia boat" is central to the love story I have been attempting to construct:

Where was he?
In the magnolia boat.
Often talking to herself when receiving guests,
Feeling more lost while combing her hair,
This beauty still broods over his charms.   [*LJS*, 1:262]

By engaging in biographical interpretation on this level, I am of course not saying that Ch'en's poem is solely about his life experience. As Octavio Paz writes, "It is clear that an author's life and work are related, but . . . the life does not entirely explain the work, nor does the work explain the life," because "there is something in the work that is not to be found in the author's life, something we call creativity or artistic and literary invention." [35] One of my aims in this book is to explore that "something in the work" which contributes to the enigma and symbolic power of poetry.

Earlier I mentioned that, as a devoted lover and heroic martyr, Ch'en Tzu-lung's life dramatically marks the intersection of love and loyalism, the two main concerns of late-Ming literati. But, more important, his poetic works, too, are characterized by these two concerns. My point is that for other poets, life and work do not necessarily complement each other so well. A case in point is the Sung patriot Wen T'ien-hsiang: he had several amorous relationships with women, but his poetry, lacking an emphasis on romantic love, is noted primarily for its heroic spirit. Conversely, Liu Shih was known for her resistance activities and bravery, but the subject of her poetry is largely restricted to love and tender emotions. [36] Obviously Liu Shih's patriotic spirit has influenced (and been influenced by) Ch'en Tzu-lung, but her poetic works—at least those that are extant—seem to reveal nothing of her loyalist sentiment. The historian Ch'en Yin-k'o thus had to rely heavily on Ch'ien Ch'ien-i's later poetry for his research on Liu Shih's political involvement following the fall of the Ming. [37] Clearly Ch'en Tzu-lung, compared with other poets, was a unique figure, one whose work explores life's potential meaning and scope to the uttermost.

The remaining chapters in this book focus on Ch'en Tzu-lung's poems on love and his later poems on loyalism. Two genres will be considered in this connection: *tz'u* songs and *shih* poetry. As I have already suggested, generic choice has long exerted a decisive influence upon Chinese literature, and it reflects most powerfully the individual poet's conception of tradition and his own self-definition. On the one hand, a genre does not exist in isolation; it is always related to other genres in the tradition that are either its distant ancestors or rivals. On the other hand, a poet's generic choice reflects his own attempts, consciously or unconsciously, to capture some inner values that are uniquely personal. Sometimes, in the case of a strong poet, the personal style can be more powerful than conventional rules, so that eventually his own style will become a generic code for others to appropriate.[38] To a large extent, the whole late-Ming debate of the T'ang style versus the Sung style, and of *shih* versus *tz'u,* is no more than a competition of generic expectations. Both in his poems and his works of literary criticism (especially remarkable for their breadth and variety), Ch'en Tzu-lung strives to establish, or revive, a lyric code based on true and durable emotions.[39]

PART 2

The Poetry of Love

FOUR

Tz'u Songs
of Passion

The poetic genres with which Ch'en
Tzu-lung and Liu Shih experimented together were extraordinarily diversified, as much by their content as by their form. But the *tz'u* (song lyric) form was by far the most important genre for them throughout their relationship, and it accounts for the largest part of their love poems. This is not surprising, if we consider the fact that from the very beginning the *tz'u* was thought to be the proper genre for representing the most delicate aspect of human emotions. In sharp contrast to the more elevated and authoritative *shih,* the *tz'u* was generally dominated by the theme of romantic love, as has been noted by James J. Y. Liu.[1] As Anne Birrell has observed, though in a different context, "The idea that Chinese poetry does not deal with love is a myth."[2] Especially in early *tz'u,* where the intensity of emotional content constitutes its primary generic quality, romantic love inevitably became a special concern for Chinese poets. Thus, it seems perfectly natural that Ch'en Tzu-lung and Liu Shih would choose the *tz'u* form as the primary vehicle for expressing their private feelings for each other.

Viewed historically, however, the two poets' choice of genre was quite exceptional. The *tz'u* form, which reached its glorious peak in the Sung dynasty, had been in constant decline during the Yüan and Ming, and for more than three hundred years it was viewed almost as a dying genre. By the late Ming, it was extremely rare for a poet to devote himself to the writing of *tz'u.* The reason *tz'u* had fallen out of favor was that as a genre it had gradually come to be overshadowed by its "neighboring" genre and generic rival, the *ch'ü*. The words *ch'ü* and *tz'u* did not originally designate poetic forms at all but were borrowed terms whose root meaning is more or less "song lyric." The *ch'ü* as a genre arose from drama; and *ch'ü* cast in the form of dramatic arias were called *chü-ch'ü*. But as a pure verse form, they were called *san-ch'ü*.[3] As with *tz'u*, the musical element in *ch'ü* is intrinsic to the genre both technically and aesthetically: the *ch'ü*, too, is characterized by lines of unequal length and a set of prescribed tones and tunes. But compared with *tz'u*, it allows a far more extensive use of colloquial language. Moreover, the structure of a *ch'ü* is more flexible than that of a *tz'u* because the poet, while composing a *ch'ü* to a tune, is allowed to add "padding words" (*ch'en-tzu*) to extend the length of a line, sometimes considerably. Other technical requirements of the *ch'ü* genre are highly complex and varied, often further complicated by the use of the "song-sequence" (*t'ao-shu*). A *t'ao-shu* is a series of songs set to the same mode, arranged according to a special sequence-pattern prescribed by the mode. The song-sequence allows a poet to compose a string of arias on a particular theme, which is singable and could form part of a lyric play. Judging from his few extant works in the genre (*CTLS*, 2:619–21), we know that Ch'en Tzu-lung was skillful in composing the song-sequence style of the *ch'ü*, a form extremely popular with late-Ming literati.

It would be misleading to claim that under the powerful influence of the *ch'ü*, the Ming poets had stopped writing *tz'u* poetry. Individual collections of *tz'u* as well as anthologies and critical texts on *tz'u* continued to be published in the Ming,[4] but according to Ch'en Tzu-lung few Ming poets produced *tz'u* poems that were distinguished by graceful writing and intense lyrical sensibility, qualities that used to characterize the *tz'u* genre. In fact, the early Ch'ing poet Wang Shih-chen said that the Ming *tz'u* suffered from a general lack of "profound aesthetic sense" except for Ch'en Tzu-lung's "elegant and beautiful" *tz'u* (*THTP*, 1:684–85). Most critics attributed the problems of the Ming *tz'u* to the literati's lack of clarity concerning the generic qualities of *tz'u*, for Ming *tz'u* often read more like the colloquial and straightforward *ch'ü* than the traditionally more elegant and refined *tz'u* (*THTP*, 2:711, 3:2461). Several Ming authors of *tz'u* songs were primarily *ch'ü* writers—for example, both Yang Shen and T'ang Hsien-tsu were well-known *ch'ü* poets who only occasionally experimented with *tz'u*. Thus, critics felt that the *tz'u* poems of these *ch'ü* specialists were not really *tz'u*, either in terms of syntax or rhythmical structure.

Another reason for the general confusion about the two genres is that, starting in Yüan times, many poets and critics used the term *ch'ü* to refer to *tz'u*.[5] The problems of terminology were greatly compounded in the Ming as more and more southern *ch'ü* tunes adopted the same titles as *tz'u*.[6] Worse still, most Ming poets who composed *tz'u* failed to follow the original metrical patterns and became less and less sensitive to the special musical element intrinsic to the genre. Thus, in his famous prosodic manual *Tz'u-lü*, the Ch'ing scholar Wan Shu (fl. 1680–92) deliberately excluded from his collection all the new *tz'u* tunes invented by Ming authors, judging them to be too much like *ch'ü* tunes (*THTP*, 3:2425).

A literary purist, Ch'en Tzu-lung strove to recapture the original spirit of *tz'u* that he believed was first embodied in the elegant works of the Southern T'ang (937–75) and the Northern Sung (960–1127) but had been unfortunately lost after the Southern Sung (1127–1279). In his preface to *Yu-lan ts'ao*, an anthology of *tz'u*, Ch'en says:

> From the time of the two Southern T'ang rulers [Li Ching and Li Yü] to the Ching-k'ang years [1126–27] of the Northern Sung, there were eminent *tz'u* poets in every age. Some of these poets' works were distinguished by exquisite refinement and delicate elegance, fully expressing the feelings of love and sorrow. Some were distinguished by spontaneous style and lofty sentiment, exploring the pleasant image of longing and beauty. Whatever their style, the content of these *tz'u* songs is based on genuine feeling, and the words used reflect meaningful intent. . . . Such were the best examples of the *tz'u*. However, since the Southern Sung, this mode of song lyric has gradually gone astray. Those who used the *tz'u* to express their feelings produced works that were rather tasteless and offensive. There were others who, in an attempt to please the vulgar, became inferior and shallow themselves, and were almost indistinguishable from dramatic entertainers . . . not to mention the *tz'u* writers of the Yüan dynasty who always "filled in words" heedlessly. Since the founding of the Ming dynasty, many talented authors have emerged—their prose essays were modeled after the masterpieces of the Han, and their *shih* poems vied with the fine works of the K'ai-yüan [in High T'ang]. But only in this "minor genre,"[7] *tz'u*, have we fallen behind. [*AYTK*, 1:279–80]

Ch'en Tzu-lung felt that, aside from the "unhealthy" influences of *ch'ü* colloquialism, the most serious flaw of the Ming *tz'u* was its failure to express authentic (*chen*) feelings. Given the original emotional emphasis of the *tz'u* genre, such a generic degradation was indeed unwarranted. Besides, considering the fact that the concept of *ch'ing* (romantic love) played such a crucial part in late-Ming cultural and literary activities, it would indeed have been a mistake not to call for a rebirth of the *tz'u*, the lyric of emotion par excellence. In the case of Ch'en Tzu-lung, his impulse to revive the original spirit of *tz'u* led him to organize the Yün-chien School of *Tz'u*, which eventually rescued the genre from prolonged neglect and abuse and again raised it to the level of a reputable poetic form.[8] In time his school was to dominate the literary scene of the late Ming and set the models for imitation.

Aside from Ch'en Tzu-lung himself, the Yün-chien school produced many outstanding *tz'u* poets, chief among them Hsia Wan-ch'un, Li Wen, Sung Cheng-yü, and Liu Shih. All these authors modeled their works after the "delicate and restrained" style of *tz'u* as established by the Five Dynasties and Northern Sung poets. The *Yu-lan ts'ao*, an anthology comprising the works of the so-called three masters of Yün-chien (Ch'en Tzu-lung, Li Wen, and Sung Cheng-yü), had apparently set for others a model unrivaled at the time. One of Ch'en Tzu-lung's students, Chiang P'ing-chieh, attempted to carry out the spirit of the Yün-chien school even after the fall of the Ming and eventually published an anthology of *tz'u* (entitled *Chih-chi chi*) bringing together his own works and those of his two students,[9] in obvious imitation of the *Yu-lan ts'ao* by the three masters of Yün-chien. Like Ch'en Tzu-lung, Chiang P'ing-chieh admired the Five Dynasties (907–60) *tz'u* poets. But unlike Ch'en Tzu-lung, who always had a high opinion of the Northern Sung poets, Chiang and his students had perhaps gone too far in denouncing all the *tz'u* poets in the Sung, Northern and Southern alike. As it turned out, during the turmoil of the dynastic transition Chiang P'ing-chieh and his circle of friends became the most powerful disseminators of the aesthetic tenets of the Yün-chien school. If anything, they were proud of being followers of a poetic school (which they called "our party," or *wu-tang*) that stressed "technical excellence" and the "recovery of *tz'u* music."[10] The irony is that while they tried to propagate the Yün-chien approach and had obviously succeeded in promoting their own *tz'u* poems (which were later incorporated into Wang Ch'ang's famous *Ming tz'u tsung*),[11] they had also unwittingly distorted the original position of Ch'en Tzu-lung—so that generations later, even to this day, many scholars, including the Ch'ing poet Wang Shih-chen, have criticized the Yün-chien school for its "complete rejection of the Sung *tz'u*" (*THTP*, 2:1980). As I shall demonstrate later in this chapter, such criticism is entirely unfounded. Ch'en Tzu-lung was most fervent in recognizing the achievements of Northern Sung poets, especially Ch'in Kuan (1049–1100), whom Ch'en and Liu had chosen as their model.

It may seem logical that in their relationship Liu Shih, being some ten years younger than Ch'en Tzu-lung, was in literary matters the disciple and Ch'en the master. But Liu Shih's literary training was almost certainly acquired before she met Ch'en. Especially in the area of *tz'u* and *ch'ü*, proficiency was traditionally associated with the courtesan culture. And it is only natural for us to assume that Liu Shih greatly influenced Ch'en Tzu-lung's *tz'u* revival movement. Support for this view is evidenced by numerous poetic exchanges between Liu and Ch'en written in the *tz'u* form. These "exchanged" *tz'u*, composed according to fixed tune patterns, function much as letters, revealing a particular immediacy of a personal relationship. In fact, while *tz'u* seemed largely to have been ignored by male Ming authors, it had become for many late-Ming women the major (and highly effective) vehicle for expressing their sensibilities. And Liu Shih was only one of many female writers of *tz'u* who published their works.[12] Moreover, from the beginning, the *tz'u* genre was thought to be associated with femininity because early *tz'u* lyrics were expressly written for professional courtesan singers. But even though courtesans played a vital role in the tradition and *tz'u* continued to be viewed as an inherently feminine genre, most *tz'u* writers before the seventeenth century were men,[13] with the rare exceptions of Li Ch'ing-chao and Chu Shu-chen in the Sung. Not until the late Ming did large numbers of women become conscious of their poetic vocation as *tz'u* writers, as may be demonstrated by the high quality of *tz'u* songs by female poets recorded in Ch'en Wei-sung's *Fu-jen chi* (Works of women) and later *tz'u-hua*.[14] In other words, women like Liu Shih were no longer just "singers"; nor were they mere objects of representation in *tz'u*. They were instead poets and even published authors. In all this process Liu Shih was an exemplary woman writer who turned her life experience into literary experience in *tz'u*, creating a new emotional realism that literally defines the conception of femininity.

It is most unfortunate that in his authoritative *Ming tz'u tsung* (Collection of Ming *tz'u*), the highly respected Ch'ing scholar Wang Ch'ang failed to include many excellent *tz'u* poems by late-Ming women, thus greatly distorting the truth of an unprecedented literary phenomenon in early seventeenth-century *tz'u*.[15] Even Liu Shih's outstanding accomplishment in *tz'u* was not acknowledged until much later in the Ch'ing (*THTP*, 4:3454). But such distortion was not entirely sexist, for it seemed to be symptomatic of the problems of early Ch'ing *tz'u* criticism, which tended to ignore the achievements of those very late-Ming poets who were responsible for the revival of the *tz'u* poetry. The problem might have been due to political censorship or simply to the loss of manuscripts during the crisis of dynastic transition from Ming to Ch'ing. I shall return to this subject later in my discussion of the problems of censorship and literary periodization.

The greatest accomplishment of Ch'en Tzu-lung and Liu Shih lies in their restoration of the quality of emotional realism originally characteristic of the *tz'u* genre. Their *tz'u* poems, serving as a kind of secret communication between them, tell the story of a passion felt by two equally talented authors. By so doing, they have (consciously or unconsciously) laid their hands on what is unique and essential in the *tz'u*. But at the same time their special gift for the concrete and the sensory has enabled them to create a new style of elegant beauty in *tz'u*, making them at home both in the world of classical rhetoric and in that of the Ming aesthetics of love. We are reminded of the Northern Sung poet Ch'in Kuan (1049–1100), who, even after his mentor Su Shih (1037–1101) had broadened the horizons of *tz'u* by establishing a school of "heroic abandon," continued to cultivate a sophisticated style of "delicate restraint" absorbing the traditional sensory quality of *tz'u* and his personal poetics of passion.[16] And true enough, Ch'in Kuan's *tz'u* provided Ch'en Tzu-lung and Liu Shih with just the right kind of inspiration and direction. Many of their love *tz'u* were set to tunes used or invented by Ch'in Kuan and adopted the same rhythmic structures and rhyme patterns. Moreover, they explored the same style of spontaneous expression and sensory imagism as did Ch'in Kuan. Clearly their *tz'u* songs of love were modeled on the work of Ch'in Kuan.[17]

To be sure, there were many reasons for Ch'en and Liu to choose Ch'in Kuan as their model. First, temperamentally they shared with the Northern Sung poet an attitude toward life that united romantic love and patriotic sentiment. Although Ch'in Kuan was best known as a poet of love lyrics (to the point that he became the ideal symbol of the poet-lover in Ming fiction), he was in his earlier days famous for his "heroic vision" and his profound interest in "books on military tactics."[18] In Ch'in Kuan passion was expressed in different forms according to the poet's different life situations—a special phenomenon that can offer grounds for comparison with Ch'en Tzu-lung. Second, Ch'in Kuan's attitude toward courtesans and women in general was different from that of his *tz'u* predecessors—because his *tz'u* emphasized the emotional constancy of women and his own respect for them. Courtesans in his *tz'u*, such as P'an-p'an and Cho-cho in the "T'iao-hsiao ling" series (*CST*, 1:464–67), were not coquettish or wanton entertainers; instead, they were virtuous women and devoted lovers, not unlike the historical Wang Chao-chün and the fictional Ts'ui Ying-ying. Indeed, Ch'in Kuan's profound emphasis on women and genuine love seemed to anticipate the late-Ming notion of *ch'ing*, and it is understandable that Ch'en Tzu-lung and Liu Shih were especially impressed with his *tz'u*. Besides, Ch'in Kuan's style of elegant expressiveness—which came from the tradition of the Southern T'ang poet Li Yü (937–78) and later exercised a great influence on the Sung woman poet Li Ch'ing-chao [19]—was totally compatible with the original generic principle of *tz'u* poetry.

That Ch'en Tzu-lung and Liu Shih should find in Ch'in Kuan a perfect source of imitation for their poetic apprenticeship in *tz'u*, even after the genre had suffered a decline of nearly three centuries, explains the enormous power that is released when the lyrical sense of a genre is reawakening. Ch'en and Liu must have been extremely perceptive in singling out Ch'in Kuan as their model poet in *tz'u*, for it was not until more than two centuries later that the famous Ch'ing critic Feng Hsü (1843–1927), known for his ambitious anthology of sixty-one Sung poets (*Sung liu-shih-i chia tz'u-hsüan, 2 chüan*), declared that Ch'in Kuan's poems are "*tz'u* of the true heart" (*tz'u-hsin*), unsurpassed by those of any other poet: "*Tz'u* poems by other poets were works of talent. But Shao-yu's [Ch'in Kuan's] were *tz'u* of the true heart; they came from his inner self. The secret of his *tz'u* cannot be learned" (*THTP*, 4:3587). It may have been the "*tz'u* of the true heart" in Ch'in Kuan that touched the hearts of Ch'en Tzu-lung and Liu Shih. In order to better explain Ch'in Kuan's poetic achievement and his strong influence on late-Ming *tz'u* poetics, I shall first quote what was thought to be his most famous (though not necessarily the best) *tz'u*, "Man t'ing fang":

> Mountains touched by light clouds,
> Sky adhering to withered grass,
> The painted horn's sound breaks at the watch-tower.
> Let me stop my travelling boat   4
> And share a farewell cup with you.
> How many fairyland memories—
> To look back is futile,
> Only scattered and tangled mists remain.   8
> Beyond the slanting sun:
> A few cold dots of crows,
> A stream winding round a solitary village.
>
> My soul is lost,   12
> At this moment when
> My perfume bag is secretly untied,
> And gently you give me your silk girdle.
> I'm afraid all this has won me the name   16
> Of a heartless lover in the Courtesan Quarter.
> Once gone, when shall I see you again?

In vain have I brought tear-stains to our lapels and sleeves!
My heart saddens,   20
When I gaze at the tall city-wall.
The lights are up—it is already dusk.[20]   [CST, 1:458]

This poem became so popular among contemporary readers that the thirty-year-old Ch'in Kuan instantaneously won the nickname "The Man of 'Mountains Touched by Light Clouds,'" after the opening line of the poem (THTP, 3:2018). What distinguishes Ch'in Kuan's tz'u song from the works of his predecessors is the power of emotional realism achieved by a new elevated style of elegance. The poem is about the poet's sorrow at the inevitability of separation from his beloved courtesan and about the intimate moments they shared before parting. It is also about a tragedy of love thwarted by external circumstances, in this case the poet's political failure and resulting exile. Overcome by a flood of emotion, the poet sheds tears in front of his beloved (line 19). The poem's focus on this image of the sentimental male lover has important implications. For it is a primary convention in the poetry of the Chinese literati—except in the sao and fu traditions, in which courtship usually occurs metaphorically between a man and a goddess—that it be the female persona, not the poet himself, who expresses longing and frustration during the separation. Besides, Ch'in Kuan's straightforward expression of passion and realistic depiction of intimacy (lines 12–15) would have been considered vulgar by the standard of classic poetry, according to which there should always be "an aesthetic distance" between the self and the expression of love.[21]

One is readily reminded in this regard of an earlier Sung poet, Liu Yung (987–1053), who, in a bold and critical revision of the literati tradition, began to adopt in his love poetry an explicit voice with a male perspective. But, because Liu Yung tended to use many colloquial expressions, his tz'u were often criticized as being "shallow and vulgar" and even "as low as dust."[22] In Ch'in Kuan's tz'u, however, the rhetorical devices make a more classical impression—despite the urgent, impulsive tone, it exhibits a predominance of elegant refinement typical of the elevated literati style. Through the principle of mixed styles Ch'in Kuan is able to express the personal and the universal together and to absorb both sensory realism and classical rhetoric. Furthermore, the repeated display of the careful fusion of feeling and scene serves to explain why Ch'in Kuan's tz'u was able to assert itself in the respectable tradition of the orthodox tz'u in the Northern Sung. It is not surprising that Ch'in was later recognized by Ch'ing critics as the exemplary tz'u poet, he who managed to capture "the genuine spirit" (pen-se) of tz'u.[23]

However different their circumstances, the ways in which Ch'en Tzu-lung's style is reminiscent of Ch'in Kuan's *tz'u* are very striking. A case in point is Ch'en's farewell poem to Liu Shih, which was deliberately set to the tune "Man t'ing fang," a tune noted for its gentle and melodious music and said to be especially suitable for representing romantic feelings.[24] Ch'en's poem was obviously written to match Ch'in Kuan's "Man t'ing fang," as I shall suggest below. Like Ch'in Kuan's song, Ch'en's piece mediates romantic passion through realistic description and at the same time stylized manipulation of literary convention:

> "*Man t'ing fang*": A Song of Farewell
>
> Purple swallows whirled by the strong wind,
> Green plums in the rain,
> Together we seek the tear-stains on the fragrant grasses.
> From the beginning we knew   4
> Our union would be short-lived.
> About the time of our parting,
> Beyond the green willows,
> Our souls lost—   8
> Before we mentioned them,
> Welling tears soaked your red sleeves,
> All left unsaid, except a few words.
>
> My feelings sadly tangled and confused—   12
> Once we depart,
> You will waste away in front of the jade mirror,
> Your silk skirt no longer fitting your thin waist.
> I think of you, drifting somewhere, all alone,   16
> Beyond scattered mists and water I seem to hear you,
> But when I dream of you, of your haggard face,
> Clouds of Mount Ch'u still stand between us.
> It will be nothing but this: 20
> Grieving with the flowers, saddened by the willows;
> Like you, I'll be afraid of the dusk.   [*CTLS*, 2:617]

In terms of sentence structure, vocabulary, and imagery, there is a strong similarity between Ch'en Tzu-lung's poem and Ch'in Kuan's "Man t'ing fang." Several words and images used in Ch'en's piece are borrowed directly from Ch'in's, though placed in a different context. For example, *t'i-hen* (tear-stains) in line 3, *hsiao-hun* (souls lost) in line 8, and *fen-fen* (tangled and confused) in line 12 come from Ch'in Kuan's lines 19, 12, and 8, respectively. What is most noteworthy is that both poems end with the word *huang-hun* (dusk). In both, there is a vivid sensory depiction of a parting scene, carefully embedded in a concrete personal experience. In both tender love is thwarted by outside forces, and a sense of pervasive helplessness reigns. For both poets, the straightforward but elegant expression of the inner turmoil of love enriches the overall power of their *tz'u*.

But it would be a mistake to see Ch'en Tzu-lung's "Man t'ing fang" song simply as an imitation of Ch'in Kuan's *tz'u*. In Ch'en, the greater degree of emotional urgency, the idea of suffering through passionate love, and the subtle use of personal allusions in the text (especially those drawn from the context of the poet's own poems) all brought about a new poetics typical of the late-Ming style. The tragic reality of Ch'en and Liu's separation impels the poet to express himself with the utmost intensity, one which comes close to the heightened rhetoric of the Ming lyric drama. Unlike Ch'in Kuan's poem, which starts with the conventional drinking scene of farewell (line 5) and only later leads into a sentimental scene of shedding tears (line 19), Ch'en's "Man t'ing fang" introduces right at the outset the dramatic moment of a tearful episode, which even permeates nature with tear-stains (line 3). The first stanza focuses on the suffering reality of the woman and reaches its climax in silence (line 11). And the second stanza expresses feelings of desperate yearning entirely from the male point of view. In vigor, directness, and the diversity of perspectives, the poem is almost like a scene from a romantic play in which the hero and the heroine are presented in the foreground.

On another level, it is equally essential to recognize that in Ch'en Tzu-lung's poem the oneness of the lovers, in spite of the inevitability of their separation, is based on the late-Ming conception of *ch'ing*. Whereas Ch'in Kuan feels sad that his departure has won him the name of "heartless lover," Ch'en Tzu-lung is concerned mainly about the welfare of his beloved after their separation: "You will waste away in front of the jade-mirror / Your silk skirt no longer fitting your thin waist" (lines 14–15). Perhaps it was this sincerity of love on the part of Ch'en Tzu-lung which so deeply touched Liu Shih that almost ten years after their separation (and three years after her marriage to Ch'ien Ch'ien-i) Liu remembered Ch'en's "Man t'ing fang" poem with keen appreciation: in 1644 she inscribed a friend's painting with the closing lines of Ch'en's poem (*LJS*, 1:287):

> It will be nothing but this:
> Grieving with the flowers, saddened by the willows;
> Like you, I'll be afraid of the dusk.

Interestingly, later scholars, unaware of the special circumstances surrounding these lines, took them to be the work of Liu Shih and consequently assigned the authorship of the "Man t'ing fang" *tz'u* to Liu Shih herself.[25]

Certainly it is no accident that Liu Shih had such a special liking for Ch'en Tzu-lung's "Man t'ing fang" *tz'u*. For its last lines are especially charged with personal allusions and snippets of shared texts. The end of the poem is in no way an end: it is but an invitation to more shared dreams and memories of passion. It is not about a departure, but about a return to the center of an important lyrical context. The three dominant images— the flowers, the willows, the dusk (lines 20–22)—are organized around thoughts of intimacy that refers back to the love poems of Ch'en Tzu-lung and Liu Shih. Certainly, on the surface, these images sound like typical expressions of melancholy and ennui in *tz'u* poetry.[26] But the real meaning behind these seemingly simple words is not so simple. Contained in the closing lines of Ch'en's poem is in effect a solemn promise from the poet to his beloved—he pledges to think of her (symbolized by the flowers and the willows) as long as the slanting sun continues to appear at sunset.

By relating the image of the dusk to his unfailing passion the poet is reminding his beloved of the many *tz'u* songs he wrote for her concerning their intimate life together and of how in these songs the sunset scene stands out almost like a metaphorical link between them (for example, *CTLS*, 2:608, 609, 612, 613, and 616). The following quotation from his song "Yü mei-jen" (The beautiful Lady Yü), perhaps a subtle reference to Liu's nickname "Mei-jen" (Beautiful One), is typical in this connection:

> The lingering coldness penetrates the remaining snow on the tip of the
>   branches,
> Shadows of her like slender shades of flowers.
> The fair one, silently standing, quietly melts my soul.
> All day, we look into each other's eyes without a word, till the *dusk* falls.
>
> [*CTLS*, 2:609]

And Liu Shih herself recalls a delightful sunset scene that took place in the Southern Villa:

> Where was he?
> At the Autumn Stone Crab-apple Hall.
> Fun was playing hide-and-seek
> Round after round, no need to linger for long.
> Again, how many sunsets have gone by! [*LJS*, 1:263]

Thus the image of dusk in Ch'en's farewell poem to Liu represents just one more attempt to convey the lovers from the present moment to memories of the past, from reality to dream.

Again, like his *fu* poetry, Ch'en's *tz'u* songs often allude to time and place, using the most objectively referential words to evoke a kind of metaphorical meeting between dream and reality. If the image of dusk represents a reminder of time (and a mediation between present and past), then the repeated references to the Red Chamber (that is, the Southern Chamber), where the lovers took their emotional voyage together, signify a place of shared secrets and dreams. The image of the Red Chamber is immediately recognizable in the following two poems exchanged between Ch'en and Liu, both set to the tune "Huan hsi sha":

"Huan hsi sha": The Fifth Watch
(Ch'en Tzu-lung)

As I half-recline on a pillow in the mild chill, tears silently flow;
My sorrow is like a dream, my dream like sorrow,
The sound of the bugle has just reached the little Red Chamber.

A breeze stirs the fading lamplight, rustles the embroidered curtains,
Flowers filter the faint moonlight; pale is the crescent curtain hook.
Suddenly old sorrows rush into my mind.   [CTLS, 2:598]

"Huan hsi sha": The Fifth Watch
(Liu Shih)

Curtains in a dark room, guarded by the gold-lion censer that spring;
Part of my old soul is gone, never to return,[27]
Flowing bits of a flashing dream linger on.

Upon awakening, fretfully I catch sight of the little Red Chamber,
In the dim moonlight, I fear the green banks all the more,
A fragrant breeze swells by the blossom-covered garden steps.

[LJS, 1:243]

These two poems must have been written sometime after Liu Shih had left the Southern Villa, perhaps in the spring of 1636. Even after their separation, the lovers continued to exchange poems with increasing frequency. The similarities between Ch'en's and Liu's "Huan hsi sha" songs are unmistakable—both refer to the little Red Chamber and both contain images of the dream, the wind blowing, the curtain, the dim moonlight, and flowers. The Red Chamber is the pivotal image shared by the two poems; what is uniquely significant about this pivotal image is its dreamlike quality. In fact the Red Chamber has literally become a symbol of the dream, and both poems are about the state of stupor upon awakening, when dream and reality merge. (Is the Red Chamber real or just a dream?) To Ch'en, the dream is like a path between the visible and the invisible—it is always there, giving him a lingering sense of sorrow (line 2). To Liu, the dream is like a haunting shadow; it reminds her of her present loneliness (line 3). The total impression created is that both dream and reality have equal claim to their existence and form two complementary worlds. But the poems are deliberately ambiguous about the boundary between dream and reality. For example, we cannot be certain whether the scene Ch'en visualizes—that of the wind blowing against the fading lamplight, the faint moonlight shining upon the flowers—is from his dream or reality or both (lines 4–5). And Liu seems to be lingering between dream and reality as she wakes to a dim garden scene in which flowers are blown by a mild breeze. In fact, love itself has become a dream, a store of illusory images and symbols.

Both Ch'en's and Liu's "Huan hsi sha" songs are modeled after Ch'in Kuan's *tz'u* set to the same tune:

A mild chill permeates the little chamber,[28]
The gloomy morning is like the deep autumn—I can do nothing about it.
Only the faint mist and the flowing stream on the serene painted screen.

Blossoms flying as they please, light as dreams,
The endless silky rain as fine as sorrow.
A pearly curtain quietly hung, small is the silver hook.   [*CST*, 1:461]

Ch'in Kuan's poem emphasizes the image of a little chamber, and Ch'en and Liu follow suit. The images of flowers and the curtain too are echoed in Ch'en's and Liu's poems. Especially in Ch'en's song, the verbal borrowings are obvious—for example, *ch'ing-han* (mild chill) in line 1 and *lien-kou* (crescent curtain hook) in line 5 are taken almost verbatim from Ch'in's lines 1 and 6. Most notably, Ch'en's line "My sorrow is like a dream, my dream like sorrow" is a recasting of Ch'in's famous couplet in lines 4–5: "Blossoms flying as they please, light as *dreams* / The endless silky rain as fine as *sorrow*."

But in sharp contrast to Ch'in Kuan's poem, which seems to be based on the conventional image of the female persona engaging in an "inner-chamber lament" (*kuei-yüan*),[29] Ch'en's and Liu's exchanged poems are the true dialogue of a man and a woman in love. Especially in giving the identical subtitle, "The Fifth Watch," to their poems, the lovers are telling us that their poems were written for the same occasion, around the same poetic idea. Thus, although their poems seem to be written within the familiar bounds of clichés, a closer reading shows them to be poetically unfamiliar creations,[30] evoking a richly personal frame of reference. Like the idea of the dusk, "the fifth watch" is an important time word for Ch'en and Liu. Readers of Chinese *shih* poetry will perhaps be reminded of the famous couplet from Li Shang-yin's (ca. 813–58) love poetry: "Coming was an empty promise, you have gone, and left no footprint / The moonlight slants above the roof, already the fifth watch sounds."[31] But "the fifth watch" as a recurrent image in Ch'en's *tz'u* (for example, *CTLS*, 2:612, 613, 616) turns out to be a highly personal allusion to Liu's habit of rising at the fifth watch (roughly 4:00 A.M.), a habit Ch'en considered especially admirable and consequently imitated.[32]

A poem set to the tune "Tieh lien hua," subtitled "Spring Dawn," is organized according to this very idea and can thus serve the reader as a lyrical invitation to the lovers' personal world:

> Right at *the fifth watch,* she bids farewell to the spring dream,
> Half awake, by the window curtain,
> Quietly facing the mirror, she sees clear reflections of herself.
> She looks over her phoenix-patterned shoes, half-twisted around each   4
>   other,
> Lines of tears streak down the mirror, rouge radiance glittering.
>
> Orioles sing endlessly on the branches,
> She deliberately removes her winter garment,
> And endures the cold season.   8
> Listlessly she binds her hair with jade hairpins,
> Letting the shifting shadows of blossoms sink before the window.
>
> [CTLS, 2:612]

The woman character in this poem is not unlike the conventional image of the deserted woman in the inner chamber who, alone and lonely, applies her makeup routinely in the morning.[33] Images of the tears, blossoms, and the mirror all recall the richly sensory style of the early *kuei-yüan* (inner-chamber lament) songs. But behind the superficial impression of a conventional *kuei-yüan* style in Ch'en's "Tieh lien hua" is embedded a very radical content. For the poem is really about a woman who displays a will of her own: unlike the conventional abandoned women in *tz'u*, who are often late getting up in the morning (for where there is no love, making up is not urgent),[34] Ch'en's female character (Liu Shih) conscientiously gets up at the fifth watch, "deliberately removes her winter garment / And endures the cold season." Clearly the resolute woman character of Ch'en's poem is not a mere object of description as in the conventional *tz'u;* she was in real life a talented writer of *tz'u* herself. No less than the male poet-lover, Liu Shih concentrated on her self-expression, even to the point of self-dramatization.

The influence of Liu Shih's poems on Ch'en Tzu-lung's *tz'u* poetic (and vice versa) may be gauged by a brief look at what is perhaps Liu's most ambitious song-series, the one entitled "Meng chiang-nan" (see appendix 2), in which the poet created through a series of twenty *tz'u* songs a living "allegory" for her relationship with Ch'en. Ch'en's *tz'u* set to the same tune will be treated as a "double" of Liu's song-series, for each of the two texts is in fact the pre-text of the other.

To begin with, Liu's creativity lies not in inventing any particularly new devices but in reverting to the original *tz'u* rhetoric, which had been unpopular, if not entirely forgotten, for nearly three centuries. Originally, during the T'ang and Five dynasties period, the subject of a *tz'u* poem usually corresponded to the meaning of its tune title. But after the Sung the subject of the poem gradually lost its thematic connection with the *tz'u* pattern. Now, by deliberately choosing those tune titles that match the content of her *tz'u*, Liu Shih was making a significant move to revive the purer, classical style of *tz'u*. The tune title of her song-series, "Meng chiang-nan," literally means "Dreaming about the south." This title serves to express the main theme of the twenty songs in the series, which are essentially about "dreams" (*meng*) of the Southern Villa (*nan lou*). But the songs are also about the metaphorical bond between dreams and reminiscences, the Southern Villa serving as their common point of reference. Interestingly, the convergence of dreaming (*meng*) and reminiscing (*i*) in Liu's songs is based on the literal meaning of the tune title: for the tune "Meng chiang-nan" was also called "I chiang-nan" (Remembering the south). Clearly Liu Shih was conscious of this alternate tune title, especially because the refrain in the first ten poems of her song-series, "he is gone," is an imitation of the "I chiang-nan" song by the T'ang poet Liu Yü-hsi, which begins with the line "The spring is gone" (*CTWT*, 1:22).

For Liu Shih, to love is to remember, to recover past moments of pleasure and pain. There is in each of the twenty songs a certain idea of memory or a certain unforgettable site in the Southern Villa that keeps recurring. With a past to sustain her, all the external references—such as images of the painted chamber, the Isle of Egrets, the Crab-apple Hall, the orchid boat, and so forth which systematically appear in the second lines of the individual songs—have become reminders of a human relation. The power of memory makes everything present at once, but it is in dreams that she can forget the pain of separation, as she says in song 9:

He is gone,
Gone, yet dreams of him come even more often.
Recalling the past: our shared moments were mostly wordless,
But now I secretly regret the growing distance.
Only in dreams can I find self-indulgence.   [LJS, 1:260]

In her supremely pleasurable dream, her self seems extended and transformed, so that upon waking she is "bewildered" like Chuang-tzu's butterfly (song 1), not knowing who is doing the dreaming and who is being
dreamed about.

The remembrance of the past is like a dream; in its lived duration the
poet experiences a void of time and space that changes and enlarges her
perceptions. As if by magic, the interior recollection takes her back to
the perfect world of the moonlight (song 13), the magnificent banquet
(song 15), and the Lake of Misty Rain (song 17). In particular, the poems'
constant moving back and forth between the inner chamber and the outer,
natural scene reflects the free, dreamlike quality of her memories.[35] What
surges up in her moments of reminiscence is a recurrent picture of an
incense-burning scene describing what seems to be the lovers' first intimate
night spent in the Southern Chamber: "The duck-censer burned low, the
fragrant smoke warm / Spring mountains winding deeply in the painted
screen" (song 11). And "behind the rosy curtain" there is "a single wisp
of incense" (song 10). The incense smoke is a symbol of the ecstatic state
of love, not only because it physically captures the lingering and fanci-
ful aspect of love but also because the animal designs on the censer are
those that represent the ritual of a conjugal union.[36] For example, song 6
describes the feeling of conjugal bliss symbolized by the harmonious coexistence of mythical animal designs on the censer:

Phoenix pecked at the scattered tiny red beans,
Pheasants, joyfully embracing the censer, gazed at us.

These lines were apparently inspired by Tu Fu's famous couplet describing the joy of a harvest in the town of P'i-mei: "Grains from the fragrant
rice-stalks, pecked and dropped by the parrots / On the green *Wu-t'ung*
tree branches where the perching phoenix aged."[37] In Liu Shih, however,
the animal images originally conceived by Tu Fu as coming from nature
have all become art objects symbolizing the emotional union of the lovers.

But the incense smoke also symbolizes the ephemeral nature of the poet's
dreams. In the "Huan hsi sha" song quoted above, she says, "Curtains in
a dark room, guarded by the gold-lion censer that spring / Part of my old
soul is gone, never to return." And here at the end of the "Meng chiang-

nan" song-series, she tells the inevitable and terrible reality of waking up:
"A parrot dream ends in a black otter's tail / Incense smoke lingers on
the tip of the green spiral censer" (song 19). According to Ch'en Yin-k'o,
the parrot perhaps refers to Liu Shih herself, while the black otter may
symbolize Ch'en Tzu-lung's wife, who, as I noted earlier, apparently came
to the Southern Villa to force Liu Shih to leave (*LJS*, 1:265). Whatever the
true meaning of these animal images, the pleasure afforded by the poems
is thus enhanced by the tension between dream and reality and between
desire and fear, all symbolized by the provocative presence of the lingering
incense fragrance.

To Liu Shih's song-series, Ch'en Tzu-lung responded with a two-stanza
tz'u, each stanza set to the tune "Wang chiang-nan" (Gazing the south-
ward), another name for "Meng chiang-nan."[38] Ch'en's song is subtitled
"Thinking of the Past," and it also uses the image of the censer (in line 4)
to evoke a sweet memory of the past:

> Thinking of the past,
> Flowers and moon were hazy,
> A jade swallow hairpin on her lush hair, stirring in the breeze,
> The golden lion censer burned low behind the embroidered curtain,   4
> Half-intoxicated, I leaned against the elegant beauty in red.
>
> Unbounded grief,
> Her tidings out of reach.
> The frail willow, thrice in slumber; spring dreams distant and vague.[39]   8
> A remote mountain corner, like the sorrow of her brows at dawn.
> Helpless, I turn to the water that flows east.   [*CTLS*, 2:606]

The "golden lion censer" inside is a metaphorical correspondence to the
dim moonlight scene outside. Like the flowers and moon (line 2), the incense smoke appears to be "hazy" both in dream and reality. In Ch'en, as
in Liu Shih, there is always a tendency to create a principle of contrast—
a contrast between the inside and the outside, the present and past. It is
mainly through contrast that a metaphorical convergence of the different scenes of memory occurs. In his "Huan hsi sha" song cited earlier,
Ch'en uses the same principle of contrast by comparing a "fading lamplight" scene and the image of flowers filtering "the faint moonlight" (lines
4–5). And his "Shao-nien yu" song, subtitled "Spring Love," is especially
notable for the contrast, and convergence, of the inner and outer romantic
scenes:

> A garden full of clear dew, soaking the bright flowers,
> Hand in hand we walked in the moonlight.

> The penetrating chill of the jade pillow,
> Faint fragrance in the icy silk curtain,
> Helpless with overwhelming love.   [CTLS, 2:603]

But to return to his "Wang chiang-nan" *tz'u:* While the first stanza dwells on memories of the past, the second focuses on the sorrows of the present. On its most obvious stylistic level, the second half of the poem is modeled after Li Yü's famous image describing his sorrows at having lost his kingdom, the Southern T'ang: "How much grief can I bear? / About as much as a river full of the waters of spring flowing east" (*CTS,* 12:10047).[40] It also recalls Ch'in Kuan's "Ch'ien-ch'iu sui" *tz'u* in which the forty-seven-year-old Sung poet laments the sorrows of his political failure: "The spring is gone / The flying blossoms everywhere, my sorrow is like the sea" (*CST,* 1:460). But Ch'en's "Wang chiang-nan" song is explicitly about the poet's agonies of love, though borrowing the language of suffering from Li Yü and Ch'in Kuan previously used in political contexts. Furthermore, Ch'en Tzu-lung is not talking just about his own feeling of misery; he is painfully concerned about the mental agony of his beloved:

> A remote mountain corner, like the sorrow of her brows at dawn,
> Helpless, I turn to the water that flows east.   [ll. 9–10]

Indeed, the poet's "unbounded grief" bespeaks his fidelity to his beloved.[41] Such fidelity is also the true expression of *ch'ing.*

Ch'en Tzu-lung and Liu Shih's equation of passion with suffering reminds us of the pervasive theme of lovesickness (*hsiang-ssu ping*) typical of Chinese romantic plays. In these works the hero and heroine actually become ill over their pining for each other.[42] The image of women suffering from the painful experience of love is of course entirely conventional in the Chinese poetic tradition: it can be traced back to the "Nineteen Ancient Poems" of the Han. But the image of the male lover and the amorous lady mutually exchanging feelings of lovesickness was first developed in the Yüan drama and did not become predominant until the Ming. The psychic state Ch'en Tzu-lung describes in many of his *tz'u* is in some degree typical of the tradition of drama. For example, in his "Chiang ch'eng tzu," subtitled "Getting Up Ill When the Spring Is Over," he confesses to having symptoms of lovesickness:

> Sick in bed, with the curtain rolled up, at the fifth watch toll,
> The morning cloud is gone,[43]
> Fallen red petals are swept away.
> The heartless spring beauty
> Gone—when will we meet again?

It gives me a thousand streams of tears.
I cannot ask her to stay,
Bitterest of all is the suddenness.   [CTLS, 2:616]

The contrast between Ch'en's and Liu's ways of expressing the feeling
of lovesickness is illuminating. Whereas Ch'en often portrays himself in
tz'u as a helpless lover physically suffering from the unredeemed pain of
separation, Liu Shih, despite undergoing a tormenting process of searching
for her lover in her dreams and in her hopes, tends to emphasize the everlasting power of true love that can somehow transcend human tragedy.
For the sake of comparison, let me quote one of Liu Shih's most famous
tz'u, the "Chin-ming ch'ih," subtitled "On the Cold Willow":

Unceasing regret! The river's cold waves,[44]
No feeling in the evening sun.
At this moment, at the Southern Shore, come the whistling winds,
They sweep up   4
The lonely shadow of these frosty branches.
Still remembering
Willow catkins in former times,
Especially at evening,   8
Between the misty waves and setting sun.
Looking on the passing travelers,
These slender branches waver purposely as if dancing,
Always stirring thoughts of sorrow,   12
Making me languish and waste away.
They recall the beautiful "Poems on the Yen Terrace."[45]

Spring days turned into autumn rains,
I think of your charms in those days,   16
So much secret hurt and pain.
Even if there were
Painted boats swirling round the riverbank,
It would be gloomy everywhere,   20
Only the water and clouds are the same as before.
Remembering the past:
Bits of the east wind were
Blocked off by the double-layer curtain,   24
The sorrow of my brows remained.
How I wish to invite the plum spirit in:
At evening, by the dim moonlight,
We could quietly speak of deep longing and love. [LJS, 1:336–37]   28

The poem is written in the form of *yung-wu tz'u* (*tz'u* poetry celebrating objects), which allows Liu Shih to express her feelings symbolically

through the description of the willow, both as an object (*wu*) and as a category (*lei*). It soon becomes clear to the reader that the connection between the symbol (the willow) and the person symbolized (the poet herself) is established by a device of symbology of names, a device also used in Ch'en's and Liu's *fu* poetry, as discussed in chapter 3. Here the symbology of names is based on the fact that Liu Shih's "Liu" literally means "the willow." The word "Liu" appears in the poem's subtitle, and her other name, "Shih," occurs at the beginning of the poem (line 3). In Chinese poetry, especially the *tz'u*, willow catkins happen to symbolize the wandering, drifting existence of the courtesan. Contemplating the tragic outcome of her love relationship with Ch'en, and of the harsh reality of her drifting from Sheng-tse to Sung-chiang and then back to the Sheng-tse courtesans' quarter, Liu Shih must have found the willow a perfect symbol of herself—a symbol which evokes rich associations of personal experience. Indeed, our knowledge about the symbolic connection between Liu Shih and the willow forces us to consider many of Ch'en Tzu-lung's poetic utterances in a new light. For example, in his "Wang Chiang-nan" *tz'u* cited above, Ch'en Tzu-lung speaks of a thrice-in-slumber willow, alluding to the "human willow" in the garden of Emperor Wu of the Han. By this simple device of allusion, the poet leads us into the depths of his symbolism, a symbolism based not only on the metaphorical equivalence between Liu Shih's life and the drifting willow catkins but also on the allegorical use of her name. (In chapter 6 I shall explore in depth the many symbolic meanings of the willow as found in Ch'en Tzu-lung's later *tz'u* poetry.)

A primary means of symbolization in Liu Shih's "Chin-ming ch'ih" song is the device of allusion, which provides an important structural principle for the poem. Generally, an allusion in a *yung-wu tz'u* works primarily as an image intimately linked to the aesthetic presence of the dominant symbol (for example the willow), which in turn becomes a metaphor of the poet's self. Reading the allusions, readers in the *yung-wu tz'u* convention are expected to infer something more, or other, as the true meaning of the poem, all the while exploring as many symbolic meanings as possible. For example, the first obvious allusion in Liu Shih's song occurs in line 14, which refers to the "Four Poems on the Yen Terrace" by the late T'ang poet Li Shang-yin. Li Shang-yin's four poems are said to be about his romantic longings for a singing girl with whom he was passionately in love. The girl was apparently "snatched away" by a powerful warlord, and Li Shang-yin's poems were written in remembrance of this tragic love affair. However, because of the political connotation of the poem's title, which alludes to the Golden Terrace of King Chao of Yen (reigned 311 B.C.–279 B.C.), traditional commentators since the Ch'ing have chosen to read Li's four poems as embodying some sort of moral or political significance, though no one has been able to provide any convincing allegorical readings.[46]

How did Liu Shih interpret Li Shang-yin's Yen Terrace poems, which affected her so much (lines 13–14)? It turns out that, again, the symbology of names is at work here: not only is the name Willow essential to the symbolic structure of Liu's *written* poem, but it has also become the locus of the poet's own *reading* experience. Li Shang-yin's four poems were important to Liu Shih mainly because Liu identified herself with an ideal T'ang reader named Willow Branch (Liu Chih). In the preface to his poem-series entitled "The Willow Branch," Li Shang-yin tells the story of a courtesan called Willow Branch who fell desperately in love with the poet after reading his "Four Poems on the Yen Terrace."[47] (Many commentators, including the modern scholar Yeh Ts'ung-ch'i, believe that the courtesan Willow Branch was also the intended subject of the Yen Terrace poems, although the poet Li Shang-yin had deliberately altered the facts in order to hide a personal secret.[48] Such an interpretation, however, has not been accepted without question.)[49] What is relevant to us as readers of Liu Shih's poem is that the poet, being a true lover herself, has become another Willow Branch who has reached a full understanding of the works of Li Shang-yin, a champion poet of love poetry in the *shih* form. To put it more simply, Liu Shih was an ideal reader who was able to appreciate both the author's manifest content and the latent content in the text that cries out to be understood sympathetically. Perhaps, also, by writing her own love poem for Ch'en Tzu-lung, Liu Shih was in a way hoping Ch'en would decode the surface texture of her poem and prove himself, like her, an ideal reader.

At the end of her "Chin-ming ch'ih" song, Liu Shih tells her lover explicitly what her secret dreams are: "How I wish to invite the plum spirit in: / At evening, by the dim moonlight / We could quietly speak of deep longing and love." What she does not spell out clearly is another crucial allusion that is at the center of her symbology of names: that the image of the "plum spirit" (line 26) is a subtle reference to *Mu-tan t'ing* (*The Peony Pavilion*), a romantic play by the Ming dramatist T'ang Hsien-tsu, in which the hero's name, "Liu Meng-mei," literally means "Willow Dreaming of Plum."[50] *The Peony Pavilion* is a play about the power of dreams and love: Tu Li-niang dreams of a handsome youth carrying a willow branch who takes her to a peony pavilion in the garden and makes love to her. She subsequently dies of lovesickness, but before her death she asks to be buried under a plum tree, a symbol of herself. Liu Meng-mei, the youth of Tu Li-niang's dream, later falls in love with Tu's self-portrait and is visited at night by Tu's spirit. Tu is eventually brought back to life because of the power of her love (*ch'ing*). Now, by using an allusion drawn from a romantic play, Liu Shih has intensified the associative power of her *tz'u* song, for even a seemingly simple image like the "plum spirit" begins to carry a larger meaning of *ch'ing*. It is the expressive function of allusions, long celebrated in the hermeneutic tradition of the *yung-wu tz'u*, that brings Liu Shih's poem in close contact with greater sensibility and imagination.

But the image of the "plum spirit" in Liu Shih's *tz'u* is meaningful at another level: it reminds us of the meeting of lovers in another romantic play by T'ang Hsien-tsu, *Tzu-ch'ai chi* (The story of the purple hairpin).[51] In the beginning of the play, the heroine, Huo Hsiao-yü, and the poet Li I fall in love on a New Year's Eve when plum-blossoms are veiled by faint moonlight (scene 8).[52] At the end of the play, as the lovers are reunited after a long and frustrating separation, it is the "tan-yüeh mei-hua" (moonlit plum-blossom) scene that they recall vividly in their intimate poetic exchanges (scene 53, 3:1801). In Liu Shih's *tz'u*, it is precisely these images of the plum and moonlight that are associated with her memories and dreams of love: "How I wish to invite the plum spirit in: / At evening, under the dim moonlight / We could quietly speak of deep longing and love." Clearly, the poet portrays her love and herself as characters in a play. On rereading Ch'en's and Liu's many exchanged *tz'u*, such as the "Huan hsi sha" songs cited earlier in this chapter, we discover with sudden pleasure that all the recurrent images of the flowers and moon are closely related to this private symbolism of love, providing a powerful intertextual impact.

That Liu Shih should have chosen T'ang Hsien-ts'u's *Tzu-ch'ai chi* as the pivotal allusion in her "Chin-ming ch'ih" deserves our special attention. For T'ang Hsien-tsu's play opens with a *ch'ü* song that specifically celebrates the late-Ming notion of *ch'ing*. The song concludes with a telling couplet:

> In this world, where can one find examples of love's longings?
> Just see how people like ourselves are devoted to love.

It was this affirmation of *ch'ing* that inspired T'ang Hsien-tsu to create in his *Tzu-ch'ai chi* a new version of the Huo Hsiao-yü story: the original T'ang *ch'uan-ch'i* tale tells of the betrayal of Huo Hsiao-yü by her heartless lover, the poet Li I; but T'ang Hsien-tsu turns Li I into a faithful and passionate lover. In C. T. Hsia's words, the play by T'ang Hsien-tsu is a "passionate orchestration of the theme of love."[53] The sad part of the story is that the lovers have to be separated right after their marriage, as Li I has earned the Principal Graduate (*chuang-yüan*) degree and is ordered by the emperor to assume a position at the frontier. The play thus celebrates the lovers' persevering devotion to each other and their "mutual avowal of undying love."[54] Liu Shih obviously identified herself with the heroine Huo Hsiao-yü, both with her romantic sentiment and with her helpless situation during the couple's long separation. Moreover, Huo Hsiao-yü is portrayed in the original T'ang *ch'uan-ch'i* tale as the illegitimate daughter of the prince of Huo, raised for the vocation of a high-class courtesan.[55] Herself a courtesan with an ambiguous background, Liu Shih must have found in Huo Hsiao-yü an apt fictional character for self-identification. And I believe that especially in her *tz'u* poetry, Liu Shih was always trying to find metaphorical equivalents to her life in the female images she read in contemporary drama and fiction.

There was another reason Liu Shih had a particular liking for T'ang Hsien-tsu's *Tzu-ch'ai chi*: the play was written in an elegant and somewhat paratactic style that, in Hsü Shuo-fang's words, "strongly resembled the *tz'u*."[56] As Ch'en Yin-k'o has observed, several lines in Liu Shih's "Chin-ming ch'ih" *tz'u* are adapted from the text of *Tzu-ch'ai chi* (*LJS*, 1:337–38). For example, the opening lines of the poem and lines 18–19, which concern the riverbank scene, are partially borrowed from two *ch'ü* songs in scene 25 of *Tzu-ch'ai chi* (3:1675), a crucial farewell scene that captures with lyrical directness the lovers' mutual oath of love. That particular scene in the play is entitled "Che liu Yang-kuan" (Plucking the willow at Yang Kuan), an ingenious choice of allusion for Liu Shih's *yung-wu tz'u* on the willow. Even the play's title, *The Story of the Purple Hairpin*, can be read as a metaphorical description of Liu's own love experience: in the play, the jade hairpin is the pledge of love between Huo Hsiao-yü and Li I (scene 8, 3:1613–18). Similarly, the jade hairpin is a recurrent image, indeed a pivotal image, in Ch'en's and Liu's *tz'u* poetry: it appears most poignantly in Liu's "Meng Chiang-nan" song-series (song 3) and Ch'en's response to Liu in his "Wang Chiang-nan" *tz'u* (line 3). By repeatedly using the image of the jade hairpin, a symbol of conjugal love, Ch'en and Liu clearly suggest they will forever be "husband and wife."[57]

Let us consider another dimension of Liu Shih's "Chin-ming ch'ih": the song is in fact modeled after a *tz'u* by the Sung poet Ch'in Kuan that bears the same tune title and uses the same rhyme. The tune "Chin-ming ch'ih" was first used by Ch'in Kuan, and Ch'in's song is one of the few examples in Sung *tz'u* whose tune titles coincide with their contents. "Chin-ming ch'ih," literally, "gold bright pond," was the name of a real pond west of the Sung capital K'ai-feng, and in his song Ch'in Kuan described the beautiful scenery near the pond, which he visited around the year 1092. The song opens with a spring scene of willow catkins:

> The Jade garden, the Gold Pond,
> The blue gate, the purple road,
> All covered by the snowlike willow catkins.[58]

Later, after Ch'in Kuan was exiled from the capital, the Gold Bright Pond became for him a symbol of the happy past. In his "Ch'ien-ch'iu sui" song dated 1095, perhaps the saddest of all his *tz'u*, the forty-six-year-old Ch'in Kuan contrasts the earlier happy days he spent near the Gold Bright Pond (which he called the West Pond) and his present suffering as a political exile.[59]

In obvious imitation of Ch'in Kuan, Ch'en Tzu-lung composed a *tz'u* set to the "Ch'ien-ch'iu sui" tune, subtitled "With Remorse":

> The Chang-t'ai willow branches, wavering toward the west,
> Your slender hands I used to hold,
> Under the flowers' shadow,
> As we cared for each other . . .
>
> Lotus blossoms flanking a pair of lamps,
> Clouds of hair adorned with kingfisher hairpins I embraced,
> The gold embroidered pillow,
> With whom can I share these now?   [*CTLS*, 2:616]

Ch'en's description of the willow at the beginning of this song, however similar to Ch'in Kuan's in his "Chin-ming ch'ih," is of a wholly different mode of expression. Whereas Ch'in Kuan's account is purely descriptive, Ch'en's is largely symbolic. For Ch'in Kuan was still working under the Northern Sung convention of *yung-wu tz'u* as a descriptive mode, while Ch'en Tzu-lung (and Liu Shih for that matter) had the benefit of learning from the Southern Sung poets a symbolic mode of *yung-wu tz'u* that represented a new rhetoric of imagistic association with a primary goal of self-expression.[60] Thus, although the opening line of Ch'en's "Ch'ien-ch'iu sui" song describing the wispy, unhindered willow catkins near the Chang-t'ai gate of the Lo-yang capital clearly reminds us of Ch'in Kuan's description of the Gold Bright Pond willow, the poem quickly leads in a different direction. It turns out that Ch'en's song is an affirmation of the metaphorical nature of the willow—that the "willow branches" are the "slender hands" of his beloved, Liu Shih. What distinguishes Ch'en's rhetoric from that of the Southern Sung *yung-wu tz'u* is the referential quality of his metaphorical equivalences. The link between Liu Shih and the willow (*liu*) is mediated not only through their qualitative similarity but also through a most objectively referential common denominator, the word "Liu," for which "willow" is a pun. Metaphor, in other words, is the cause, not the product, of this "allegorical" *yung-wu* procedure. To a large extent, this mixture of allegorical referentiality and metaphorical reflection characterizes the new poetics of late-Ming poetry.[61]

Despite their differences, both Ch'in Kuan and Ch'en Tzu-lung were praised by *tz'u* critics as representing the "genuine spirit" (*pen-se*) of *tz'u*.[62] I think this traditional judgment, which sounds perceptive and to the point, is too general to be fully understood and needs to be made more specific. First, we must consider what the modern poet-critic Wang Kuo-wei (1877–1927) pointed out as the distinguishing aspect of Ch'in Kuan's *tz'u*—that is, the quality of "grieving intensity" (*ch'i-li*) as seen in lines 4 and 5 of the following "T'a-so hsing" *tz'u*:[63]

Fog veils the tower,
Faint moonlight dims the ferry,
Eyes strain, but the Peach Blossom Spring is nowhere to be found.
How can I bear to be shut up all alone in this inn against the spring chill? 4
The cuckoo's cries, the sun's rays at dusk.[64]

Sending a plum-blossom by a courier,[65]
Letters to be carried by the fish,[66]
All kindle my profuse feeling of grief. 8
The Ch'en River should stay in the Ch'en Mountain,
For whom did it flow into the Hsiao and Hsiang? [CST, 1:460]

The message Ch'in Kuan spells out in this *tz'u* song is certainly not simple: it is a uniquely personal expression of suffering through a few contrasting images. The poem was written in 1097 soon after Ch'in Kuan had been further demoted and exiled to another remote place called Ch'en-chou. Thus, it reveals the concentration of the lonely poet's mind on the reality and cause of his distress. Confronting his unfulfilled dream of the Peach Blossom Spring (line 3) and with no way of escaping (symbolized by the ferry in line 2), the poet finds even the simple idea of sending a letter extremely painful (lines 6–7).[67] For the poet, written communication with the loved ones at home only reminds him of his lost happiness and of the unbearable physical separation between them. But Wang Kuo-wei was apparently impressed by Ch'in Kuan's ability to translate his feeling of

suffering into sensory imagery, creating an admixture of mental distress
and pictorial realism.

Being admirers of Ch'in Kuan, both Ch'en Tzu-lung and Liu Shih composed their own *tz'u* songs set to the "T'a-so hsing" tune, adopting the
rhyme scheme of Ch'in's song. Their "T'a-so hsing" *tz'u*, both subtitled
"Chi-shu" (Sending a letter), were obviously written as poetic exchanges:

[Ch'en to Liu]

How many heart's longings?
The bird-patterned letter paper cut in half.
Once finished, she folded it close to her breast,
Before leaving, she read it again—many lines of tears,   4
Adding a few words, she burst into sobs.

Far apart, our souls melt;
My feelings hard to express.
I can't help thinking of you, in my most vivid memories.   8
Come back to join this heart-broken man,
Open the letter, and you will find the red mark gone.[68]   [*CTLS*, 2:610]

[Liu to Ch'en]

The shadow of flowers, a streak of moonlight,
Beginning with sorrow, ended with regret.
Not many tears were left when I started this letter.
Once finished, it is suddenly swept away by the wily wind,   4
The wily wind shatters my feeling.

Behind the half-rolled curtain, the faint lamplight,
As if in a dream,[69]
My soul melts as I catch sight of you.   8
When you open my letter, do read thoughtfully,
My brief dream was hard to capture in words.   [*LJS*, 1:243]

In these dramatic imitations of Ch'in Kuan's *tz'u*, the *idea* of sending letters
is transformed into the *act* of sending and receiving letters. And the cause
of separation and suffering is also different here: whereas Ch'in Kuan's
"grieving intensity" stems from political failure, that of Ch'en and Liu is
caused by lovesickness. Ch'en remembers his lover Liu Shih primarily as
a writer of letters, like the talented woman (*ts'ai-nü*) in a typical romantic
play, who took great care to choose the letter paper for the occasion and
"folded it close to her breast" (see Ch'en, lines 2, 3). The rhetorical transformation of a purely lyrical song into a lyric-dramatic song-set (written
as poetic dialogue) should be seen as virtual proof of Ming drama's strong
influence on the *tz'u*. To Ch'en and Liu, the *tz'u* meant a genre in which

lovers can speak to each other directly and confidentially about the innermost secrets of their hearts, including the physiology of their lovesickness.
In other words, the *tz'u* is not simply a form of self-expression; it is a
rhetorical artifice written to be heard, a lover's aria in the drama of genuine human passion. It is a true "song," intended at the same time to be
expressive and esoteric.

But the textuality of Ch'en's and Liu's song-letters is not confined to
its reference to Ch'in Kuan's "T'a-so hsing." Far from being simply an
allusion borrowed from an earlier model *tz'u*, the idea of sending a letter also comes from *Tzu-ch'ai chi*, the romantic play by T'ang Hsien-tsu
I discussed above in connection with Liu Shih's "Chin-ming ch'ih" *tz'u*
on the willow. In fact, the subtitle of Ch'en's and Liu's songs, "Chi-shu"
(Sending a letter), is drawn verbatim from the farewell scene (scene 25)
of *Tzu-ch'ai chi*, the very scene that has inspired Liu Shih's writing of
her *yung-wu tz'u*. For that particular farewell scene in T'ang Hsien-tsu's
play ends with the two words "chi-shu." Huo Hsiao-yü sings before her
separation from Li I:

> Tell him not to part with his sword when he goes to the frontier,
> When spotting a courier, ask him to send me letters [*chi-shu*].
>
> [scene 25, 3:1677]

And at the end of the play (scene 53), the chorus sings of the lovers' ability
to exchange poems and "understand each other's feelings" (*chih-yin*):

> Surely every talented man can write poetry,
> But how unusual to find a woman who understands his sentiments.

Now, by assuming the roles of the talented man and gifted woman exchanging letters, Ch'en Tzu-lung and Liu Shih are no doubt working
through an original but stylized use of the literary convention in lyrical
drama. Their dialogue in *tz'u* literally dramatizes the daydreaming lovers'
hope, reflecting their awareness of the artifice of their imaginings—imaginings of letters being opened, being read, being understood. Most notably,
the image of Ch'en Tzu-lung's nearly self-annihilating passion for his beloved is the product of a highly dramatized process based on the popular
image of the sentimental male lover in Ming drama.

To be sure, the rhythm and the elegant language typical of Ch'in Kuan's
tz'u are always present in Ch'en Tzu-lung's and Liu Shih's minds and help
to determine their unique style of *tz'u*. But on the other hand, they have
also learned the vigor of expression and dramatic potentialities from contemporary *ch'ü* drama, without being seduced into producing colloquial
tz'u that may read and sound like *ch'ü* (as many Ming poets had done

and as the Sung poet Liu Yung did several centuries earlier). The result is a harmonious union of a classical style and contemporary realism—with diction appearing more elegant and refined than in earlier Ming lyrics and content becoming more bold and dramatic than in traditional *tz'u*. It engenders a new, refined style which does not scorn the everyday reality of love (*ch'ing*). It is the principle of mixed styles in Ch'en's and Liu's song lyrics that defines the heart of the Yün-chien Revival of *tz'u*.

To a great extent, the *tz'u* had returned to its original status of being the *ch'ü tzu tz'u* (dramatic song lyric), totally in keeping with its primary musical function and emotional tone. Perhaps this was all it took for Ch'en and Liu to engender a true revival of the genre at a time when the "genuine spirit" (*pen-se*) of the *tz'u* had been forgotten for well over three hundred years.

1. Ch'en Tzu-lung's tomb in Sung-chiang, China. Renovation completed in November 1988.

2. A portrait of Ch'en Tzu-lung, carved on a stele at Ch'en's tomb (based on a seventeenth-century portrait). Newly inscribed by Ku T'ing-lung.

3. Emperor Ch'ien-lung's stele canonizing Ch'en
Tzu-lung posthumously as Chung-yü (Loyal and Noble).

4. The Ch'in-huai River in Nanking today.

河東君半訪初君東河繪室秋余清

景小堂野

5. A portrait of Liu Shih by Yü Chi (1739–1823).

清

女士柳如是

樓閣仕女圖軸

縱　五尺五寸七分
巾　二尺八寸八分

華藴閣君藏

6. A painting by Liu Shih.

7. Calligraphy and painting by Liu Shih.

8. Calligraphy by Ch'en Tzu-lung.

9. The Yüan Chiang Pavilion built in honor of Ch'en Tzu-lung in 1778 by imperial order of Ch'ien-lung. New inscription by Ku T'ing-lung refers to Ch'en's poem on Hsia Yün-i.

FIVE

Shih Poetry

of Reflection

Like any Chinese poet, Ch'en Tzu-
lung had a clear sense of generic distinctions. As a leader of the Yün-chien
school of *tz'u* and a diligent advocate of the classical *shih,* Ch'en must
have felt especially strongly about the genre differences between *tz'u* and
shih. But it is not simply that Ch'en writes differently in these two genres;
it is that he has attempted to express different aspects of love in poetry,
each corresponding to what he perceives as the distinct generic configurations of *tz'u* and *shih*. For Ch'en believed that generic constraints should
be both formal and thematic.

First of all, the dominant image of the beloved as a goddess in Ch'en's
shih poetry presents a sharp contrast to the flesh and blood, worldly
woman depicted in his *tz'u* poetry. In other words, the image of the *ts'ai-nü*
(talented woman) in *tz'u* has been transformed into that of the *shen-nü*
(divine woman) in *shih,* and their differences are due largely to discrimi-
nations of subject matter and style between the two genres.[1] Traditionally,
the Chinese used the following stylistic criterion to distinguish between
shih and *tz'u:* "*shih* is sublime, while *tz'u* is seductive" (*shih* chuang *tz'u*
mei). However general and simplistic this traditional view may seem, it
did play an important part in Ch'en Tzu-lung's poetic discourse. Ch'en's
acquiescence to the tradition, however, does not occur without reflection
on that tradition: by turning his beloved into a goddess in his *shih* poetry,

Ch'en Tzu-lung has literally created a "sublime" personification of the genre, putting the genre several degrees higher than *tz'u*. The basis of his love poetry in *shih* is still the concept of *ch'ing*, but *ch'ing* is treated here from a radically different viewpoint. Sensual (and even erotic) these *shih* poems are, without doubt, but their sensuality is very much abstracted and idealized as compared to the *tz'u* songs of passion. It is a profoundly reflective poetry well suited to the grand style of the orthodox *shih*.

To a certain extent, the image of the goddess used as a figure for the palace lady or the courtesan is conventional in the *shih* tradition,[2] a device no doubt adapted from the earlier *fu*. Perhaps this is why Liu Shih calls herself a "divine woman" (*shen-nü*) in her *shih* poem to Ch'en Tzu-lung (for example, "Early Autumn," *LJS*, 1:306). But simply to recognize this technique as coming from *shih*'s generic convention is an oversimplification. For behind the question of the generic quality there is something unmistakably personal about the recurrent image of the goddess in Ch'en's *shih*. On its most obvious level, his *shih* poetry containing the goddess image is a lyrical equivalent of his elaborate *fu* that often detail, through dazzling images and lengthy narration of an imaginary quest, the truth of his love relationship with Liu Shih. For example, the following *shih* poem, written perhaps in the autumn of 1633, seems to prefigure his "Ts'ai-lien *fu*" (*Fu* on picking the lotus), a *fu* already discussed in chapter 3.

> *On an Autumn Night during a Heavy Rain,*
> *Yen-yu and Jang-mu and I Gathered at the*
> *Residence of Courtesan Yang [Liu Shih], Who*
> *Mentioned She Was Quite Ill and Dispirited;*
> *The Three of Us, All Feeling a Bit Out of*
> *Sorts, Weren't Able to Drink*

Heartbroken in two different places, afflicted with the self-same passion,
Wind and rain, envious of her beauty, fill the whole town.
The parrot was startled out of a bad dream,
Better not to send the departed soul near the cuckoo.[3]   4
Amber girdle-pendant, cold in the gloomy autumn,
Tears on the lotus pillow, bits of jade on the floating leaves,
There's no sorrow that hasn't been exhausted in Ts'ao Chih's *fu*.
I went to the Western Grave-mound, and wept over the emerald filigree   8
    ornament.[4]

[*CTLS*, 2:425]

The rhetorical interplay between referential and metaphorical elements is nowhere more evident than in this poem—for the unusually long title speaks directly of factual data, while the poem proper is characterized by compact imagery and implicit meaning. The circumstantial title guides the readers to the poem's intended reference, but the symbolic associations in the poem provide a quality of lyrical enigma, constantly inviting the reader to discover new levels of significance. It is this interplay of exposure and concealment that gives the poem its ultimate power and beauty.

In the title, the poet indicates that his poem is about Liu Shih—apparently she was still using her original surname, Yang. The title speaks of "illness" but does not specify the nature of the ailment. Not until reading the poem proper does the reader discover that the illness is lovesickness, revealed figuratively through an allusion to Ts'ao Chih's "*Fu* on the Goddess of the Lo." In his lyrical conception, the poet has apparently become a Ts'ao Chih, a human lover in desperate search of the beloved goddess. Like Ts'ao Chih, he offers his girdle-pendant to the goddess as a pledge of love (line 5). And like Ts'ao Chih's goddess, Liu Shih is intimately linked with the lotus ("Tears on the lotus pillow, bits of jade on the floating leaves"). Indeed, she has become a lyrical sign pointing metaphorically to the figure of the lotus-goddess in Ch'en's "*Fu* on Picking the Lotus," in which the lovers' courtship is mapped out figuratively through the use of a recurring symbol. If the lengthy, elaborate description of the journey in quest of the goddess—a 166-line *fu* that tends to move away from the center of lyrical compactness—seems centrifugal in its motion, then the brief and concentrated image of the goddess in the 8-line *shih* represents lyricism as a centripetal force.[5]

Such a *shih* is really a "miniature *fu*" embodying a totality in itself. The same structure is found in many of Ch'en Tzu-lung's *shih* poems: each work, however short and compact, seems to serve as a lyrical variation on the "same" theme concerning the divine woman. But this does not mean that a *shih* poem takes shape by a simple subtracting of some narrative-descriptive elements of the *fu;* rather, it is a completely new creation, representing a different aesthetic value and different rhetorical significance. Unlike his *fu* on the goddess, which focus on the progressive movement of a journey, Ch'en's *shih* poems on the same subject abandon linearity in favor of imagistic juxtaposition and personal reflection. Private insight and the subjective focusing of inner contemplation are more keenly apparent in *shih* than in *fu.* For example, in his *shih* poem "On the Autumn Pool," the governing principle behind the poem's description of a love relationship remains the same from beginning to end—it consists of internalizing, condensing, intensifying, compressing, and making all images center on the poet's private reflection on his own emotional experience:

Wind ripples the scaly white waves of West Pond,
Bright clouds embroider the evening with many streaks of red.
The cold rain is like silk drawn up into the blue sky,
The pale reflection on the lake, the chill moonlight.   4
Fragrance and dampness permeate the tiered boat at dusk,
As I prepare to enter the round toad-moon floating in the mist.
Silver lamplight shines upon the water, the dragon is sad,
Tipping a cup, I sprinkle it on no human road.   8
The fair one enchantingly faces the erratic wind,
Embracing the heart of autumn in the river's reflection.
Her skirt shaped like an immortal's garment, dancing with the calm,
    blue water.
Red carp splash east of the lotus flowers.   12
She plucks the rosy clouds, fashioning them into phoenix stationery,
Casting small words of "spring silkworms" into the autumn waters.[6]
The River Goddess of Hsiang plays a jasper zither: sounds in a mirror,
Our love knots tied: night after night, we make the lotuses our haunt.

[CTLS, 1:221]

In a mere sixteen lines, the poem (though written in the Ancient Style form, rather than the more compact eight-line Regulated Style of *shih* as in the previous poem cited above) manages to achieve a complex world of imagistic suggestiveness, indeed assuming a greater load of associative energy than would a much longer *fu*. In a personal note on the poem, Ch'en Tzu-lung explained that he composed the poem at West Pond, during an outing with his friends Yen-yu, Jang-mu, and Liu Shih (*CTLS*, 1:221). But the poem turns out to be dominated by a feeling of mystery transcending the living world, giving us infinite space for imagination. For the poet writes as if he has walked into the inside of the moon (line 6), and the imagery seems to be that of a fairy tale. The River Goddess of the Hsiang, the phoenix stationery made of rosy clouds, the heart of autumn reflected in the river—all these allude to the world of fairies, a world entirely unlike that of the concrete realities in Ch'en's *tz'u*.

But at the center of Ch'en's *shih* poem are the images of the mirror and the reflecting pool that inspire the erotic sensibility of desire. The "sounds in a mirror" (line 15) are metaphorically linked to the reflection in the water (line 10), creating an auditory and visual metaphor of the lovers' intimacy. Like the erotic experience itself, the act of mirroring has become that of echoing, an intriguing mixture of fact and fantasy, the real and the fictive. On the surface, the poet is again using Liu Shih's nickname Ying-lien (Pitying My Reflected Image) figuratively to create a rhetoric of intimacy: the word "lien," which means "love," becomes a linguistic and thus symbolic equivalent of the word "lotus" (pronounced the same as *lien*), which appears at the poem's conclusion. In fact, the lotus-pond image in line 12 clearly encourages such a reading.

We should note that the West Pond, the main subject of description of the poem, was also known as the White-Dragons (Pai-lung) Pond,[7] which reminds us of Ch'en's name Tzu-lung (Child-Dragon). Thus, the line "Silver lamplight shines upon the water, the dragon is sad" (line 7) can be read as the poet's own formula for self-reflection, indeed, as a deliberate parallel to Liu Shih's name, Ying-lien. In a way, Ch'en the lover has become the duplicated image of Liu the beloved. By echoing her language of self-reflection he announces his own equivalence to the goddess's mirror-image. This point takes on greater meaning when we realize that Liu Shih wrote a similar poem on a similar occasion, obviously a poem to match Ch'en's. Liu's piece is entitled "Written While Climbing a Buddhist Temple in the Dragon Pond as the Wind Was Blowing—to Rhyme with His Poem" (*LJS*, 1:54). The poem vividly recalls Ch'en's "On the Autumn Pool": it too centers upon the illusory image of a reflecting pool, making it metaphorically associated with the gleaming reflection of a "jade mirror" (*yü-ching*). Ch'en's name "Dragon" appears as part of Liu's poem title, while Liu's own name, Ying-lien, is carefully embedded in the poem's opening and closing lines. The poem captures the mirror's double nature of being real and fictional.

The mirror's complex duality—reality and fiction, the tangible and the intangible, fact and otherworldly ideal—is portrayed even more vividly in a poem entitled "The Frosty Moon," which Ch'en Tzu-lung wrote perhaps after Liu Shih had left him in 1635:

The fair one gave me a mirror engraved with a pair of dragons,
And said, "Like the bright moon, it preserves my pure heart."
Its frigid light, like a reflection of her at our parting,
A shame it's turned into these dense, frosty flowers.   4
I clasp the mirror in search of her image—nowhere to be seen,
By the frost I gaze at the moon—so many mournful sounds.
Red silk all over the river, the dragon woman is awake,
I wouldn't begrudge two gold pieces to buy it.   8
The warm fragrance is dense, like the misty fog,
I cut out the frost and moon to make a cold coverlet.
The chill of the coverlet itself is bearable,
But the chill of the dream is hard to bear.   12
Phoenixes are separated by thousands of miles,
The chariot of the wind and the steeds of the clouds all come in pursuit
    of them,

My sorrowful soul, disoriented, is all the more confused,
Making me sigh deeply, incessantly, even now.   [*CTLS*, 1:231]   16

The mirror, which contains the "pure heart" of the beloved, is a perfect
pledge of love. In essence and form, the mirror—round, translucent, endlessly reflecting—is like the omnipresent moon, a symbol of constancy. It
follows that the beloved, nowhere to be seen, has perhaps been turned
into an elusive moon goddess, forever inaccessible to her human lover—
despite his journey to mythical realms in search of the goddess (line 14).
The theme of a lengthy quest for a goddess is of course one of Chinese
poetry's most ancient conventions,[8] and it definitely reminds us of European courtly love poetry, in which the lover elevates his lady to the status
of a goddess and attempts to win her through persistence and homage.

But Ch'en's poem is not only a quest for the goddess; it is also, what
is more important, a description of the intricate powers of inner reflection, recognition, and identity—presented metaphorically by the image
of the mirror. By focusing on the reflection in a mirror, Ch'en explicitly
directs us not to read the quest theme in the traditional way established
by the ancient poets of *sao* and *fu*.[9] The powers of the mirror come from
an "irreducible honesty" which forces the viewer to see what he "cannot
otherwise see."[10] What happens when the poet looks into the mirror? Sur-
prisingly, Ch'en Tzu-lung does not see his own reflection, as one expects.
He notices only that the image of the beloved goddess is "nowhere to be
seen," for she has been turned into the "dense, frosty flowers" (line 4).
In other words, she has become "flowers in the mirror," the proverbial
symbol of illusion. Somehow the poet defines himself through his *relation* with this new flower image in the mirror, an image reminding him
of the "frosty moon" (which is also the poem's title). Thus, what is reflected is not the subject's own image, but a reflection of self-reflection
based on introspection and imagination. Indeed, the mirror itself has become the poet's perfect metaphor for poetic interiority and self-absorbed
contemplation.

Ch'en's particular liking for mirror metaphors has a basis in real life.
According to reliable biographical sources, Liu Shih developed an infatua-
tion with mirrors and accumulated a large collection of them—in fact,
after her death many Ch'ing poets composed verses in remembrance of
her treasured mirrors (*LJS*, 1:271). For Liu Shih the mirror evidently was
not simply a possession; rather it served her, as it did Ch'en Tzu-lung, as
an important symbol. For example, on the back of one of her mirrors, Liu
Shih wrote, "When the sun shines upon it, lotus blossoms appear / By the

pond, it brings out the full moon" (*LJS*, 1:272). It was the self-transposing power of the mirror—the power of being able to change itself into the water and moon—that was meaningful to Liu Shih.

In Ch'en Tzu-lung's fantasy, however, water (an extension of the mirror image) often serves as a metaphor for tragic isolation—especially in those poems written after his separation from Liu Shih. In particular, the theme of separation by a wide river dominates Ch'en's love poetry in the *shih* form. The river stretches out of view and is transformed into something intangible. It symbolizes the poet's consciousness of a tragic situation beyond man's control. On this side of the river, life is constituted by the feeling of loneliness; on the other side of the river is the loving yet elusive goddess constantly beyond reach. In his poem "The Evening of the Double-Seventh: In Imitation of Hsieh T'iao," the poet imagines that he and his beloved have become the constellations of the Herdboy and the Weaving Maid, legendary "star-crossed lovers" separated forever by the Heavenly River (the Milky Way):[11]

In early autumn, I discern the clouds and trees,
In the setting sun, a slight chill sets in.
I stroke the leaves on the jade steps,
And pluck the divine fragrant flowers.   4
Emerald lotuses grow on an autumn islet,
A medley of flowers stirs in the dusky fragrance.
The twilight mist and dew are fine and enchanting,
At this moment, we gaze out at each other from our ornate chambers.   8
I stretch my neck in anticipation of our meeting,
Who knows how long the road is?
The Jade Cord stars are beautiful in the thin mist,
The Milky Way is vast and distant.   12
A lonely magpie at the Tiao-ling Park
Leaves me no bridge with which to cross the river.
The clear sky is quiet and cloudless,
The vermilion bird clothed in lovely garments.   16
Stalks of orchids are graceful in the dark night,
All the more unforgettable in this gentle wind.
Greeting the cool breeze, I embrace the "cloud and rain."
Like the scene at the southern slopes of the Shaman Mountain.   20

[*CTLS*, 1:125]

According to tradition, the Herdboy and the Weaving Maid, separated all year round, are allowed to visit each other on the seventh day of the seventh lunar month, upon which day magpies would come in great flocks to build a bridge for the unfortunate lovers. What makes Ch'en's poem especially sad is that not even on this evening of all evenings can the poet be reunited with his beloved because only a single magpie appears, leaving him "no bridge with which to cross the river" (line 14). The poet suffers the anguish each lover must suffer in the face of frustrated desire, a frustration symbolized by the unfeeling, endlessly extending river.

Ch'en's poem is modeled after the poetic style of the Six Dynasties poet Hsieh T'iao (464–99), a fact Ch'en acknowledges in the poem's title. What Ch'en owes to this earlier poet, I believe, is the no-bridge-to-get-across image, which he has borrowed from Hsieh's famous poem entitled "On My Way Back to the Capital. . . . A Poem for My Colleagues in Ching-chou" (HCHW, 2:1426).[12] In this poem, Hsieh T'iao laments the pain of separation from Prince Sui, a dear friend from whom he was forced to separate because of political pressure from the emperor. But in Ch'en Tzu-lung's poem, this traditional theme of friendship—which has perhaps encouraged generations of commentators to read the conventional story of the Herdboy and the Weaving Maid as topical allegory referring to the ruler-minister relationship[13]—is now converted back to that of romantic love. And the poem ends poignantly with an allusion to Sung Yü's "Kao T'ang fu," a fu detailing the erotic meeting in a dream between King Hsiang of Ch'u and the Goddess of the Shaman Mountain, who had been transformed from the Spirit of the Morning Cloud (Chao-yün),[14] a name that immediately recalls Liu Shih's nickname, "Cloud-Beauty" (Yün-chüan). Thus, only in his dream can Ch'en Tzu-lung see the vision of his goddess again. Only in his memory can he overcome the boundaries of space and time and reach the other side of the river.

On the other hand, nothing is more painful than the pain of memory, like an impassable gulf constantly reminding us of the distance between the present and the past. Inevitably it is on the night of the Double-Seventh, at the annual reunion of the Herdboy and the Weaving Maid, that an earthly lover suffers most from the pain of memory. For example, in Ch'en's shih poem entitled "Written on the Eve of the Double-Seventh, the Year of Wu-yin, During An Illness," we find images of the familiar symptoms of lovesickness resulting from the tormenting experience of recollection:

> Once again, I'm ill as the festival approaches,
> The Autumn Wind stirs the pure waves,
> Blue clouds cluster as the moon sinks,
> A magpie from the Tiao-ling Park traverses the stars.[15]
> Your charming smile in the distant bright chamber,
> Pale moonlight floods the cool mats.

4

How unbearable: on this night we are both ill,
Painfully recollecting the past, with one Heavenly River between us.   8
[*CTLS*, 2:359]

Thus, the "Heavenly River," or Milky Way (line 8), has literally become the seat of reflection, like the shining surface of the mirror. It offers a correspondence between the imaginary land and reality, between the mystic union and human love. And the feeling of tenderness reaches its peak through this metaphor of the Heavenly River, which unites idealized divine passion with the most earthly expression of desire. This point becomes especially meaningful when we note that Ch'en's poem on the Double-Seventh was composed the same year (that is, in the Year of Wu-yin, 1638, three years after their separation) he wrote the long, important preface for Liu Shih's first collection of poems, the *Wu-yin ts'ao* (see chapter 3). By openly establishing their relationship in literature, Ch'en and Liu were surely trying to overcome the pain of separation in life.

Whereas in his *tz'u* Ch'en perceives himself to be endlessly suffering from the pain of separation, in his *shih* poetry the river/separation motif is not always a form of pessimism. In *shih* the oneness of the lovers provides an optimistic perspective, and indeed a solution, to the problem of separation. One of Ch'en's most plainly autobiographical poems, "Everlasting Longing," describes a faith in the eternity of the lovers' oneness, a kind of affirmation and realization derived from self-reflection:

The fair one, in the past, stood before the spring wind,
An enchanting flower about to speak, but silenced by the thin mist.
When happy, she leaned her slender waist against the embroidered
    pillow,
When sad, she played mournful strings with her pale hands.   4
The fair one is now in the autumn wind,
By the blue clouds in the remote distance across the river.
Writing fills her rosy-cloud stationery, but she would not send it,
Even Purple Mermaid must be envious of the charming Moon Lady.   8
"I advise you not to journey into that dream;
The roads between the sky and sea are rugged, highly uneven.
Even if you were to ride a wind to the Jade Palace,
Jade-tower immortals would speak to you disdainfully.   12
Traces of my fragrance at our parting still linger on your sleeves,
If the fragrance has feeling, it will be like that of old.
I only hope your heart knows its old friend.
Need we always lean against each other by the fine-worked window?"   16
[*CTLS*, 1:262]

Here the poet imagines that his beloved—now the Moon Goddess presiding over the Jade Palace "in the remote distance across the river"—has asked her messenger, Purple Mermaid, to send him a letter in order to reassure him of the permanent value of their undying love. This attitude of sturdy stoicism seems to be a lyrical recasting of a somewhat "prosaic" communication in *fu* between the lovers shortly after their separation. In works entitled "*Fu* on Parting" and "Imitation of *Fu* on Parting," respectively, Liu Shih and Ch'en Tzu-lung made the following exchange:[16]

[Liu to Ch'en]

Even bosom friends like us have to part from each other,
Though we are now separated, our love will surely grow stronger.
Let us walk the same path till old age,
And preserve our hearts' fortitude and purity.   [*LJS*, 1:321]

[Ch'en to Liu]

As long as our hearts do not change,
Even if separated by thousands of miles, we'll remain one.
For delight's sake, need we always share the same coverlet and canopy,
And always heave a long sigh before the bridge?[17]   [*LJS*, 1:324]

It is in Ch'en's *shih* poem "Everlasting Longing," however, that the idea of eternal love acquires a dimension of convincing depth and intensity. This poem is again built upon an evocation of the divine world of the goddess, a world that transcends human space and time. And the redeeming power of this celestial world over the temporal and spatial limits of human passion brings about the triumph of this eternal love. Indeed, Ch'en's poem echoes the coda of Po Chü-i's (772–846) famous "Song of Unending Sorrow," in which the eternity of love can be affirmed only after the spirit of Yang Kuei-fei is turned into the Fairy of Eternal Fidelity in a distant Fairy-Mountain Palace:

Now with deep emotion, she takes out their old pledges.
Sending back, through the envoy, a filigree coffer and a gold hairpin.
Keeping one branch of the hairpin, and one part of the coffer,
Breaking the gold of the hairpin, dividing the coffer into two:
"Let our hearts be as firm as this gold and this coffer—
In Heaven or on earth, we shall meet again."   [*CTS*, 4819]

Thus, the rhetorical meeting point of the beloved and the goddess is not simply a metaphorical resemblance but that of a shared third term: the supreme power of *ch'ing*. This *ch'ing*, transcending time and space, was at the center of the late-Ming sublimation of love. Since *ch'ing* is man pursuing true love and compassion in order to redeem himself, it is in the world of eternity (symbolized by divine woman) that *ch'ing* appears in its purest manifestation. In *shih* poetry, where sincerity is paramount, this pure image of the beloved goddess would surely appear to have absorbed the male lover's attention to the exclusion of everything else. But at the same time, hidden in the vivid description of the imaginary world of the enchanting fairies, we can detect in Ch'en's poem a highly rationalized act of stoical self-reflection—"I only hope your heart knows its old friend / Need we always lean against each other by the fine-worked window?" The poet's realization of a new sense of courage in the face of the tragic reality of separation calls to mind Su Shih's (1036–1101) well-known statement on the universal problem of separation:

> For human beings there are sorrows and joys, separations and unions,
> For the moon, there are cloudy and clear skies, waxing and waning phases,
> These things can never be perfect, from of old.
> I only wish that we could live long enough
> To share this beautiful moon across a thousand miles.[18]   [CST, 1:280]

All this has a bearing on the complex and intricate meanings of *ch'ing* which characterize Ch'en Tzu-lung and Liu Shih's notion of love. To a certain extent, Ch'en and Liu were simply following a "motto for lovers" set up earlier by the Sung poet Ch'in Kuan, who in his *tz'u* song "Ch'üeh-ch'iao hsien" in celebration of the long-enduring love between the Herd-boy and the Weaving Maid, makes the following pivotal statement:

> When *ch'ing* between two lovers is long and enduring,
> Need they be together day and night?   [CST, 1:459]

Ch'in Kuan's innovative perception concerning love—which had markedly revised the age-old tone of lamentation characterizing poetry on the Double Seventh legend[19]—no doubt helped shape the late-Ming notion of *ch'ing*. The best proof of Ch'in Kuan's influence can be found in Ming drama, especially in T'ang Hsien-tsu's *Tzu-ch'ai chi* (Story of the purple hairpin), in which the heroine Huo Hsiao-yü, suffering from a serious case of lovesickness on the eve of the Double-Seventh, is given counsel by her wise mother, Pao Ssu-niang:

> When people are in love,
> If the love is long and enduring, based on solemn oath,
> Need they be together day and night?
> And always delight in clinging to each other?   [scene 33, 3:1706]

Obviously it was from Ch'in Kuan's "Ch'üeh-ch'iao hsien" *tz'u* that T'ang Hsien-tsu's play took its elements of emotional stoicism.

But Ch'en Tzu-lung's contribution lies elsewhere. With Ch'en, literature is genre-determined. Whereas Ch'in Kuan had introduced a new, sublimated idea of love in his *tz'u,* perhaps under the influence of his mentor Su Shih,[20] Ch'en Tzu-lung might have considered such a theme and style unfit for the *tz'u,* a genre specifically reserved, in his view, for the concrete *realities* of human passion. On the other hand, he was apparently attracted to the elements of sublimity present in some of the *tz'u* poems of Ch'in Kuan and Su Shih. Ch'en Tzu-lung's response and his solution to the problem of stylistic configurations are based on genre distinction: he has incorporated Ch'in's and Su's thought of emotional stoicism, with its morals and ideals, into his own *shih,* while at the same time keeping the highly realistic and sentimental character of his *tz'u* poetry intact. When we compare Ch'en's *shih* poem "Everlasting Longing" with his "T'a-so hsing" *tz'u,* subtitled "Sending a Letter" (discussed in chapter 4), the stylistic differences between the two genres are especially noticeable. Both poems are about sending and receiving love letters—but, whereas the former is characterized by a calm and willing acceptance of physical separation from the beloved, the latter focuses on the burning and chilling of lovesickness suffered by a tearful, "heart-broken man" and indeed is thus an emotional outburst of pain and anxiety. Moreover, the idealistic schema of the unattainable goddess who inspires the human poet from afar—a schema highly central to his *shih* style—is totally absent from his love poetry in the *tz'u* form, in which a very different kind and level of style is required. Most interesting, as far as generic discrimination is concerned, Ch'en and Liu complemented each other perfectly. Like Ch'en, Liu developed in her *tz'u* a love poetry characterized by emotional realism and passionate abandon of feeling. And Liu's *shih* poetry on the same subject, like Ch'en's, conveys the idea of sublimity and calm reflection, to the extent that she compares herself to the nature-loving recluse T'ao Ch'ien (365–427).[21] Their keen awareness of generic propriety and self-conscious choice of rhetorical devices make Ch'en Tzu-lung and Liu Shih, more than any other figures of their time, ideally qualified to promote a poetic renaissance in the late Ming.

PART 3

The Poetry of
Loyalism

SIX

Loyalism as
Love in
Tz'u Poetry

By 1645, ten years after Liu Shih had left Ch'en Tzu-lung, major cities in the lower Yangtze delta like Nanking and Sung-chiang had all fallen to the Manchus. Ch'en shaved his head, disguised himself as a monk, and managed to take refuge in a Buddhist temple called the Water-Moon Monastery. From then until his death in 1647 he was actively involved in various underground resistance activities. By that time Liu Shih, then married to Ch'ien Ch'ien-i, had also shaved her head and become a Buddhist, though perhaps for personal, rather than political, reasons (*LJS*, 2: 802–03).

It was during the fugitive period between 1645 and his eventual martyrdom that Ch'en produced what several Ch'ing critics regarded as the most "sorrowful" and "beautiful" verse in *tz'u*.[1] This part of Ch'en's work has been most familiar to later critics, causing them to see Ch'en exclusively as a patriotic poet. But one crucial fact about Ch'en's poetry that has been ignored by scholars and readers is that his later *tz'u* songs of loyalism bear a striking stylistic resemblance to his earlier *tz'u* songs of love. To a large extent, the language of loyalism in his patriotic *tz'u* has been borrowed from the language of love, and there is an almost point-for-point correspondence between the two kinds of poetry—a correspondence that can only make us as readers see the later *tz'u* as an intentional "rewriting" of the earlier *tz'u,* an attempt to combine in one language these two major forms of human passion. The following two *tz'u* songs, one on love and one on loyalism, demonstrate to perfection the emotional intensity and sensory power of expression they share:

"T'ao-yüan i ku-jen": Rainy Dusk from the Southern Chamber

From the little chamber, I gaze afar across the plains:
Holding the curtain aside, I see a sail on the Southern Shore.
May I ask, where does the evening wind blow
The spring of strewn blossoms?   4

The road of *hsiang-ssu* [love's longings] is immeasurable,
But how far precisely is the horizon?
Don't listen to the whispers of charming orioles,
My grief reaches its height in the rain of pear blossoms.   8

[CTLS, 2:602]

"Tien chiang ch'un": My Feelings on a Spring Day During a Storm

The beauty of spring fills my vision,
An east wind, as usual, blows red blossoms past.
In these spells of mist,
Flowers alone are hard to preserve.   4

Hsiang-ssu [love's longings] in my dream:
The road of the noble sons of my old country.
Spring has lost its master,
Where the cuckoo cries,
Tears are stained with rouge in the rain.   [CTLS, 2:596]   8

The first poem, most likely composed in the spring of 1636, describes the poet's longing for his beloved Liu Shih. The second, written perhaps in the spring of 1647, mourns the fall of the Ming dynasty. Despite their entirely different themes, the language and images employed in the two poems are much the same. In both the poet uses the term *hsiang-ssu* (love's longings), a term commonly reserved for the description of sensual love and lovesickness. Further, both poems exhibit a sense of helplessness typical of men suffering from the pain of memory. Even the objects of reminiscence are named in a similar fashion—the beloved in the love poem is called "*ku*-jen" (which is part of the tune title), meaning "my *old* sweetheart"; and that of the political poem is called "*ku*-kuo," "my *old* country" (line 6). The means by which such feelings are provoked are also the same: it is through the associative power of sensory images of fallen flowers and of wind and rain that the poems convey their vivid sense of emotional intensity. These pivotal images work like symbols, constantly kindling our imaginative associations—so that the "rain of pear blossoms" symbolizing the tears of the poet's beloved corresponds metaphorically to the cuckoo's tears of blood "in the rain," a symbol for the suffering soul of the Ming emperor.[2]

Essential to Ch'en Tzu-lung's unique poetics is his method of revisionary interpretation, of reinterpreting loyalist feelings as a form of romantic love. According to this self-interpretative procedure, his earlier *tz'u* poems on romantic love have become the predecessors of his later *tz'u* on loyalist sentiment. In fact, not only his *tz'u* poetry but his life also is being reinterpreted, so that his life—both public and private registers—is now being viewed in retrospect as a full manifestation of *ch'ing*. Such a scheme of interpretation may be compared to the notion of *figura* in the medieval European exegetical tradition. Erich Auerbach defines *figura* as "something real and historical which announces something else that is also real and historical,"[3] for it is the purpose of the figural interpretation to establish "a connection between two events or persons in such a way that the first signifies not only itself but also the second, while the second involves or fulfills the first."[4]

Although figura in the West is reserved primarily for biblical interpretation—it is used to interpret figures and events in the Old Testament as prefiguring those of the New Testament—it can be called on to contribute to our discussion of Ch'en Tzu-lung's *tz'u* poetics. What makes the notion of figura especially applicable to our late-Ming poet is the fact that figural interpretation claims historical concreteness for both events under consideration, unlike allegory, which typically focuses on what the sign *signifies* and thus largely diminishes the concrete historicity of the *sign* itself.[5] Since we can claim with confidence that love and loyalism were both real experiences for Ch'en, they were thus like two poles of a figure, each signifying and fulfilling the other. Moreover, like the two terms in a figural interpretation, love and loyalism in Ch'en are important because of their "temporality"—one representing the past and the other the present.[6] Through the figural union of love and loyalism, his present life poignantly reveals the past's meaning—a meaning not available to the past self of Ch'en Tzu-lung—and simultaneously draws on the past to enlarge the meaning of the present. Viewed from a larger perspective, love and loyalism are both contained in a "supratemporal" unity, the timeless world of idealized *ch'ing*. This assertion of unity would have been particularly satisfying for the intellectuals of the late Ming.

As we saw in chapter 2, late-Ming literati desired to merge these two forms of *ch'ing* so that any reference to one would necessarily implicate the other, a conception radically different from the traditional separation of romantic love from moral heroism. But Ch'en Tzu-lung's contribution lies in turning a cultural phenomenon into a new poetics of *tz'u,* thus establishing a method of revisionary interpretation in the aesthetic tradition itself. Indeed, Ch'en's accomplishment seems to parallel John Donne's innovative merging of sexual and religious language in seventeenth-century English poetry.[7]

The stylistic features of Ch'en Tzu-lung's loyalist poems in the *tz'u* form are strongly reminiscent of those of Li Yü's (937–78) *tz'u.* Li Yü, one of the greatest *tz'u* poets in the Chinese tradition, was the last ruler of the Southern T'ang. He lost his kingdom to the Sung emperor in 975. Early in 976 he was taken to the Sung capital and remained under house arrest there until his death two and a half years later.[8] The sharp contrast between past and present in his life (and thus between happiness and sorrow) provided Li Yü with a basis for his intensely lyrical style of *tz'u.*[9] Sensory visualization and subjective voice characterize his song lyrics, as in this "Wu yeh t'i" *tz'u,* which may have been written during his last years in captivity:

> The forest flowers have lost their spring red
> Before their time!
> Nothing can be done about the cold rain of morning and the wind of night.
>
> Rouge tears
> Are enchanting—
> When shall I see you again?
> Indeed life is full of sorrow, like a river endlessly flowing east.[10]
>
> [*CTWT,* 1:224]

Reading this poem, we are immediately reminded of Ch'en Tzu-lung's "Tien chiang ch'un" *tz'u* cited above, in which the mingling images of fallen flowers and rouge-tears of rain also corresponded to the poet's sorrowful feeling.

Perhaps by imitating Li Yü's style of *tz'u,* Ch'en Tzu-lung was secretly comparing his own life experiences to Li Yü's. Like Li Yü, Ch'en portrayed himself as a lover in his early poetry. And like Li Yü, Ch'en met with a reversal of fate in midlife due to a political crisis, thus becoming keenly aware of the nature of suffering. Both of these poets felt a strong need to express their loyalist feelings in *tz'u* poetry, to make their *tz'u* a living testimony to their hearts and souls. The similarities in their lives and works are so strong that some critics, for example, T'an Hsien, even regarded Ch'en Tzu-lung as Li Yü's reincarnation (*hou-shen*).[11] The only major difference between them, according to Hu Yün-yüan, is that Ch'en's poetry expresses a more intensified feeling of grief:[12] "Ch'en's *tz'u* lyrics are permeated with lamentation and lingering sorrow, and they can be compared to Li Yü's [Hou-chu's] many fine verses on his past. However, Li's image of 'washing his face in tears' falls far short of Ch'en's 'shedding blood and burying the soul.' "[13]

One crucial difference between the two poets, however, has escaped the traditional scholars' attention: whereas Li Yü's love songs are noticeably different from his patriotic songs in terms of rhetoric and style,[14] Ch'en Tzu-lung's *tz'u* on love and loyalism share the same rhetorical methods. In the case of Li Yü, love poetry in *tz'u* tends to be descriptive or dramatic, with the poetic voice often assuming an objective point of view.[15] In sharp contrast, his poems mourning the fall of his country seem to be characterized by a strong expressiveness that is anything but objective. In other words, unlike Ch'en Tzu-lung, who consciously combined love with patriotism, Li Yü separated these two themes and these two kinds of human feeling.

To return to the stylistic devices of Ch'en Tzu-lung's *tz'u:* the shared poetics of love and loyalism often reflects actual circumstances in the poet's life. For example, the image of rain is predominant in both Ch'en's love and loyalist song lyrics, as may be seen in his "T'ao-yüan i ku-jen" and "Tien chiang ch'un" *tz'u,* in which both the subtitles and the poems themselves suggest a symbolic meaning for the rain (or tears of rain) image. But, as it happens, this poetic device, which dominates the imagistic textual web of the poems, is based on actual external circumstances—for spring in South China was (and still is) invariably a prolonged rainy season. And it seems that Ch'en and Liu wrote many of their love songs during those months, as is reflected in the subtitles of several of their *tz'u* lyrics: "The Spring Rain," "The Wind and the Rain," "Listening to the Raindrops," among others (*LJS*, 1:266). Similarly, many of Ch'en's loyalist *tz'u*—chief among them his two final pieces, one on the Cold Food Festival and the other on Tomb-Sweeping Day (*CTLS*, 2:611, 616)—were written during the rainy season, as was noted by Wang Yün, a student of Ch'en Tzu-lung: "[When he composed those poems], it was raining for an entire ten-day period. Master Ch'en [Tzu-lung] went to visit Yin Yüan-su (a *chung-han* official) at his Villa, and later he stopped at the house of Ch'ien Yen-lin in Wu-t'ang. Because of the rain, I was unable to accompany him on either occasion."[16]

Thus, it is only natural that a creative poet like Ch'en Tzu-lung would make the image of rain, originally a mere description of reality, partake of the symbolic in his *tz'u* poetry. What further distinguishes his recurrent use of the rain motif from the conventional rain image in *tz'u* is its telling and constant association with the theme of the Cold Food (*Han-shih*) Festival. Again this motif appears in both his love poems and his loyalist poems. The most notable examples can be found in his "Mu shan hsi" *tz'u* (dated ca. 1636) and "T'ang to ling" *tz'u* (dated 1647), both of which contain the rain image and are subtitled "Cold Food Festival":

"Mu shan hsi": Cold Food Festival

Blue clouds, fragrant grass,
A brocade of plains and rivers as far as the eye can see,
Kingfisher-green illuminates the cold pond.
In the drizzling rain   4
Willows are pale and yellow.
As the moon appears, all sounds are cut off.
In stocking feet, she walks on the blossoms' shadows.
Peach blossoms in full bloom,   8
Pear blossoms thin—
She touches them all with slender hands.

This day last year,
I recall, in the small garden,   12
Drinking into the night and becoming tipsy,
She cast away her amorous heart,
Her red sleeves dangled quietly.
The beautiful spring now is just the same,   16
But that happy dream is already a world apart.
It is sunset,
And evening again:
We have left the east wind behind.   [*CTLS*, 2:616]   20

"T'ang to ling": Cold Food Festival

Hearing at this time about our late emperor's burial, I felt something I couldn't bear to express.

Blue-green grass surrounds the fragrant woods,
The cold pond swells with deep water.
At fifth watch, wind and rain block the distant mountain from view,
Quivering flowers in the rain, tears upon the blossoms,   4
They can't be blown away,
Both are hard to bear.

A pair of ornamental designs embroidered with golden threads;
On the sandy flats, a lacquered coach creeps along;   8
Beyond the palace ladies' tombs, the dark shades of the willow.

I look back at the pine-and-cypress path to the Western Grave-mound,
Heartbroken,
I tie a lover's knot.   [*CTLS*, 2:611]

Though written more than ten years apart, the two poems were composed
shortly before the Cold Food Festival in the third lunar month, when
people put out their fires and eat cold food.[17] Each poem opens with descriptions of scenery surrounding the "cold pond," using highly similar
vocabularies and sensory images. Flower imagery in the first stanza of each
poem serves as a symbolic equivalent of emotions expressed in the second stanza. And most critical, the predominant rain image in both poems
seems to suggest the theme and mood of reminiscence so often associated
with Chinese festivals. Grace Fong has observed that "Chinese poets over
the centuries have had a penchant for composing festival poems," for festivals have "become times when they may feel a strong longing for friends
and loved ones."[18] In Ch'en Tzu-lung, the Cold Food Festival is a key setting for many of his poems in remembrance of love—for example, "The
Cold Food Rain" and "The Cold Food" quatrains (*CTLS*, 2:583; 1:241),
written between 1635 and 1640. Thus, Ch'en's "Mu shan hsi" *tz'u* cited
above represents just another effort to interweave the Cold Food Festival
motif with the theme of reminiscence of the beloved.

But Ch'en's "T'ang to ling" *tz'u* mourning the death of the Ming emperor surprises us with the same rhetoric of love. The emperor, as we find
him in the poem, inspires love that is unambiguously sensual—the poet
says, "Heartbroken / I tie a lover's knot." Moreover, the second half of
the poem is adapted from an old love poem attributed to the fifth-century
courtesan Su Hsiao-hsiao:

> I ride in a lacquered coach,
> My love rides a black steed.
> Where shall we tie our love-knots?
> Under the pine and cypress of the Western Grave-mound.[19]

Legend has it that Su Hsiao-hsiao was buried under the Hsi-ling Bridge by
the West Lake in Hangchow, and that after her death her lovers continually visited her tomb site. It is said that on stormy nights her singing voice
could be heard coming from the grave. The grave is generally known as
the Western Grave-mound, a place Ch'en Tzu-lung and Liu Shih seem to
have frequented, especially during the Cold Food Festival. Four years after
their separation, Liu Shih wrote with fond memories of such outings:

> Most memorable is the Cold Food path to the Western Grave-mound,
> The peach blossoms feed on the spirit of the beauty.   [*LJS*, 1:242]

And Ch'en, in a poem written expressly for Liu Shih, speaks of going "to the Western Grave-mound" and weeping "over the emerald filigree ornament" (*CTLS*, 2:425). Allusions to the Su Hsiao-hsiao legend have become a shared code in the lovers' poems in remembrance of their love.

Thus, the image of the Western Grave-mound in Ch'en's "T'ang to ling" *tz'u* may be yet another allusion to the poet's own remembrance of love, based on the characteristic recurrence of that image in his love poetry. Indeed, the whole "T'ang to ling" *tz'u* could be taken for a love song were it not for the fact that the poet has clearly indicated in his preface that the *tz'u* was composed right after he had heard about his "late emperor's burial," when he "felt something [he] couldn't bear to express."[20] It is especially revealing that Ch'en should have chosen the Cold Food Festival, a recurrent motif in his love *tz'u*, as the setting for his "T'ang to ling" *tz'u* expressing his loyalist sentiments. But the truth is that after the fall of the Southern Sung, the Cold Food Festival, a "general festival for the dead,"[21] had become a time for loyalists to offer sacrifices at the imperial tombs. For example, the Sung loyalist Lin Ching-hsi (1242–1310) wrote in one of his poems,[22]

> I still remember the annual sacrifice performed at the Cold Food Festival,
> When scions of the old ruling house carried incense on horseback.

And later, Wang Kuo-wei, a loyalist to the Ch'ing, concludes his famous poem "The I-ho Park" with poignant references to the annual Cold Food sacrifice:

> At the Ting-ling tombs, pines and cypresses grow luxuriantly,
> Reflecting on the rise and fall [of the Ch'ing], they should cry out with
>   grief.
> Yet I recall that every year on the Cold Food Festival,
> The Marquis Chu personally offers sacrifices at the Thirteen Imperial
>   Tombs.[23]

What makes Ch'en Tzu-lung's "T'ang to ling" *tz'u* fundamental to the loyalist tradition is not only that it uses the Cold Food Festival theme, but also that it refers implicitly to a tragic historical event, the so-called incident of the tombs, which took place at the end of the Southern Sung but had become for Ming loyalists a topos of their own suffering and political resistance. That the Western Grave-mound, a pivotal image in Ch'en's poem, is located in Hangchow is central to the political interpretation I am reconstructing. For Hangchow (Lin-an) used to be the capital of the Southern Sung, and the imperial tombs were on the slopes of the Yüeh mountain in nearby Kuei-chi. In 1278, on the eve of the fall of the Southern Sung and soon after the patriotic hero Wen T'ien-hsiang had been captured by the Mongols, a Tibetan lama (on orders from the Mongols) opened and looted the six Sung imperial tombs and numerous graves of high officials, amounting to one hundred and one in all.[24] The incident was so appalling that practically every Chinese scholar in the regions of Hang-chow and Kuei-chi was moved to action. T'ang Chüeh (1247–?) and Lin Ching-hsi (1242–1310) were among the most active local scholars. Out-raged and grieved by the event, T'ang Chüeh managed to enlist a group of young people, in the disguise of medicinal-herb collectors, to gather some scattered imperial bones and rebury them on Mount Lan-t'ing (Mount Orchid Pavilion), a site associated with purification rituals since the time of Wang Hsi-chih (301–79).

Later, the same Tibetan lama ordered that whatever imperial remains were found in the area should be buried together with animal bones in Hangchow with a white pagoda to mark them. The Chinese again were deeply offended. But Lin Ching-hsi managed at least to transplant six wintergreen (holly) trees from the original Ch'ang-chao palace of the Sung to the burial mounds on Mount Lan-t'ing to commemorate the eternal "presence" of the dead emperors and empresses. Many Sung loyalists, in-cluding the famous poet and scholar Hsieh Ao (1249–95), wrote poems celebrating the transplanting of the wintergreen trees.[25] And the winter-green tree subsequently became a symbol of patriotic love. As Lin Ching-hsi says in one of his poems, "Only the spring breeze knows my heart. / Year after year, the cuckoo cries on the wintergreen tree."[26]

But in literature what eventually became most memorable about the incident of the tombs was that it spurred the creation of thirty-seven "*tz'u* songs celebrating objects" (*yung-wu tz'u*) by T'ang Chüeh and thirteen other Sung loyalists. The group of protesters wrote the songs during five meetings they held secretly in places near Hangchow to mourn the tragic event. These *tz'u* were later known collectively as *Yüeh-fu pu-t'i* (New subjects for song lyrics), and there are five series of poems in the collection. Each series is set to a particular *tz'u* tune and focuses on an object—white lotus, water shield, cicada, and so forth—related allegorically in one way or another to the Sung emperors, empresses, and imperial consorts whose tombs were looted by the "barbarians."[27]

It is no accident that Ch'en Tzu-lung was the first Ming scholar to con-solidate the allegorical reading of these *Yüeh-fu pu-t'i* poems, rescuing them from the oblivion in which they had fallen since the beginning of the Ming. As a promoter of the *tz'u* revival movement and a patriot de-voted to the Ming cause, Ch'en seems to have viewed these *tz'u* songs as concrete expressions of a perfect union of moral content and stylistic beauty, in which patriotism is conveyed through the lyrical evocation of symbolism. The following statement by Ch'en evinces his intense interest in the tomb incident and the *Yüeh-fu pu-t'i* song-series:[28]

> T'ang Chüeh (Yü-ch'ien) and Lin Ching-hsi both went out [to gather bones] in the disguise of medicinal-herb collectors. T'ang Chüeh buried the imperial bones and planted the wintergreen trees on the burial mounds; T'ang's moral righteousness and upright virtue were regarded highly by the world.[29] His poems on the water shield, lotus, and cicada are all superb, and can rival the works of Heaven. These poems were unprecedented in the Sung.

I believe it was partly due to the inspiration of Ch'en Tzu-lung that the young scholar-poet Chu I-tsun (1692–1709) began to search actively for the long-lost manuscript of *Yüeh-fu pu-t'i*; Chu eventually found the collection and printed it with a preface of his own.[30] In any case, Ch'en Tzu-lung must have helped inspire the sudden popularity of scholarship concerning the incident of the tombs. For not long afterward Wan Ssu-t'ung (1638–1702) set out to gather the available historical and literary sources regarding the events of 1278 and created an extensive anthology entitled *The Forgotten Events of the Six Southern Sung Tombs*. The collection includes such early historical works as those by T'ao Tsung-i (1268–1358) and later commentaries by Ming loyalists like Huang Tsung-hsi (1610–95).[31] Indeed, it is most unfortunate that, for unknown reasons, Ch'en Tzu-lung's important contribution to the *Yüeh-fu pu-t'i* scholarship and criticism was completely ignored by early Ch'ing scholars on the subject and has therefore been forgotten by modern scholars as well.

Ch'en Tzu-lung's "T'ang to ling" *tz'u* is his most powerful (though not immediately apparent) allegorical reference to the *Yüeh-fu pu-t'i* song series. I think when Ch'en says in his preface, "Hearing at this time about our late emperor's burial, I felt something I couldn't bear to express," he is subtly comparing the circumstances concerning Emperor Ch'ung-chen's burial to the Sung incident of the tombs. For one thing, Ch'en's poem is about another tomb incident, namely, that involving the last emperor of the Ming, who was not properly buried even long after his suicide on the Coal Hill of Peking. Like the Sung loyalists, Ch'en is offering sacrifices to the spirit of his emperor on the Cold Food Festival. And all the overt images in the poem alluding to "the palace ladies' tombs" (line 9) and to Su Hsiao-hsiao's grave (lines 10–12) remind us of the Southern Sung imperial burial mounds near Hangchow and the Sung poets' unending love for their country. The pines and cypresses on the "path to the Western Grave-mound" (line 10) may be seen as symbolic equivalents of the wintergreen trees planted on the Sung imperial grave mounds. For Ch'en tells us that it is upon looking at the pines and the cypress trees that he is "heartbroken." The image of the pine tree, though a conventional image in the graveyard poems, is used here with a special purpose. It functions as a symbol of mourning for the Ming, because it was under a pine tree on Coal Hill that Emperor Ch'ung-chen hanged himself at the fall of the Forbidden City in 1644.

I believe one of the reasons Ch'en Tzu-lung especially liked the Southern Sung *yung-wu tz'u* poems regarding the incident of the tombs was their high quality of symbolic language. When he says that T'ang Chüeh's *yung-wu* poems on "the water shield, lotus, and cicada are all superb" and "can rival the works of Heaven," he is no doubt speaking of the poems' power of expressing loyalist feelings through a device of symbolism or indirection which intimates that something more than the object (*wu*) is the ultimate referent. In the first place, the Sung loyalist poets' choice of *yung-wu tz'u* as the medium for expressing their feelings about the incident of the tombs suggests they must have thought of the *yung-wu* mode, originally used for poetic descriptions, as a highly personal form (but also impersonal in its indirectness) through which to project images of their inner selves.[32] This attitude represents a deliberate effort on the part of the Southern Sung poets to create a new poetic rhetoric, claiming that the descriptive in poetry is no longer purely descriptive but must contain private feelings. Thus, the *yung-wu tz'u* eventually became a privileged mode of topical allegory—a refined device of insinuating something without saying it—that allowed the Southern Sung poets to express their loyalist sentiments through the symbolization of particular objects (*wu*). Of course, the Chinese language itself seems to embody this quality of symbolic association almost inherently, but in the *yung-wu tz'u* poetic images assume a greater load of associative energy than in other genres. In the *Yüeh-fu pu-t'i* poem-series, images such as the white lotus, the water shield, and the cicada may appear at first puzzling, but because the dense texture of the poems greatly intensifies the associative power of the imagery, readers are continually pressed to infer something more, or other, as the true meaning of the poems.

We have every reason to believe that Ch'en Tzu-lung must have found this symbolic device of the *yung-wu tz'u* extremely pleasing. He himself wrote numerous *yung-wu tz'u* both on love and loyalism, although his rhetorical devices are not entirely the same as those used by the Southern Sung poets. One thing is certain—it was not entirely owing to the moral or political content of the *Yüeh-fu pu-t'i* songs that Ch'en Tzu-lung found himself so impressed with them. Besides the *Yüeh-fu pu-t'i* authors, other Southern Sung poets such as Hsin Ch'i-chi (1140–1207) and Liu K'o-chuang (1187–1269) produced many, and indeed more famous, patriotic poems in the *tz'u* form. However, because the *tz'u* songs of Hsin Ch'i-chi and his followers adopted the style of "heroic abandon" rather than the "delicate restraint" of *yung-wu*,[33] Ch'en Tzu-lung did not hold them in high esteem. In fact, Ch'en's criticism of the Southern Sung *tz'u* as "tasteless" and "offensive"[34] likely refers specifically to the *tz'u* poems associated with the heroic abandon school. To be sure, Ch'en Tzu-lung was a stylistic purist; he did not allow mere content to dominate him.

Ch'en Tzu-lung's own *yung-wu tz'u*, which constitute a large percentage of his *tz'u* corpus, rely mainly on a form of symbolic association. In both his love poetry and loyalist poetry in *tz'u*, the *yung-wu* mode serves as a principal technique of "poetic ambiguity" that insists on creating concrete images of the object while making its referential meanings ambiguous and inexhaustible. The following "Hua t'ang ch'un" *tz'u*, subtitled "Apricot Blossoms in the Rain," exhibits a symbolic power that the Ch'ing critic Wang Shih-chen, speaking of Ch'en Tzu-lung's *yung-wu* poetics, praises as "absolutely captivating":[35]

> The lodge by the pool lightly shaded, the water level with the bridge,
> Flower-tips flirt with the rain for a while,
> Where the slight chill touches them, they are supremely enticing,
> Spellbinding at this moment.   4
>
> I remember that, beyond the Green Gate dike,
> Day after day, fragrant pollen was everywhere.
> The jade-like visage is now lonely; her faint-red blossoms flutter about:
> Unbearable are the spring nights.   [*CTLS*, 2:601]   8

The central symbol of the poem is the apricot flower. In Chinese culture, the apricot is "an emblem of the fair sex," and "the slanting eyes of Chinese beauties are often compared to the ovoid kernels" of apricots.[36] The lonely apricot which holds the poet spellbound is no doubt a metaphor for the female figure: such a device of personification whereby something nonhuman symbolizes something human is central to the *yung-wu tz'u* tradition.[37] But symbolism on this level is only minimal symbolism, and readers of *yung-wu tz'u* are accustomed to go beyond personification to discover the true import of the poem. Since the Southern Sung, the *yung-wu tz'u* as a genre has always operated on the principle of association, insisting on uniting concrete images with qualities that are shared by both the symbol and the thing symbolized. Since the shared qualities are never explicitly named, they emerge only by virtue of the various imagistic associations. And it is the reader's task to find the various meanings of this relationship.

To begin with, Ch'en Tzu-lung's "Hua t'ang ch'un" *tz'u* reads very much like a love poem in which the poet seems to contrast his lonely present with memories of a romantic past (lines 5–7), leaving the reader to wander along in a world of imagination. Indeed, the image of the apricot flower has been used in his other *tz'u* poems (for example, *CTLS*, 2:598) to symbolize the femininity of the beloved. But a crucial reference to the Green Gate in line 5 dissuades us from treating the "Hua t'ang ch'un" *tz'u* as a mere love poem. The Green Gate was the name of a city gate in the Han-dynasty capital of Ch'ang-an. Since the name Ch'ang-an is often used in poetry to signify—with a suitable historical indirectness— the present seat of the emperor and his court, this allusion points to the poem's political associations. If we follow this interpretation, it becomes clear that in his poem Ch'en Tzu-lung is mourning the fall of the Ming dynasty—before the fall, the "fragrant pollen" of the apricot "was every-where"; after the fall, "the jade-like visage" is "lonely," and the "spring nights" have become "unbearable." But what does the apricot stand for? And what is the connection between the apricot and the Ming dynasty?

An examination of Ch'en Tzu-lung's use of the apricot image elsewhere in his *tz'u* poetry discloses that the image has become an internal referent, which by means of recurrence and repetition almost always refers to the palace ladies of the Ming. The opening lines of his "Shan hua tzu" *tz'u*, subtitled "Spring Sorrow," is a good example:

> Willows hazy in the morning mist,
> Apricot flowers blown to earth at the fifth watch.
> The lonely, silent moon beyond the Ching-yang Palace
> Shines on the fallen red blossoms.   [*CTLS*, 2:602]

The Ching-yang Palace in this *tz'u* provides an important referential con-text and intertextual link, for it is an allusion that brings the apricot image and other related details of the poem in close contact with historical and political significance. History informs us that the Ching-yang Palace be-longed to the Southern Ch'i dynasty, 475–502, a period during which the northern territory of China was lost to foreign rule. Every morning when the bell rang on the Ching-yang tower, the palace ladies would rush to do their toilet. Now, Ch'en Tzu-lung situates his "Ching-yang tower" allu-sion in the complex web of flower symbolism, by following the rules of the *yung-wu* tradition, which dictate that every historical allusion in the poem work as an image, linked intimately to the meaning of the dominant symbol—in this case, the apricot. The poet feels sad because the apricot blossoms (the palace ladies of the Ming) have withered and died after the dynasty's fall, and thus when the bell rings in the morning, no human presence is to be found. Only the lonely moon shines upon the fallen red blossoms. Clearly Ch'en Tzu-lung is comparing his fallen country to the perished Southern Ch'i, and his love for the apricot-flower is an allegory of his patriotic love.

To return to Ch'en's "Hua t'ang ch'un" *tz'u:* through the poem's sub-title, "Apricot Blossoms in the Rain," the poet is articulating a concept central to his political allegory. What he wishes us to infer is the fact that his poem was written around Tomb-Sweeping Day, only a few days after the Cold Food Festival. The apricot usually begins to bloom around that time, and there is usually rain accompanying the blooming of the flowers. (For this reason, such rain is often called "the rain of apricot blossoms.") Tomb-Sweeping Day is also a time for remembering the dead, and this association puts the poem squarely in the tradition of political allegory. The poem is thus mourning the death of the Ming dynasty; it is not a simple love poem. But the power of the poem still lies in its symbolic suggestiveness.

Sometimes, because of the vague symbolic meanings in Ch'en Tzu-lung's *yung-wu tz'u,* the boundaries between his love poetry and loyalist poetry are extremely fluid. This is true especially with those *yung-wu tz'u* on the willow, a topic we touched upon in chapter 5 in connection with Ch'en's and Liu's love poems. Like the apricot flower, the willow is "the emblem of the fair sex." [38] Moreover, since the willow has become the "conventional euphemism for the courtesan," [39] it is particularly pertinent to Liu Shih. In Ch'en's love *tz'u,* Liu Shih is often compared to the willow catkins that are forever drifting and lonely. [40] It is the notion of the past as being irreversible that gives the image of wandering catkins such a poignant feeling of regret and sorrow. For the poet laments the fact that despite his unchanging love he can do nothing but watch his beloved drift away. In this view of things, most of Ch'en's *yung-wu tz'u* on the willow can be read as tokens of his longing for Liu Shih. For example, the following "Huan hsi sha" *tz'u,* subtitled "On the Willow Catkins," is replete with such implications: [41]

> By the hundred-foot Chang-t'ai, they are tossed around by the wind,
> Through layers upon layers of curtain, they sport with the spring radiance.
> I pity their drifting about, but can do nothing about it—just let them drift.

The faint sun rolls, fading under the shadow of blossoms,
A soft wind sends them west of the jade chamber,
At the edge of the world—few know of my secret heart.   [*CTLS*, 2:597]

The first line of the poem alludes to Chang-t'ai Street in the Han city of Ch'ang-an, where rows of willows used to shade the singing girls' quarters in the spring. Thus, at first glance, it seems that the poem was written for the courtesan Liu Shih.

However, given the enormous suggestive powers of the *yung-wu* mode, it is entirely possible that in the "Huan hsi sha" *tz'u*, Ch'en Tzu-lung is making a symbolic connection between the drifting willow catkins and the fallen Ming. And, by analogy, his beloved Liu Shih can be seen as a symbol of the old dynasty to which the poet is forever attached. Or the poet may be using the willow as a symbol of himself, a lonely loyalist who has drifted from one place to another after the fall of his country. That the willow did become a reflexive symbol for Ming loyalists can be amply supported by the many *yung-wu tz'u* of the literati scholars following the fall of the Ming. For example, the renowned loyalist poet Wang Fu-chih (1619–92) wrote about "the withering willow" in his "Tieh lien hua" *tz'u*, subtly comparing himself to the dying willow and bringing in as a secondary theme the mourning cries of the cicada, a vital allusion to the "cicada poems" in the Southern Sung *Yüeh-fu pu-t'i*.[42] And, as late as the nineteenth century, Yang Feng-pao (1754–1816), "one of the most thorough premodern students of Ming loyalism,"[43] composed a song-series of *tz'u* entitled "On the Autumn Willows by West Lake" supposedly to lament the fall of the Ming.[44] In the *shih* genre, though to a lesser degree, one encounters the same recurrent use of the willow image as an allegorical displacement of loyalism. Wang Shih-chen's famous poem-series "On the Autumn Willow" mourns "the desolation of a scene transformed" and tells us how his heart is "overcome with regrets." In his preface, Wang suggests that his poems are topically allusive, following the well-established tradition of political allegory: "In the past, the Prince of Chiang-nan felt sad at the sight of fallen leaves.[45] The Minister of War of Chin-ch'eng plucked a willow branch and wept.[46] I am by nature a man of sorrow, and full of emotions. I express my feelings through the willows in imitation of the chariot officer in the 'Small Odes.'[47] I air my autumnal grief after the fashion of the faraway people at the bank of the River Hsiang."[48]

In Ch'en Tzu-lung's *yung-wu tz'u* on the willow one is impressed by the ambiguous, unbounded nature of its symbolism, often threatening to break its allegorical boundaries. For we can never be sure whether a particular willow poem, especially an undated one, is about his beloved Liu

Shih or about himself as a loyalist or both. The fact that he portrays loyalism as a sensorily realistic form of intimate love also tends to blur the distinction between the two themes. What makes our exegetic context even more complicated is the real possibility that the poet, as a loyalist who was "adrift" after the dynasty's fall, might have regarded himself as meeting the courtesan's fate.[49] In his imagination, the beloved courtesan Liu Shih could very well have become the symbol of his self-extension. Viewed in this light, any specificity of willow = beloved or of willow = loyalist would begin to "step out on us."[50]

In fact, ambiguity as a poetic device was later to be favored by the *tz'u* critics of the Ch'ing engaged in allegorical interpretations. As Chou Chi (1781–1839) puts it in the preface to his anthology of Sung *tz'u*, "Without knowing allegory we cannot understand *tz'u* poems; yet if we concentrate only on the allegorical meaning, we will never escape from it."[51] Chou Chi implies that good allegory should not be too explicit because the ideal reader is "like a man standing on the edge of a pool admiring the fish" and wondering "whether it is a bream or a carp."[52] And I believe that in his willow poems, Ch'en Tzu-lung has deliberately created a similar sense of ambiguity. For example, his "Huan hsi sha" *tz'u* ends with a line that enhances the general mood of suggestiveness and reticence, while at the same time guiding readers to its possible meanings: "At the edge of the world— few know of my secret heart." Ch'en's device of implicit meaning is to a certain extent a recreation of the traditional *tz'u* aesthetics as prescribed by the Sung critic Shen I-fu (?–after 1279): "The concluding lines should be open-ended, conveying an impression of endless overtones" (*THTP*, 1:279).

Ch'en Tzu-lung's *yung-wu tz'u* was highly regarded by the Ch'ing poet and critic Wang Shih-chen. Commenting on Ch'en's "Huan hsi sha" *tz'u* on the willow, Wang exclaims, "This *tz'u* captures that which is beyond the mere appearance of things, a supreme form of *yung-wu*" (*CTLS*, 2:597). Wang even used his favorite term, *shen-yün* (literally "spiritual resonance"), what he believed to be the ideal state of poetry, to describe the general style of Ch'en's *tz'u*.[53] By definition, *shen-yün* is a rhetorical device of suggestion in *shih* that is meant to convey "ideas beyond words."[54] Or, as Richard Lynn explains, *shen-yün* is "that quality in poetry which expresses, in an indirect and tenuous way, personal mood, atmosphere, or tone."[55] Whether or not Wang Shih-chen's formation of the *shen-yün* concept in *shih* poetry was directly inspired by Ch'en Tzu-lung's *tz'u* poetics, one can never know. But it is undeniable that Ch'en's *tz'u*, looked upon so highly by Wang, must have provided the younger poet ample opportunity for critical reflection, if not actual technical guidance. Most interesting, Wang Shih-chen seemed to be especially fond of two kinds of *yung-wu tz'u* by Ch'en Tzu-lung: those on love and those on loyalism. These *tz'u* were considered by Wang to have the highest quality of *shen-yün,* and the reasons are not difficult to find. First of all, love and loyalism were the two most important things in Ch'en's private life. And it is only natural that the manifest content of his *yung-wu tz'u* would encourage a symbolic interpretation concerning the poem's latent content. Moreover, the *yung-wu* poems on love and those on loyalism have in common a predominant idea of impermanence and loss, both symbolized by falling flowers and willow catkins—images well suited for conveying the idea of endless overtones in poetry.

The symbolic device of Ch'en Tzu-lung's *yung-wu tz'u* is of course strongly reminiscent of the Southern Sung *yung-wu tz'u,* of which the *Yüeh-fu pu-t'i* song-series is representative. And, significantly, Wang Shih-chen also used the term *shen-yün* to describe the general quality of endless suggestiveness in the Southern Sung *tz'u.*[56] But on closer scrutiny, one notices stylistic features that distinguish Ch'en's *tz'u* songs from those of the Southern Sung. First, unlike the Southern Sung *yung-wu* songs, which exhibit a general lack of connectives between images and lines, Ch'en's *tz'u* poems are characterized by a flowing syntax and the impression of an easy style. Whereas ambiguity in the Southern Sung *tz'u* may be caused largely by the mosaic of seemingly disjointed images, the ambiguity in Ch'en's *yung-wu* songs results mainly from the rich symbolic associations of the object (*wu*) itself, whose referential meanings we may approximate but never exhaust. In other words, there seems to be a strange, even contradictory combination of hypotactic syntax and implicit meaning in Ch'en's *yung-wu tz'u.* But such an apparently contradictory style is precisely what private symbology is all about—for however flowing and uninterrupted the syntax is and however linked the images seem to be, if the symbolic dimension is meaningful only to the poet's private perception, the general impression of the poetic voice would appear to be implicit rather than explicit.

Ch'en Tzu-lung's lyrical voice in *tz'u* also recalls the subjective, emotional tone of Li Yü's song lyrics, as I suggested earlier in this chapter. It is unmistakably clear even at a single glance that both poets preferred the rhetoric of mixing flowing syntax with sensory suggestiveness. Moreover, with regard to form, Ch'en Tzu-lung obviously favored the shorter *hsiao-ling* form in *tz'u*—of which Li Yü was a master—over the longer, more elaborate *man-tz'u* form that had dominated the *yung-wu* mode since the

Southern Sung.[57] But unlike Li Yü's more or less straightforward *tz'u*, Ch'en's *hsiao-ling* songs are often characterized by the *yung-wu* dimension, turning his subjective experience of reality into allegorical symbols.

Perhaps it was the richly symbolic nature of Ch'en Tzu-lung's *yung-wu tz'u* that led later commentators to read his love poetry exclusively as allegories of loyalism and to completely overlook the fact that there was a *real* basis in his songs of love. Needless to say, the idea that love was a prefiguration of loyalism in Ch'en's *tz'u* poetry was also wholly ignored. Throughout the centuries, commentators have insisted that the only way to read Ch'en Tzu-lung's *tz'u* is as moral and political allegory:

> Ch'en Tzu-lung (Ta-tsun) expresses his allegorical meanings through the symbol of "fragrant flowers and the fairest." One should always keep this in mind when reading Ch'en's collected works of *tz'u*, the *Hsiang-chen ko.*[58]

> I often regretted that the *tz'u* poems of Ming were either casual works of social intercourse or frivolous evocations of inner-chamber affairs. Ch'en Tzu-lung (Ta-tsun) was the only Ming poet [in *tz'u*] who followed the moral teaching of *feng* and *sao*,[59] and succeeded in maintaining the orthodox tradition of *tz'u* composition [*CTLS*, 2:618].

Of course these commentators were merely following the hermeneutic strategy of the Ch'ang-chou school of *tz'u* prominent from the end of the eighteenth century, according to which love poems in *tz'u* should always be seen as allegorical references to some moral or political phenomenon.[60] Chang Hui-yen (1761–1802), the founder of the Ch'ang-chou school, even claimed that a purely descriptive *tz'u* poem about a lonely woman, such as the "P'u-sa man" by Wen T'ing-yün (ca. 812–ca. 870), should be read as political allegory referring topically to specific contemporary events. For Chang believed that only by focusing on allegory could *tz'u* poetry be respected as a serious literary genre equal to *shih* and *fu*. Indeed, throughout the Ch'ing, the one critical trait essential to scholar-poets was allegorism in *tz'u*—that is, the reading of *tz'u* as political allegories in the manner of the Han Confucian exegesis in the *Shih-ching* (Classic of poetry), though now with fresh urgency. The phenomenon obviously reflects the overall consciousness of political pressure under the rule of the foreign-born Manchus, who were always quick to root out political subversion. In the meantime, under the influence of this exegetical tradition, the Ming loyalists in the Ch'ing also began to write *tz'u* poems to the same allegorical patterns that they read in (or read into) the work of others.[61] That is to say, persecution gave rise to a special technique of writing, and *tz'u* had become for poets the most suitable genre for expressing subtle and secret feelings in defense of their loyalism.

But, certainly, to read Ch'en Tzu-lung's love poems in *tz'u* categorically as political allegory (as has been done by traditional and modern commentators alike) would be anachronistic. As I outlined above, Ch'en's love poems are true love poems, although love is often connected with loyalism. Moreover, what sometimes distinguishes his love songs from his loyalist songs is that historical allusions are either missing or replaced by personal allusions, although his willow poems remain ambiguous in their meaning. In any case, the use of figural presentation and symbolism in Ch'en's *tz'u* was obviously based on aesthetic and philosophical, rather than political, considerations. It seems that at the time Ch'en was writing his loyalist poems in *tz'u*, from 1644 to 1647, literary censorship and persecution did not yet pose as severe a threat to the Ming loyalists as it did later to the Ch'ing literati, and thus Ch'en did not need to use allegory as a means of self-protection. However, the fact that Ch'en had developed a figural relationship between love and loyalism in his *tz'u* must have to some extent helped shape the allegorical approach in the Ch'ing *tz'u*. For one thing, Ch'en's song lyrics argue most convincingly that, while *tz'u* was the most suitable genre for capturing the intimate feelings of love and sensuality, patriotism could be seen as a form of love, totally in keeping with the essence of *ch'ing*. And if we want to present loyalism allegorically—that is, to reveal it and at the same time hide it—the most effective and most readily comprehensible image for us to use in a *tz'u* form would of course be that of romantic love.[62] To modern readers like us, Ch'en's style reveals most clearly evidence of the reawakening sensory apprehension of things and emotions that was typical of the late Ming and had made its way into the *tz'u* tradition.

SEVEN

Tragic Heroism in
Shih Poetry

Ch'en Tzu-lung's conception of style
and theme in *shih* poetry is again different from that of his *tz'u*: unlike
his political poems in *tz'u,* in which loyalism is figurally connected with
romantic love, his *shih* poems on the same subject are peculiarly lacking in any figural or allegorical approach. In *shih* poetry, Ch'en's power
of expression led to a more direct and literal expression of his loyalist
sentiments without the need for adopting the symbolic *yung-wu* mode
which is central to his *tz'u* poetics. And this directness of expression in
Ch'en's *shih,* no doubt related to the ancient view of poetry as expressing the "heart's intent" (*chih*), supports a very radical content, a content
characterized by moral heroism and the existential concern about life and
death—in sharp contrast to the main focus on passionate love in *tz'u.* Indeed, in his *shih* poetry on loyalism, Ch'en has become an existentialist,
always anxious to define his moral choice and the meaning of his suffering by bravely confronting the existential questions. What Richard Sewall
calls "the tragic vision"—that is, the vision that impels the individual man
of action to face "the irreducible facts of suffering and death" and to "fight
against his destiny"[1]—is clearly embodied in this kind of poetry. In other
words, in Ch'en's *shih* poems, we see that the idea of suffering is closely
related with that of the noble, and that the image of the poet as tragic hero
signifies a new role of *shih* poetry in turning tragic heroism into an aes-

thetic principle. In this chapter, we will look at a few examples of Ch'en Tzu-lung's *shih* poetry in order to examine this image of the poet.

The classic image of the Chinese loyalist in *shih* is in one important respect unique: students of Chinese poetry have long regarded the loyalist not only as a man of quiet suffering, but as a traveler wandering despondently through the buried ruins of the fallen capital, urgently asking the reader to read his "heart within."[2] In the ancient anthology of poetry, the *Shih-ching* (Classic of poetry), there is just such a devoted official: a loyalist of the Chou who visits the ruins of the old capital, now completely covered by millet fields:

> That millet bends under its weight,
> Its grain is in sprout,
> I walk with slow, slow steps,
> My heart within is shaken.   4
> Those who know me
> Would say my heart is worried;
> Those who do not know me
> Would ask what I am seeking.   8
> Gray and distant Heaven—
> What man brought this about?[3]

Despite this poem's lack of internal indication that it is to be read in a loyalist frame of reference, Chinese scholars and poets since the Han (206 B.C.–A.D. 220) have insisted on reading it as specifically referring to the sorrows and reflections of a Chou loyalist.[4] Though seemingly far-fetched, such a tradition of reading has consequently led later poets to establish a tradition of writing that refers repeatedly to this ancient poem as something like a historical source. The following poem by Ch'en Tzu-lung, from a series of poems entitled "Various Feelings on an Autumn Day," definitely belongs to such a tradition:

> Mountains and rivers fill my vision; grief as far as I can see.
> Again I linger in the millet fields of the Chou plains.
> Red maples, splendid trees, beautiful throughout the autumn,
> White geese, tawny clouds, coming from thousands of miles away.   4
> Evening rain falls on the thicket near the luxuriant park,[5]
> At dusk deer descend the Hsü Terrace.[6]
> Rolling up my sleeves, I alone ascend the tomb of Yao-li,[7]
> I wail at the Hsin Pavilion as I raise my cup.[8]   [*CTLS*, 2: 525–26]   8

A comparison with the ancient poem from the *Shih-ching* serves to show to what extent stronger emotions—that is, emotions expressed in gesture, words, and cries—have become the reality of life for the Ming loyalist. Whereas the *Shih-ching* poet talks only about worries of the heart (*hsin-yu*, line 6), Ch'en Tzu-lung uses such strong words as "grief" (*ai*, line 1) and "wail" (*t'ung-k'u*, line 8) to express the extent of his sorrow and anger. In other words, Ch'en puts himself on stage. By sacrificing at the tomb of an ancient loyalist, Yao-li, he was upholding both the principle of his own loyalism and the cult of the loyalist hero. (The *Shih-ching* poet had no such option.) This explains why in his forthright utterances, Ch'en's individual character seems to be manifest in all its force, obviating the need for us to ask whether we know his heart within. Indeed, we behold an intensified image of a suffering loyalist, see it in a dramatic directness that rarely could have been possible in earlier *shih* poetry.

Wailing was a characteristic behavior of the typical Ming loyalist. In his play *The Peach Blossom Fan*, K'ung Shang-jen uses an important scene entitled "Wailing for the Emperor" to depict the sorrow and despondency of the Ming officials. As soon as they hear that Emperor Ch'ung-chen has died, they all kowtow "in the direction of the north and wail aloud,"[9]

> My emperor,
> My Emperor Ch'un-chen,
> My Imperial Master who has just died . . .

In comparison, the famous story about the Eastern Chin (317–420) loyalists who gathered in the Hsin Pavilion—one source of Ch'en Tzu-lung's poem—gives a much more restrained picture of human sorrow: "On their free days those gentlemen who had crossed the Yangtze River would always invite each other to go for an outing to Hsin Pavilion, where they drank and feasted on the grass. Once Chou I, seated among the company, sighed and said: 'The scenery is just as good as in the North, but these are the wrong mountains and rivers.' They all looked at each other and shed tears."[10]

Conscious of the tradition of antiquity, Ch'en Tzu-lung concludes his poem with a reference to the Hsin Pavilion incident, but in a new mode of expression: "I wail at the Hsin Pavilion as I raise my cup." This, of course, is not to suggest that the ritual of wailing was nonexistent before Ch'en's time, but there is no denying that in literature the Ming loyalist's expression of grief differs drastically from that of the earlier loyalists. For there is in Ch'en's poem a new tragic sense of life that seems to reach its climax in the mere act of wailing itself. One is reminded of the Hebrews' wailing at the wall, the ultimate expression of grief over inexplicable pain.

The Hebrews' experience is considered tragic mainly because of its "unde-served suffering."[11] Similarly, we feel that the Chinese loyalist's suffering and calamity, brought about by the dynasty's fall, are equally undeserved and merit our sympathy. The helplessness of the loyalist in the face of the political calamity makes us feel that he is, as A. C. Bradley would say of a tragic hero, "terribly unlucky."[12] But here the tragic and the heroic diverge. The loyalist's grief and suffering make him a tragic figure; but it is his resistance that turns him into a hero.[13]

When we realize that Ch'en Tzu-lung's poem "On an Autumn Day" was written in 1646 following a major defeat of the Loyalist army in the Lake T'ai area,[14] we can understand his pain. And the battle explains why Ch'en visited the ancient sites of the Wu district in the first place. All his references to the Wu, which used to occupy the Nanking area, serve as in-direct allusions to the fall of the Ming court in Nanking. (The Hung-kuang emperor of the Ming was enthroned in Nanking in 1645, and Ch'en served briefly at the fugitive court there.) In his poem, Ch'en not only mourns the tragic fact of the Ming fall but, more important, he also reaffirms his heroic loyalty to his lost country. He does so by calling attention to the example of a famous retainer, Yao-li, whose determination to avenge and die for his lord, King Ho-lü of Wu, is celebrated in history. Indeed, Ch'en's *shih* poetry is often marked by a special emphasis on the heroic strength of the ancient assassin-retainers, an emphasis which recalls Ssu-ma Ch'ien's classic view: "Some [of these assassin-retainers] succeeded in carrying out their duty and some did not. But it is perfectly clear that they had all determined upon the deed. They were not false to their intentions."[15]

To Ch'en Tzu-lung, it was precisely this quality of sincerity in a hero that brought positive, creative meanings to human suffering and despair. In his poem on another assassin-retainer, Ching K'o (?–227 B.C.), en-titled "Song of the Yi River" (*CTLS*, 1:303), Ch'en is especially success-ful in describing the sense of majestic grandeur typical of the tragic hero. The historian Ssu-ma Ch'ien depicts Ching K'o setting off on his mis-sion to assassinate the tyrant Ch'in Shih-huang, knowing that the attempt is doomed to fail and yet all the while bravely singing the mournful but heroic "Song of the Yi River" echoed in Ch'en's much later song-title. Heroism, as Ch'en Tzu-lung defines it through this memorable episode from history, is a matter of devotion and sacrifice, even to the point of suicidal and futile action. Such an approach to the question of loyalism no doubt gave Ch'en the courage to die for his country later. Thus, follow-ing Ch'en Tzu-lung's martyrdom in 1647, the Ming loyalist Hou Fang-yu (whose personal life was fictionalized in K'ung Shang-jen's *Peach Blossom Fan*) compared Ch'en to the ancient hero Ching K'o in his poem "Nine Lamentations: On Ch'en Tzu-lung" (*CTLS*, 2:794).

Returning to Ch'en's poem "On an Autumn Day," we note another aspect of the poet's feeling that gives the poem its particular depth and poignancy, and that is also a clue to the Chinese sense of the tragic vision. It comes from the ancient conception of the Confucian gentleman as a man who has many cares and is capable of enduring intense sorrow. The *I-ching* (*Book of Changes*) commentary defines such an attitude as a consciousness of "suffering" (*yu-huan*), one which gives dignity to the burdens of humanity.[16] Perhaps this theme accounts for Ch'en Tzu-lung's particular liking for an edition of the *I-ching* annotated by the Sung loyalist Hsiung Ho: the concept of *yu-huan* appears in the opening passage of the book's preface.[17]

Translated into poetry, the consciousness of suffering, or the notion of *yu-huan*, opens up new and redeeming implications. The poet, as a man of sorrows, embraces not only the tragic reality in life but also the vision of an aesthetic totality which provides a sense of magnitude and catharsis, so that we feel suffering itself is being given a kind of purity and grandeur. Indeed, it is because of the soothing power of this poetic vision that Chen's poem "On an Autumn Day" provides us with a sense of melancholy equanimity, despite the intensity of the poet's sorrow. We see in the poem that, paralleling the tragic reality of life, nature's movement continues—trees are as splendid as ever in the mountains and birds still return joyfully (lines 3–4).[18] Such enduring faith in nature is the foundation of Chinese lyricism, a lyricism that transcends the ultimate limits of man's temporality. Only in this higher sphere of lyricism can a poet truly experience the profound tranquility of "self-reflection."[19] The center of this lyricism lies not in the act of philosophizing, but rather in that of aesthetic contemplation.

But, as a poet, Ch'en Tzu-lung does not always view nature as calming and joyful. Whereas his eight-line poems in the Regulated Style of *shih* (such as that discussed above) tend to focus on the soothing grace of serene nature, his works in the Ancient Style (especially the "song form," the so-called *ko-hsing t'i*) are more likely to center on images of war and death and their corresponding metaphors of devastation. This may be so because the Ancient Style verse, having an "open-ended" format rather than a prescribed eight-line structure, lends itself to more descriptive details. For example, some time after the fall of the Ming, Ch'en Tzu-lung wrote what we may call a war-and-death poem in twenty lines, entitled "The Song of the Cuckoo":

Mount Wu lies far and secluded, at the top of the blue clouds,
Vines and creepers extend in the chill of the spring wind.
Hidden springs gurgle, striking against the mournful jade,
Jasper blossoms flutter, falling in the red brocade torrent.   4
Weasels leap in the mist; crows peck at trees.
The River Goddess in delicate beauty stands near slender bamboos.
By the shady pine, the disarrayed grass and fragrant asarum,
Loudly someone sings and howls, gazing at the melancholy spring.   8
The call of the cuckoo breaks the streaked stone,
Facing the sky, it cries forth blood, staining the white clouds.
Flourishing boughs and fragrant trees have all changed their colors,
Hundreds of birds squeak mournfully in search of their flock.   12
Don't seek divine reasons for the myriads of worldly matters,
Sparrows, toads, ospreys, and hawks, joyful and sad by turn.
In those days, a man lived in the Golden Hall with jade tables,
Now, in the empty mountains, his feathers are stripped away.   16
Kings Yü-fu and Pieh-ling, how many years ago?
Sleeping Dragon and Leaping Horse are both gone.[20]
The only thing left to do is to hold the Yang-t'ai goddess's hand,
To question Heaven at the walls of the Ch'u temple, where ink is   20
    dripping wet.[21]   [*CTLS*, 1:299–300]

In this poem, the constant juxtaposition of mountain scenes and river scenes has acquired a new meaning, diametrically opposed to the traditional, idealized concept of the harmony of above and below, mountain and river, and so on.[22] It is true that the opening lines of the poem seem to promise an ideal and orderly world of rich sensory experience—the distant hill pairing off with hidden springs, mountain creepers with riverside blossoms, and blue clouds with red brocade torrent—a colorful world which the River Goddess enjoys in timeless eternity (line 6). But as the poem progresses, this seemingly perfect and beautiful world undergoes an unhappy transformation: "Flourishing boughs and fragrant trees have all changed their colors" (line 11). Worse still, heaven and earth are shaken, everywhere stained with the cuckoo's tears of blood (lines 9–10).

In fact, the whole poem is built upon the image of blood, symbol of political tragedy and human sacrifice and of death itself. The title of the poem, "The Song of the Cuckoo," alludes to the tragic story concerning Wang-ti, king of Shu, whose soul turned into a cuckoo after his death, constantly weeping tears of blood. Ch'en Tzu-lung chooses the image of the cuckoo to refer to the soul of the Ming emperor, whose blood has completely changed the colors of heaven and earth and destroyed the harmony of mountains and rivers.

The symbolism of blood also applied to the individual souls of the people, especially to those thousands of men and women who committed suicide for the Ming cause. Indeed, what may seem like a beautiful, richly evocative image of the spring in the beginning of the poem—"Jasper blossoms flutter, falling in the red brocade torrent" (line 4)—is actually permeated with horror and human tragedy. The image of jasper blossoms is a subtle reference to "jasper blood," a common metaphor for blood shed for patriotism. It comes from the legend of Ch'ang Hung, a minister of the ancient Chou dynasty whose blood was thought to have transformed into jasper three years after his death.[23] Ch'en Tzu-lung, then, took over this conventional symbolism and set it in a new context—the blood shed by the numerous Ming martyrs has now turned the river into a "red brocade torrent." This image of the bloodstained water is both elevated and gruesomely literal, directly reflecting the historical fact that thousands of people south of the Yangtze threw themselves into the river at the end of the Ming.[24]

"The country is broken, but the mountains and rivers remain," says the great T'ang poet Tu Fu.[25] Now Ch'en Tzu-lung's depiction of a landscape overturned and made chaotic by human misfortunes rewrites and reverses the line in which Tu Fu had voiced the Chinese nature poet's special brand of stoicism. To Ch'en, "the country is broken" and the mountains and rivers have *not* survived. Indeed, Ch'en offers, in another poem, a minimal rewriting of the same Tu Fu verse: by taking the "water" element away from the character for "river" (*ho*) and replacing it with the element "human," he makes the line say, "The country is broken—and my home, where is it?" (*CTLS*, 2:397) In "The Song of the Cuckoo," Ch'en carries this strategy to paradoxical lengths. Dragon and horse are associated, in Chinese folklore, with water and mountain, respectively, so the line "Sleeping Dragon and Leaping Horse are both gone" (line 18) can be read as meaning that rivers and mountains too have vanished in the catastrophe. But Sleeping Dragon and Leaping Horse may also refer to two ancient heroes, Chu-ko Liang and Kung-sun Shu (see note 20). The paradox can be resolved only by taking the two phrases as epithets designating the two great men of antiquity who, like King Arthur in the English legend, are "gone" and unavailable in their country's time of need.

"The Song of the Cuckoo" is therefore about the poet's despair in the midst of unalloyed misery. Ch'en observes that hundreds of mountain birds "squeak mournfully in search of their flock" (line 12). And the Ming prince who used to live "in the Golden Hall with jade tables" is now "in the empty mountains" with "his feathers stripped away" (lines 15–16).[26]

Throughout the poem there are descriptions of affliction and hardship that seem to refer specifically to actual events of the resistance movement following the fall of the Ming—most probably a movement led by the prince of Lu in 1646 which suffered extremely heavy casualties before the prince himself escaped to a seaport.[27] Indeed, the content of the poem matches what the historian Lynn Struve says of that event: "Very few active Lu supporters surrendered, most of them meeting martyr's deaths or escaping to carry on the fight from the Ssu-ming Hills or the coastal zone."[28]

It has often been said that the tragic is absent from traditional Chinese poetry.[29] But it might be more exact to say that for traditional Chinese poets the tragic was contained in the conception of history itself. This is so because, in Chinese literature, "tragedy" is only a theoretical, not a specific, literary genre; and readers generally obtain their tragic sense from reading history. In other words, the tragic experience as registered in the historical records often became the model for the idea of the tragic in literature. As in Ch'en's poem, the Ming loyalists refused to accept the fate assigned to them by the natural movement of the dynastic change; their tragic sense of life stemmed not only from their own sufferings, but also from their stubbornness, their irreducibility—the same qualities that characterized earlier loyalists in history. Like Lynn Struve, who inscribed her book on the Southern Ming "for those Ming martyrs who 'knew it was no use, but went on anyway,' "[30] Ch'en Tzu-lung was in a way addressing his poem to the many Ming heroes who lived out their stubborn ideal of loyalism, refusing to yield to the dynamics of history. However, seeing that attempts at restoring the Ming again and again ended in defeat ("Kings Yü-fu and Pieh-ling, how many years ago?" line 17),[31] Ch'en could not help feeling bitter and anguished, even angry. In his extremity, the poet ends the poem by questioning the judgment (or indifference) of Heaven.

The act of questioning Heaven, rooted in the Ch'ü Yüan legend, is obviously a political statement on the part of Ch'en Tzu-lung. In the original "Tien-wen" (Heavenly questions) ascribed to Ch'ü Yüan (d. 315 B.C.?), the questions addressed to Heaven are not exclusively political by nature—rather they concern mainly cosmological and astronomical matters, with a special focus on problems of mythology.[32] What characterizes Ch'en's heavenly questions is a new attitude of defiance, directly questioning the tragic destinies Heaven has imposed on the virtuous, but helpless loyalists. It reminds one of Job's questioning of God in the Bible, where the question of suffering has gained a personal and dramatic dimension. No other form of complaint or accusation can better convey the intensity of the poet's anguish and isolation. Ch'en feels so justified in his questioning that he has even invited the Mountain Goddess of Ch'u, the Yang-t'ai Maiden, to join him in challenging Heaven (lines 19–20). His new style of heavenly questions, with all its political relevance, has apparently provided inspiration for later Ming loyalist-poets. For example, the famous scholar Wang Fu-chih used his commentaries on Ch'ü Yüan's "T'ien-wen" to question indirectly the legitimacy of the Manchu rule, suggesting that a regime without *tao* (moral principle) could never survive long.[33]

Elsewhere Ch'en Tzu-lung reveals even more clearly what Heaven means to him. For he conceives of Heaven as a witness, not only to his sufferings but also to his innermost ambition in life—the *chih* which defines the ultimate value for the Chinese individual. This conception of Heaven is not new in the literature of the Chinese, as I shall demonstrate below. However, Ch'en represents the fullest development of this crucial mode of self-expression observable in loyalist poetry. His series of seven poems entitled "At Year's End: Modeled after Tu Fu's Seven Songs of T'ung-ku" provides the most extraordinary example:[34]

Song 1

Loyalist of the Western Capital, now a wanderer in Chiang-nan,
As I walk and sigh by the great marsh, my hair has gone gray.
The raging north wind shatters the pillars of earth,
At year's end, battered feathers in the cold of winter.   4
The warm, bright sun does not shine,[35]
Even if I carve out my heart, throw it on the ground, no one cares.
Alas, song the first! Its notes reach the clouds,
I look aloft at the blue Heaven, but it appears not to hear.   8

Song 2

Wearing shabby clothes and a black cap, I live in the wilds,
Selling hot cakes while playing a flute, now I mingle with cheap laborers.
A penumbra, I do not recognize anyone in sight,[36]
Jackals and wolves fill the road, my heart is crushed.[37]   4
The world has become distant, to whom shall I tell my heart?
I regret not having died for my country sooner.
Alas, song the second! I'm shedding red tears of blood,
For the Bright and brilliant Ming, a white rainbow pierces the sun.[38]   8

Song 3

Comet-like bullets bombarded the Golden Terrace,[39]
Everywhere people cried and grieved, mourning for the emperor.
The yellow flag, the purple chariot canopy, all dim in color,
The death of Lord Shan-yang, how painful![40]   4

A palace official, ashamed before Heaven and earth,
Still lived a stolen life, no different from slaves and hired men.
Alas, song the third! The whole world in confusion,
The Demon of Drought leaps freely while ghosts cry at night.   8

Song 4

How sad! I drift from place to place, lamenting my lonely roots,
My mother died in my early childhood; I was raised by Grandma, who
   pitied me.
Since retiring from office, I have not provided her with comfort,—not
   even for a day,
Suddenly she died in my care; how I mourn for her wandering soul.   4
Cypress road, hibiscus field, all are covered by icy snow.
With tears dried up, I slept by the barren grassland, full of bitter sorrow.
Alas, song the fourth! I'm back on the road again,
Cold wind piercing, the white sun at dusk.   8

Song 5

Dark clouds fall in ruins, the Southern Sieve stars without light,[41]
The verdant tomb on Mount Chung colored by T'ung-shan's blood.[42]
To die for one's country—there's no harm in dying in the marketplace.
To be eaten by crows and hawks, or by mole crickets and ants—   4
   is there any difference?[43]
Was he not the great official and authority?[44]
How dare one talk about honor and integrity in front of him?
Alas, song the fifth! The gibbons full of sorrow at night,
Where can the shamans summon your soul?   8

Song 6

To each other we gave what we valued most—fine jade and white silk,
I was the melilotus, you were the orchid.[45]
When the chariot of our lord was broken, and the nine caldrons
   submerged by water,[46]
P'eng Hsien joined the vast sea, in the cold of River Hsiang.[47]   4
Why did I alone become the worthless mugwort?
I slap my chest, stamp my foot, crush my heart.
Alas, song the sixth! I'm choked with sobs.
The flood dragon wanders about, the sea water all dried up.[48]   8

Song 7

Throughout my life, I've pursued virtue and gallantry with passion,
Now, crestfallen and holding my breath, I dwell among the weeds.

I know full well that to die for one's country is no easy matter,
In avenging Han and restoring Ch'u, I have toiled in vain.[49]   4
My life is suddenly almost over,
What a pity, this seven-foot frame will be as light as a goose feather.[50]
Alas, song the seventh! Songs now and forever.
The blue Heaven pales on my account.   8

Ch'en's exceptionally vivid description of the many shades of personal feelings reveals the way he perpetuates, yet largely diverges from, the ancient tradition of the *Shih-ching*. Like the poet of the "millet poem" in the *Shih-ching* (cited earlier in this chapter), Ch'en addresses Heaven in a plaintive tone, seeking sympathy and understanding (songs 1, 7). But unlike the *Shih-ching* poem, in which the persona's view of Heaven remains unchanged throughout the poem (as seen in the refrain, "Gray and distant Heaven— / What man brought this about?"), Ch'en's poem-series indicates a psychological progression from a distrust of Heaven to a belief in Heaven's sensibility. In the beginning of the series the poet cries, "Alas, song the first! Its notes reach the clouds, / I look aloft at the blue Heaven, but it appears *not* to hear." Yet the poem-series ends in a more contemplative tone, viewing Heaven as a humane witness with sympathetic feelings: "Alas, song the seventh! Songs now and forever. / The blue Heaven pales on my account." It is precisely in song 7, the last in the series, that the poet finally reveals his *chih*, the life vision he hopes will eventually redeem him—despite his relapses into despair. If Ch'en spoke like a doomed man, it is only because he feared his *chih* would never be realized in his lifetime. No tragedy obtains in mere suffering itself; what is tragic is that the sufferer's moral dignity cannot be allowed to reach fulfillment.

In Ch'en Tzu-lung, the idea of *chih* has acquired a new meaning in poetry—*chih* is not simply one's highest ideal in life; it is rather a vision of death. In this new meaning of *chih*, men are constantly defining and redefining existential concerns and always coming near to making an ultimate choice in which the strength and weakness of the individual are laid bare. It is in this sense that one's definition of *chih* as well as the subsequent fulfillment of it can reach tragic dimensions. When Ch'en Tzu-lung says, "I know full well that to die for one's country is no easy matter" (song 7, line 3), he is of course talking about honorable death. He is resolved to die, but death is a thrust of destiny that raises the deepest issues for each individual: whereas heroic death is greater than Mount T'ai, common death can be as insignificant as a feather (line 6). If one must die, it is best to die like a hero, to fulfill death honorably as in fulfilling a significant action. What the Sung patriot Wen T'ien-hsiang said in his famous poem "Crossing the Ling-ting Sea" represents the ultimate fulfillment of this *chih:*

> In all the ages past, has anyone failed to die?
> Let's leave our loyal hearts to shine upon history.[51]

Thus, by dying heroically, one's vision of death becomes the vision of "a greater life"—one that transcends the tragedy of physical death by bringing "humanity" (*jen*) into completion, as expressed in Wen T'ien-hsiang's "Elegy Sewn between My Sash and Garment."

As mentioned above, Ch'en Tzu-lung and his contemporaries in the Restoration Club cultivated a code of honor based on patriotism. It is no accident that two of the most notable martyrs of the Ming—Huang Tao-chou and Hsia Yün-i—were closely associated with Ch'en, the former being his teacher and the latter his best friend. And songs 5 and 6 in his poem-series focus, respectively, on these two heroes. Huang Tao-chou served as grand secretary in the Lung-wu regime in Fu-chien, being the "most esteemed civil officer" in the fugitive court there.[52] Then, in early 1646, during a skirmish with the Ch'ing troops in the Chiang-hsi area, Huang was captured and later executed in Nanking. A story has it that on the way to his execution, Huang passed by a Tung-hua gate in Nanking that was near the imperial tomb of the founder of the Ming. Huang refused to proceed any further, saying, "I would like to die here, since it is near Emperor Kao-tsu's tomb." Ch'en's poem alludes to this event in the line "To die for one's country—there's no harm in dying in the marketplace."

As for Hsia Yün-i, his death was equally heroic—he drowned himself in 1645 after the fall of his hometown, Sung-chiang, where he and Ch'en Tzu-lung had been involved in a battle against the Manchus. Being Ch'en Tzu-lung's closest friend, Hsia Yün-i represented for the poet the symbol of moral heroism, a heroism realized not by words alone, but by action. In his poem-series on the funeral of Hsia Yün-i (one of his last writings), Ch'en wrote,

> His *chih,* recorded in the chronicles, is truly fulfilled,
> With action completed, his virtue of loyalty and piety is beyond doubt.
>
> [*CTLS,* 2: 531]

Emperor Ch'ien-lung must have understood what Hsia Yün-i's heroic death meant to Ch'en because the Yüan Chiang Pavilion, built in honor of Ch'en by imperial order in 1778, was named after the Yüan River,[53] an important image in Ch'en's poem-series on Hsia Yün-i's funeral.[54]

But as a loyalist who did not die immediately after the dynasty's fall,

Ch'en Tzu-lung carried his suffering much further than Hsia Yün-i—as is painfully reflected in his series of seven songs. His physical ordeal and mental suffering apparently kindled new energies in him, compelling him to keener expressive efforts. His poems contain a tension between the determination to die for the Ming cause and a feeling of shame for not being able to realize it in action sooner. It is a tension typical of the Ming loyalists, who believed that honorable suicide was the only way of preserving one's integrity in the face of the collapse of the dynasty. Some loyalists, chief among them Wu Wei-yeh, expressed their sense of failing and disgrace in the most beautiful of melancholy and anguished lyrics.[55]

What distinguishes Ch'en Tzu-lung from many other Ming loyalists is his persistence despite the repeated failures of the restoration activities. Thus, he was able to sing "songs now and forever" (song 7). And for all his occasional lapses into despair, he never stopped trying—by joining the extensive resistance movements, which involved the ultimate risk. Especially after the death of his grandmother (song 4)—that is, after the fulfillment of his duty of filial piety—he acquired a new sense of freedom that was to push him to the very limits of action, even though he knew his cause was hopeless. Such can be said to be the clear "mark of the hero."[56] What Richard Sewall says about the tragic hero can easily be applied to Ch'en Tzu-lung: "Only the strongest natures could endure this kind of suffering—persisting in their purpose in spite of doubts, fears, advice of friends, and sense of guilt. . . . Only the hero suffers in this peculiar, ultimate way."[57]

Ch'en Tzu-lung wins our sympathy because his action embraces both courage and inevitable defeat—the two main qualities of a tragic hero.[58] When confronted with an irreversible, helpless situation, such a person will not take the easy way out, will not escape from suffering, will not die before exhausting all possible means of action. In his poems he describes himself as being already at the end of his rope—"Like a Juan Chi who cried at the end of the road / And a Liang-hung who changed his name while returning home."[59] It is the power of sincerity that makes it possible for such a person to transcend suffering in the midst of suffering and to bring positive and creative meaning to the principle of loyalty. But it is a tragic vision won not without self-sacrifice, as the loyalist poet Ku Yen-wu (1613–82) says in his poem on Ch'en Tzu-lung:

> He had wings, but did not fly away,
> In the end, he was caught by those who set nets.
> Refusing to submit to the shame of being killed by the Eastern Barbarians,[60]
> He bravely followed the example of P'eng Hsien.

The double meaning of suffering—the tragic and the heroic—is itself
the main theme of Ch'en Tzu-lung's "Seven Songs." Although Ch'en indicates in the title of his poems that his series is modeled after Tu Fu's
"Seven Songs," his work represents a drastically different world of reality
quite unknown to the T'ang poet. What Ch'en owes to Tu Fu is the use
of a literary device for providing a poetic record of personal hardships.
Tu Fu wrote his "Seven Songs" in the midst of the An Lu-shan Rebellion (755–63), when war forced millions of people to leave their homes,
and his poems are therefore about his and his family's suffering during
the war.[61] Of course, Ch'en's and Tu's experiences during what might be
seen as periods of national crisis are somewhat analogous. But there is a
great difference between their main concerns: unlike Ch'en, who raises
the ultimate questions about honorable death, Tu is primarily concerned
with personal misery and his own unfulfilled political ambition, as may
be seen in the final song of his series:

> This man, who has not yet made a name for himself, has already
>   grown old,
> For three years, nearly starved, I've traveled through the deserted
>   mountain paths.
> In Ch'ang-an, there are so many young lords and noblemen,
> Wealth and position should be attained in early manhood.   4
> In the mountains I've come across friends who are also Confucian
>   scholars,
> We only talk about the past, lamenting our unfulfilled ambitions,
> Alas, song the seventh! I quietly end my song,
> As I look up to the heavens, the white sun moves in haste.   8
>
> [*CTS*, 4:2298]

Compared with the expression of *chih* in Tu Fu's "Seven Songs," Ch'en
Tzu-lung's obviously carries a much more urgent, or tragic, desire to embrace heroic values of self-sacrifice. As I mentioned, Ch'en represents the
new approach to the question of *chih* on the part of the late-Ming intellectuals,[62] a tendency started earlier by Sung loyalists. In Ch'en's new
definition of *chih*, the meaning of life depends on the meaning of one's
death, indeed, transcending what Tu Fu says about the individual's name
and position in life.[63] Such a distinct contrast is a consequence not only
of the different life-situations the two poets confronted, but also of the
redefined concept of *chih* in *shih* poetry that had arisen between the T'ang
and the Ming.

Ch'en's series of songs may have been modeled after a group of "Six
Songs" by the Sung hero Wen T'ien-hsiang,[64] a poem-series that was, in

turn, an imitation of Tu Fu's "Seven Songs." Wen wrote his poem-series sometime after he was captured by the Mongols in 1279. He was under custody during his trip north to Ta-tu (modern Peking), where he would die three years later. By then, his wife and two concubines as well as his son and two daughters had all been taken prisoner by the Mongols. Thus, his "Six Songs"—following the song style of Tu Fu's poem-series—is clearly articulated as a lament for his hardships. In poem after poem, he mourns the catastrophes that befell his wife, his sister, his daughters, his son, and his concubines. Indeed, there was no reasonable excuse for causing them to suffer, nothing in their lives to justify such misfortunes, as is made clear in song 1:

> My wife, my wife, whom I met in poverty,
> Since youth we've been married, sworn never to part.
> Amidst turmoil and separation, she fell in with tigers and wolves,
> The male phoenix, flying swiftly, has lost its mate.[65]   4
> The chicks she carried along, where did they go?
> Suddenly, my country is broken and my family gone too,
> I cannot bear to depart from you.[66]
> Heaven is everlasting, Earth eternal, all is vast and boundless,   8
> The Herdboy Star and the Weaving Maid far apart; they gaze at each
>   other night after night.
> Alas, song the first! My song is long,
> The mournful wind blows from the north, I get up and linger.

The opening lines of each of Wen's six songs—except for the concluding piece—address a certain family member, a technique Wen borrowed from Tu Fu. The entire poem-series reads like an autobiography detailing the full drama of a personal and family tragedy resulting directly from a national crisis. What is especially noteworthy is that the mood of the poems is not just one of anxiety but rather one of constant discovery. And a recurrent theme of heroism makes suffering and endurance the structural design of Wen's poetry. One gets the impression that the poet-hero, in the course of his long ordeal, has finally understood that Heaven is not always reasonable and just. But unjustified suffering must be accepted as part of the hero's mission. He is determined to carry the heroic action to its uttermost limits, exploring the farthest reaches of human capacity for sacrifice, as he confesses in the final poem:

> How I was born at a bad time,
> A lonely root that never knows the beauty of spring.
> Winter is cold, days are short—I'm ever more anguished,
> North Wind follows me amidst armored horses and dust.   4

At first, I took pity on my kindred's great mishaps,
Now in turn they should pity me.
You are in the north, alone with my children,
When I die, who will bury me?   8
In our hundred-year mortal span, what distinguishes good from bad?
Millets grew and died, all fleeting like a flash.
Alas, song the sixth! I will say no more,
But laugh and walk out of the gate—Heaven and Earth have grown old.   12

Only a true hero is able to "laugh and walk out of the gate" while confronting death. Such a strong statement is possible only when one has transformed personal suffering into a noble action—and for this reason, we feel in Wen's poems "a consciousness of greatness in pain."[67]

Certainly, learned as he was, Ch'en Tzu-lung must have been familiar with Wen T'ien-hsiang's "Six Songs." In fact, Ch'en once praised Wen's poetry for its quality of heroic spirit, a spirit that even "affects the northern stars."[68] Moreover, like Wen T'ien-hsiang,[69] Ch'en Tzu-lung was a great admirer of Tu Fu, striving to create anew the poetic greatness achieved by the High T'ang poet. In a tradition in which "the defining criteria for value were inescapably governed by past models,"[70] it is especially pertinent for a poet to link his private inner experience with that of previous poetic masters. What Ch'en has done, I believe, is combine Tu's art of rhetoric and Wen's heroic spirit. And the result is a new, elevated style that achieves greater formal control and the dignity of a tragic vision. Unlike the two song-series by his past models, which rely on formulaic repetition such as "My wife, my wife," "my sister, my sister," and so on to accentuate the vernacular ring of the poetic voice, Ch'en deliberately imbued his poem-series with a classical tone. For the poems are written as quasi–Regulated Verse, creating a tension between harsh reality and lyric vision. Besides, Ch'en does not dwell on the personal sufferings of his family members—as did Tu Fu and Wen T'ien-hsiang—but focuses instead on the examples of contemporary martyrs and especially on the essential dilemma of life and death and the problem of when to die. Still more unusual is the bitter intensity of his feeling of shame for not having died for his country earlier—a conception of heroism that differs essentially from that of Wen T'ien-hsiang. This recreation of the "Seven-Song" style in *shih,* based on past models, echoes Ch'en's quintessential poetic theory: greatness in poetry does not lie in mere formal originality (for most of the forms had already been invented and fully developed by the Ming), but rather in the individual poet's creation of profound meaning and fine rhetoric.[71]

Ch'en's *shih* poems on loyalism employ a poetics drastically different from that of his love poetry written in the same form—a phenomenon which implies that in the *shih* genre the poet intends to separate patriotic sentiments from romantic love. His *shih* poetry gives us a stronger sense of urgency, of nakedness, of the finality of a firm poetic voice—but without at the same time sacrificing the poetic elegance so typical of his style. The early Ch'ing poet Wang Shih-chen used the term *ch'en-hsiung kuei-li* (profoundly heroic and elegantly beautiful) to describe the style of Ch'en's *shih* poetry and ranked Ch'en among the greatest poets of the seventeenth century: "His poems are profoundly heroic and elegantly beautiful; few modern authors can compete with him. He was truly a champion poet of unsurpassed talent. Among his contemporaries, only Mei-ts'un [Wu Wei-yeh] was his match."[72]

That the School of Seven Masters in *shih* should have been revived in the late Ming, after having been almost completely overpowered by the schools of Kung-an and Ching-ling,[73] was owing largely to Ch'en Tzu-lung's promotion of an individual voice of tragic vision based on the restoration of classical poetry. As a leader of the Chi-she group and the Yün-chien School of Poetry, Ch'en preached the importance of recovering the past as a remedial measure for Ming literature. He firmly believed that true poetry could be reborn only from a return to its origins. The fact that the name of his literary society, Chi, means "seeds"—as noted in chapter 3 in connection with a late-Ming renaissance—is especially pertinent here. For a return to the fertile beginnings of the past and to poetic models like those of the High T'ang would bring a true rebirth of poetic creativity.

EPILOGUE

Political censorship prevented Ch'en Tzu-lung's poetry from exercising an immediate and strong influence on early Ch'ing poetry. But 250 years after his death—shortly before the collapse of the Ch'ing dynasty—Chinese poets began to single out Ch'en Tzu-lung as their model. In 1909 a group of Chinese intellectuals organized a poetry club called the Southern Society (Nan-she) as the forum for their anti-Manchu politics, in obvious imitation of the Restoration Society (Fu-she) of the late Ming. Liu Ya-tzu (1887–1958), one of the founders of the Southern Society, expressed his admiration for Ch'en Tzu-lung and his loyalist protégé Hsia Wan-ch'un, the son of Hsia Yün-i:

> Throughout my life I've followed the Yün-chien School.
> Apart from the poetry of Hsiang-chen, I read only Yü-fan.[1]

Thus, by following in Ch'en's footsteps, twentieth-century loyalist poets reacted to the troubles of their times with renewed attempts to define their own life-vision.[2] To them Ch'en Tzu-lung represented the most vivid example of a poet who lived in close relation to political crisis but struggled to go beyond it in the work of art itself.

But until recently, Ch'en's love poetry has been wholly ignored or explained away as political allegory. It is clear that changing attitudes toward *tz'u* poetics on the part of the Ch'ing literati, especially after the eighteenth century, contributed largely to this problem of neglect and misinterpretation. Most scholars and poets of the early Ch'ing still, of course, shared the late-Ming idealization of *ch'ing* and believed that romantic love was a crucial part of the character of a great man. However, from the Middle Ch'ing on, a rather different, much more Confucian and "moralistic" attitude toward love and women is reflected in poetry—partly owing to the revival of orthodox neo-Confucianism during the period.[3] With this change came a completely different view of courtesans. Whereas courtesan-poets of the seventeenth century had enjoyed a position as important as that of the gentry women poets (if not more so),[4] by the eighteenth century courtesans were virtually excluded from the world of refined letters and seldom published their poems. (Even if they did, it was rare for their works to be preserved and respected.)[5] As a result, the eminent female writers of poetry whose names have come down to us from the Middle Ch'ing on were almost invariably born into "literary and official families" (*shu-hsiang shih-huan*).[6] A courtesan whose beginnings were as obscure and insignificant as Liu Shih's would not have had much chance of achieving distinction as a woman poet in the world of Liu's successors. Thus about the time Emperor Ch'ien-lung finally rehabilitated Ch'en Tzu-lung and honored him as a poet-hero, conditions for a similar rediscovery of Liu Shih were at their most unfavorable. Under such circumstances it was only natural that Ch'ing scholars and critics would try to safeguard Ch'en's reputation as a Confucian hero by deliberately suppressing the facts of his romantic involvement with the courtesan Liu Shih—which meant putting aside the poetry the lovers exchanged or at the very least denying Ch'en's love poetry its true value.

But, although the poetic voice of Ch'en Tzu-lung in his love poetry has been misunderstood and misinterpreted, the poems themselves have survived. What once was not considered worth reading, or worth reading literally, has become for us a genuine poetry that repays rereading and reinterpretation. A fuller understanding of the context in which Ch'en's unique poetic voice arose can only enrich the (as always, intertextual) experience of reading it.

APPENDIX 1:

A BRIEF DESCRIPTION

OF POETIC GENRES

I. *Fu* poetry[1]
Emerged ca. 150 B.C.
Characteristics: Use of rhyme, caesura, and parallel lines. Preface in prose form. Length of poem varies from a few to several hundred lines. *Fu* may be descriptive or lyrical, and often read as allegories.
Major subgenres:
1. *Ku-fu* (Ancient *fu*)—*Fu* poetry before the Six Dynasties (222–589).
2. *P'ien-fu* (Parallel *fu*)—Emerged in the Six Dynasties period. Use of structural patterns based on fixed line length.
3. *Lü-fu* (Regulated *fu*)—Emerged in the T'ang (618–907). Characterized by prescribed rhyme and tonal patterns.

II. *Shih* poetry
1. *Yüeh-fu* (Ballads)
Emerged ca. 120 B.C.
Characteristics: Basically a song form, applied broadly to popular ballads and ritual hymns and also to literary imitations of the genre. Use of dialogues, formulaic expressions, hyperbole, repetition with variation, free rhythmic patterns, often in lines of unequal length.
2. *Ku-shih* (Ancient Style poetry)
Emerged ca. 200 for five-character-line verse, and ca. 500 for seven-character-line verse.
Characteristics: Poem length and tonal patterns not prescribed.

Mostly in lines of equal length. Couplets serve as independent metrical units, with the rhyme often falling at the end of the second line of the couplet. Rhyme may be constant or change in the course of the poem.

Major subgenres:

1. five-character-line *shih*
2. seven-character-line *shih*
3. *Ko-hsing t'i* (Song Form)

    Originally a form of *yüeh-fu* ballads but later identified with the *ku-shih* form. Mostly in seven-character lines, occasionally in lines of unequal length. Lyrical and narrative in nature.

3. *Chin-t'i shih* (Recent Style poetry)

    Emerged ca. 600

    Characteristics: Use of prescribed tonal and rhyme patterns, alternation of level and oblique tones in the lines of each couplet, and verbal parallelism in some couplets. All in five-character or seven-character lines.

    Major subgenres:

    1. *Lü-shih* (Regulated Verse)—eight-line verse, with strict verbal parallelism in the two middle couplets. Rhyme-words in lines 2, 4, 6, 8 (occasionally in line 1 also) should be of level tone. Considered the perfect form of poetry.
    2. *Chüeh-chü* (Quatrain)—four-line verse, freer use of parallelism. The lines sometimes carry oblique tone rhymes.

III. *Tz'u* poetry (Song Lyric)

   Emerged ca. 750

   Flourished ca. 850–1279

   Revived ca. 1630

   Characteristics: Originally a song form, set to particular tune patterns. Generally in lines of unequal length, with two-stanza or more than two stanza structure. Use of level or oblique tone rhymes.

   Subgenres:

   1. *Hsiao-ling*—Usually contains not more than 62 characters.
   2. *Man-tz'u*—Ranges roughly from 70 to 240 characters. Use of diverse stanzaic patterns.

IV. *San-ch'ü* (Dramatic Lyric)

   Emerged ca. 1250

   Characteristics: Contains lines of unequal length, often written in the form of "song sequence" (*t'ao-shu*) and incorporated into drama. Frequent use of *ch'en-tzu* ("padding words") and colloquial expressions.

APPENDIX 2:

TWENTY SONGS

BY LIU SHIH

("Meng Chiang-nan":
Thinking of Someone [*LJS*, 1:255–65])

1. He is gone,
   Gone somewhere west of Feng-ch'eng.[1]
   A thin rain dampens my red sleeves,
   New weeds lie as deep as my jade brows are low,
   The butterfly is most bewildered.[2]

2. He is gone.
   Gone from the Isle of Egrets.
   Lotus blossoms turn to emerald remorse,
   Willow catkins rise to join the zither's grief,
   Behind the brocade curtain—the early autumn startles.

3. He is gone,
   Gone from the painted chamber tower.
   No longer lustrous and beautiful, I sit idle,
   Why bother about rouge powder and jade hairpin?
   Only the wind coming at night.[3]

4. He is gone,
   Gone from the small water pavilion.

123

Would you say we "have not loved enough"?
Or that we "have little to regret"?
All I see is trodden moss.

5. He is gone,
   Gone from the green window gauze.
   All I gain is frail sickness. Lighter than a swallow,
   Pitiful is my lone self, now that we are far apart.
   Secretly we hide sweet memories in our hearts.

6. He is gone,
   Gone, leaving the jade pipe cold.[4]
   Phoenix pecked at the scattered tiny red beans,
   Pheasants, joyfully embracing the censer, gazed at us,[5]
   Apricot was the color of my spring dress.

7. He is gone,
   Gone from the shadow of the green *wu-t'ung* tree.
   I can't believe this has earned us a heart-breaking tune,
   Still I wonder why our love has failed.
   Whence this brooding grief? No need to look.

8. He is gone,
   Gone from the small Crab-apple Hall.
   I force myself to rise; the fallen petals are quivering,
   A few red parting tears still remain,
   Outside the door, willows leaning against one another.

9. He is gone,
   Gone, yet dreams of him come even more often.
   Recalling the past: our shared moments were mostly wordless,
   But now I secretly regret the growing distance.
   Only in dreams can I find self-indulgence.

10. He is gone,
    Gone, and the nights are longer.
    How can this jeweled belt warm my thoughts about the black
       steed?[6]
    Gently putting on the silk robe in chill jade moonlight,
    Behind the rosy curtain, a single wisp of incense.

11. Where was he?
    On the Isle of Smartweed.
    The duck-censer burning low, the fragrant smoke warm,
    Spring mountains winding deeply in the painted screen,
    The golden sparrow ceased to weep.

12. Where was he?
    At the middle pavilion.
    Recall once after washing his face,
    His carefree laughter seemed so unconcerned—
    Who knows for whom he smiled?

13. Where was he?
    In the moonlight.
    In the middle of the night, I clutched his priceless arm,
    Lethargic, I looked at the lotus flowers again and again,
    My inner sentiments, how hazy!

14. Where was he?
    In the magnolia boat.
    Often talking to herself when receiving guests,
    Feeling more lost while combing her hair,
    This beauty still broods over his charms.

15. Where was he?
    At the magnificent banquet.
    My perfumed arms fluttered up and down,
    Words issued in song, like profound thoughts,
    Chiefly from my faintly glossed lips.

16. Where was he?
    At the Autumn Crab-apple Hall.
    Fun was playing hide-and-seek,
    Round after round, no need to linger for long.
    Again, how many sunsets have gone by!

17. Where was he?
    On the Lake of Misty Rain.
    Water rippled by the bamboo oar, the moon shining bright in the
      lustrous and gentle spring,

Our storied boat filled with wind and daphne fragrance,
Willows caressing the delicate waves.

18. Where was he?
At the jade steps.
No fool for love, yet I wanted to stay,
Overly sensitive to any sign of indifference,
It must be that I feared love would run too deep.

19. Where was he?
Behind the curtain patterned with thrushes.
A parrot dream ends in a black otter's tail,
Incense smoke lingers on the tip of the green spiral censer,
Delicate were the pink jade fingers.

20. Where was he?
By my pillow side.
Nothing but endless tears at the quilt edge—
Wiping off secretly, but only inducing more,
How I yearn for his pity and love.

GLOSSARY

(See also bibliography for Chinese names and book titles.)

Ch'ai Hu-ch'en, 柴虎臣

Ch'an-chüan, 嬋娟

Ch'ang-chao, 長朝

Ch'ang-chou, 常州

Chang Fang-t'ung, 張方同

Ch'ang Hung, 萇弘

Chang Liang, 張艮

Chang P'u, 張溥

Chang Wan-hsiang, 張畹香

Chao-yün, 朝雲

"Che liu yang-kuan", 折柳陽関

chen, 真

Ch'en Chen-hui, 陳貞慧

ch'en-hsiung kuei-li, 沈雄瑰麗

Ch'en Shu-k'o, 陳恕可

ch'en-tzu, 襯字

ch'i-li, 淒厲

Chi-nan, 濟南

Ch'i Piao-chia, 祁彪佳

Chi-she, 幾社

"Chi-shu", 寄書

"Chiang ch'eng tzu", 江城子

Chiang Yen, 江淹

"Ch'ien-ch'iu sui", 千秋歳

Ch'ien-lung, 乾隆

chih, 志

chih-yin, 知音

Ch'in-huai, 秦淮

Chin I, 金逸

"Chin-ming ch'ih", 金明池

chin-shih, 進士

chin-t'i shih, 近體詩

chin-yü hsiao *tz'u*, 近於小詞

ch'ing, 情

Ching-ling, 竟陵

ch'ing-so, 青瑣

chiu-yüan, 舊院

Ch'iu Yüan, 仇遠

Cho-cho, 灼灼

Chou Ch'üan, 周銓

Chou Tao-teng, 周道登

chü, 曲

chü-ch'ü, 劇曲

Chu Hsi, 朱熹

chü-jen, 擧人

Chu-ko Liang, 諸葛亮

Chu Shu-chen, 朱淑真

Ch'u-tz'u, 楚辭

ch'ü tzu tz'u, 曲子詞

Chu-yü t'ang chi, 屬玉堂集

ch'uan-ch'i, 傳奇

chuang-yüan, 狀元

127

"Ch'üeh-ch'iao hsien", 鵲橋仙
chüeh-chü, 絕句
chung, 忠
Ch'ung-chen, 崇禎
Chung-yü, 忠裕
Fang Chung-lü, 方中履
Fang I-chih, 方以智
Feng Hsü, 馮煦
fu, 賦
Fu-she, 復社
Han Shih-chung, 韓世忠
Heng-t'ang, 橫塘
Ho-lü, 闔廬
hou-shen, 後身
hsia erh hui, 俠而慧
Hsia Yün-i, 夏允彝
hsiang-ssu, 相思
hsiang-ssu ping, 相思病
Hsiao Kang, 蕭綱
hsiao-ling, 小令
Hsiao-yün, 曉雲
Hsieh Ao, 謝翱
Hsieh Ling-yün, 謝靈運
Hsieh Tao-yün, 謝道韞
Hsieh T'iao, 謝朓
Hsin Ch'i-chi, 辛棄疾
Hsin-chung, 信衷
hsing-wang, 興亡
Hsiu-ju chi, 繡襦記
Hsü Lin, 徐霖
Hsü Wu-ching, 徐武靜
Hsüeh T'ao, 薛濤
Hu Yün-yüan, 胡允瑗
"Hua t'ang ch'un", 畫堂春
huai-ku, 懷古
"Huan hsi sha", 浣溪沙
Huan Wen, 桓溫
Huang Tao-chou, 黃道周
Huang Tsung-hsi, 黃宗羲
Huang Yü-ch'i, 黃毓祺
Huo Hsiao-yü, 霍小玉
"I chiang-nan", 憶江南
I-ching, 易經

I sheng chi, 倚聲集
I-tai tsan, 衣帶贊
Juan Chi, 阮籍
Juan Ta-ch'eng, 阮大鋮
Kao T'ai-an-jen, 高太安人
"Kao T'ang fu", 高唐賦
ko-hsing t'i, 歌行體
Ko Nen, 葛嫩
ku-fu, 古賦
Ku Mei, 顧媚
ku-shih, 古詩
Kuan Tao-sheng, 管道昇
Kuei-chia-yüan, 歸家院
Kuei Chuang, 歸莊
Kuei-hsiu shih-jen, 閨秀詩人
kuei-yüan, 閨怨
Kung-an, 公安
Kung-sun Shu, 公孫恕
Kung Ting-tzu, 龔鼎孳
Kuo-ch'ao kuei-hsiu cheng-shih chi,
　國朝閨秀正始集
Lan-t'ing, 蘭亭
lei, 類
Li Chen-li, 李貞麗
Li Ching, 李璟
Li Ch'ing-chao, 李清照
Li Ho, 李賀
li-ho, 離合
Li Hsiang-chün, 李香君
Li I, 李益
Li Ling, 李陵
Li Meng-yang, 李夢陽
Li P'an-lung, 李攀龍
Li-sao, 離騷
Li-tai shih-yü, 歷代詩餘
Li Ts'un-wo, 李存我
Li Wa chuan, 李娃傳
Li Wen, 李雯
Li Yü, 李煜
Liang Hung, 梁鴻
Liang Hung-yü, 梁紅玉
"Lien-hua fu", 蓮花賦
Liu Chih, 柳枝

Liu K'o-chuang, 劉克莊
Liu Meng-mei, 柳夢梅
Liu Yin, 柳隱
Liu Yung, 柳永
"Lo-shen *fu*", 洛神賦
Lu Chi, 陸機
lü-fu, 律賦
lü-shih, 律詩
Lung-wu, 隆武
Ma Chiao, 馬嬌
man-tz'u, 慢詞
Mei-niang, 美娘
"Meng chiang-nan", 夢江南
Mo-ling, 秣陵
Mu-chai i-shih, 牧齋遺事
Mu-tan t'ing, 牡丹亭
"Nan Lo-shen fu", 男洛神賦
nan-shih, 南市
Nan-yüan, 南園
P'an-p'an, 盼盼
Pan-yeh-t'ang, 半野堂
Pao Chao, 鮑照
Pao Ssu-niang, 鮑四娘
Pei-ti, 北地
pen-se, 本色
Pi-chi man-chih, 碧雞漫志
p'ien-fu, 駢賦
Pien Sai, 卞賽
P'ing-shan leng yen, 平山冷燕
Po Chü-i, 白居易
Po Hsing-chien, 白行簡
"P'u-sa man", 菩薩蠻
san-ch'ü, 散曲
san-yen, 三言
sao, 騷
"Shan hua tzu", 山花子
Shang Ching-lan, 商景蘭
"Shao-nien yu", 少年遊
Shen Ch'ien, 沈謙
Shen I-fu, 沈義父
shen-nü, 神女
shen-yün, 神韻
Sheng-tse, 盛澤

shih, 詩
Shih-ching, 詩經
shih chuang *tz'u* mei, 詩莊詞媚
shu-hsiang shih-huan, 書香世宦
ssu-kung-tsu, 四公子
Ssu-ma Ch'ien, 司馬遷
Su Hsiao-hsiao, 蘇小小
Su Hsiao-mei, 蘇小妹
Su K'un-sheng, 蘇崑生
Su Shih, 蘇軾
Sun K'o-hsien, 孫克咸
Sung Cheng-pi, 宋徵璧
Sung Cheng-yü, 宋徵輿
Sung-chiang, 松江
Sung-chiang fu-chih, 松江府志
Sung liu-shih-i chia tz'u-hsüan,
　宋六十一家詞選
Sung Yü, 宋玉
"T'a-so hsing", 踏莎行
T'ai-p'ing yü lan, 太平御覽
T'an Hsien, 譚獻
tan-yüeh mei-hua, 淡月梅花
T'ang Chüeh, 唐珏
T'ao Ch'ien, 陶潛
t'ao-shu, 套數
T'ao Tsung-i, 陶宗儀
"T'iao-hsiao ling", 調笑令
"Tieh lien hua", 蝶戀花
"T'ien-tz'u tsa-shuo", 填詞雜說
T'ing-ch'iu-sheng-kuan tz'u-hua,
　聽秋聲舘詞話
Ting Shao-i, 丁紹儀
"Ts'ai-lien *ch'ü*", 採蓮曲
"Ts'ai-lien *fu*", 採蓮賦
ts'ai-nü, 才女
ts'ai-tzu chia-jen, 才子佳人
Ts'ai Yen, 蔡琰
Ts'ao Chih, 曹植
Tso Ssu, 左思
Ts'ui Ying-ying, 崔鶯鶯
Tu Li-niang, 杜麗娘
Tung Pai, 董白
tz'u, 詞

Tsu-ch'ai chi, 紫釵記
Tsu-hsiao chi, 紫蕭記
tz'u-hua, 詞話
"Tz'u-lun", 詞論
"Wang chiang-nan", 望江南
Wang Cho, 王灼
Wang Hsi-chih, 王羲之
Wang Shih-chen (1526–90), 王世貞
Wang Shih-chen (1634–1711),
　王士禎
Wang-ti, 望帝
Wang Tuan, 汪端
Wei Lu, 衛錄
Wen Chen-heng, 文震亨
Wen Cheng-ming, 文徵明
Wen T'ing-yün, 溫庭筠
wen-ya, 溫雅
Wo-tzu, 卧子
wu, 物
Wu-chiang, 吳江
Wu Cho, 吳焯
Wu I, 吳易
Wu-ling-ch'un (Ch'i Hui-chen),
　武陵春(齊慧貞)
Wu Ping, 吳炳
Wu Sheng-chao, 吳勝兆

wu-tang, 吾黨
"Wu yeh t'i", 烏夜啼
Wu-Yüeh, 吳越
Yang Ai, 楊愛
"Yang-hua", 楊花
Yang Kuei-fei, 楊貴妃
Yang Shen, 楊慎
Yang Wen-ts'ung, 楊文驄
"Ying-hsiung ch'i-tuan shuo",
　英雄氣短說
Ying-lien, 影憐
Yü Chi, 余集
yu-ch'ing, 有情
yü-ching, 玉鏡
Yu-huan, 憂患
Yu-huan i-shih, 憂患意識
Yu-lan ts'ao, 幽蘭草
"Yü mei-jen", 虞美人
Yü-t'ang-ch'un, 玉堂春
Yüan Chiang, 沅江
Yüan-yang lou tz'u, 鴛鴦樓詞
yüeh-fu, 樂府
Yün-chien, 雲間
Yün-chüan, 雲娟
yung-wu tz'u, 詠物詞

NOTES

Preface

1 Jonathan Spence and John Wills, *From Ming to Ch'ing* (New Haven: Yale Univ. Press, 1979), xvii–xviii.

Chapter 1. The Loyalist Tradition

1 Translation by William Atwell, in his "Ch'en Tzu-lung (1608–1647): A Scholar-Official of the Late Ming Dynasty" (Ph.D. diss., Princeton Univ., 1975), 140. See also original source in *CTLS*, 2:721.

2 What Jonathan Chaves has said about "moral heroism," though in a different context, can certainly be applied to Ch'en Tzu-lung. See Jonathan Chaves, "Moral Action in the Poetry of Wu Chia-chi (1618–84)," *Harvard Journal of Asiatic Studies* 46.2 (1986): 392–94.

3 See, e.g., Wu Wei-yeh, *Mei-ts'un shih-hua*, in *Mei-ts'un chia ts'ang-kao, chüan* 58 (1911; rpt. Taipei: Student Book Store, 1975), 3:988.

4 Lin Hsiao-ming, "Ch'en Tzu-lung mu hsiu-fu chün-kung," in *Shanghai hsin-min wan-pao*, Dec. 14, 1988. See illustrations above.

5 Thomas Carlyle has a chapter entitled "The Hero as Poet" in his *On Heroes, Hero-Worship and the Heroic in History* (rpt. Lincoln: Univ. of Nebraska Press, 1966).

6 See his *Ming i-min shih* (rpt. Shanghai: Chung-hua shu-chü, 1961).

7 See Emperor Ch'ien-lung's edict reprinted in Ch'en Tzu-lung, *Ch'en Chung-yü ch'üan-chi*, ed. Wang Ch'ang, (n.p., 1803), 1a–3a.

8 *Ch'en Chung-yü ch'üan-chi* (n.p., 1803).

9 See *Ch'en Tzu-lung shih-chi*, ed. Shih Chih-ts'un and Ma Tsu-hsi (Shanghai: Ku-chi ch'u-pan-she, 1983).

10 For Wen T'ien-hsiang as a poet, see Horst Huber, "The Upheaval of the Thirteenth Century in the Poetry of Wen T'ien-hsiang," paper presented at the Association for Asian Studies Annual Meeting, Washington, D.C., March 1989.

11 William Andress Brown, *Wen T'ien-hsiang: A Biographical Study of a Sung Patriot* (San Francisco: Chinese Materials Center Publications, 1986), 45–46.

12 Ibid., 44–45.

13 Ibid., 49. For a Ming writer's view of the heroic Wen T'ien-hsiang, see F. W. Mote, "Confucian Eremitism in the Yüan period," in *The Confucian Persuasion*, ed. Arthur F. Wright (Stanford: Stanford Univ. Press, 1960), 233.

14 Wen T'ien-hsiang, *Wen T'ien-hsiang ch'üan-chi*, based on the 1560 edition of *Ch'ung-k'o Wen-shan hsien-sheng ch'üan-chi*, ed. Lo Hung-hsien (Peking: Chung-kuo shu-tien, 1985), *chüan* 14, p. 349.

15 Literally, "since I passed the civil service examination and was awarded the Classics degree." For the definition of *ming-ching*, see Charles O. Hucker, *A Dictionary of Official Titles in Imperial China* (Stanford: Stanford Univ. Press, 1985), p. 333, no. 4007.

16 The translation of these two lines is adapted from Brown, *Wen T'ien-hsiang*, 155. Huang-k'ung Beach literally means "Frightening Beach," and Ling-ting Sea means "Sea of the Wanderer."

17 Yü Ying-shih, *Fang I-chih wan-chieh k'ao*, rev. ed. (Taipei: Asian Culture Co., 1986), 106.

18 Because of the implicit nature of documents concerning Fang I-chih's suicide, this important fact was not made public until three hundred years after Fang's death, when Yü Ying-shih published his book on the loyalism of Fang I-chih. (*Fang I-chih wan-chieh k'ao* was first published in 1972.) See also the revised 1986 edition, *Fang I-chih wan-chieh k'ao*, 95–122, 205–46.

19 Yü Ying-shih, *Fang I-chih wan-chieh k'ao*, 107, 212.

20 *Wen T'ien-hsiang ch'üan-chi*, *chüan* 10, p. 251. See also Brown, *Wen T'ien-hsiang*, 223.

21 Some notable examples were Huang Tao-chou, Hsia Yün-i, and Hsia Wan-ch'un. See also Yüan Chou-tsung, ed. *Ai-kuo shih-tz'u hsüan* (Taipei: Commercial Press, 1982), 461.

22 Brown, *Wen T'ien-hsiang*, 56.

23 Laurence A. Schneider, *A Madman of Ch'u: The Chinese Myth of Loyalty and Dissent* (Berkeley: Univ. of California Press, 1980), 83–85. Of course, the myth of Ch'ü Yüan had undergone many changes even before the Ming. For example, in the work of Liu Tsung-yüan (773–819) the Ch'ü Yüan lore became closely connected with the exile theme. See William H. Nienhauser, Jr., et al., *Liu Tsung-yüan* (New York: Twayne, 1973), 36–37, 105.

24 See Tu Teng-ch'un, *She-shih shih-mo*, in *Chao-tai ts'ung-shu*, vol. 50. See also Frederic Wakeman, Jr., *The Great Enterprise: The Manchu Reconstruction of*

Imperial Order in Seventeenth-Century China (Berkeley: Univ. of California Press, 1985), 1:665–74.

25 William S. Atwell, "From Education to Politics: The Fu She," in *Self and Society in Ming Thought*, ed. Wm. Theodore De Bary (New York: Columbia Univ. Press, 1970), 358, 347. See also Hu Ch'iu-yüan, *Fu-she chi ch'i jen-wu* (Taipei: Chung-hua tsa-chih-she, 1968).

26 Atwell, "From Education to Politics," 335.

27 Ibid., 348. See also Lynn Struve, "Huang Zongxi in Context: A Reappraisal of His Major Writings," *Journal of Asian Studies* 47.3 (1988): 478.

28 See *Huang-Ming ching-shih wen-pien* (1639; rpt. Hong Kong, 1964).

29 Atwell, "From Education to Politics," 347.

30 In Ch'en Tzu-lung, *Ch'en Chung-yü ch'üan-chi*, 1b. According to Emperor Ch'ien-lung, there were some 3,600 Ming officials who died in martyrdom. (Of course, this number does not include the countless men and women who killed themselves in order to avoid "personal degradation at the hands of marauding troops." See Jonathan Chaves, "Moral Action in the Poetry of Wu Chia-chi," 387–405.)

31 For this point, see Stephen Owen's account in his *Remembrances: The Experience of the Past in Classical Chinese Literature* (Cambridge: Harvard Univ. Press, 1986), 136–37.

32 Numerous Ming loyalists, including Kuei Chuang and Ku Yen-wu (1613–82), composed poems on the story of Cheng Ssu-hsiao. There has been a controversy concerning the authenticity of *Hsin-shih* found in the Soochow well, but most scholars today accept the work as authentic. See Yang Li-k'uei, "Cheng Ssu-hsiao yen-chiu chi ch'i shih chien-chu" (M.A. thesis, Cultural Univ. Taiwan, 1977), 82–101. For a good edition of *Hsin-shih*, see Cheng Ssu-hsiao, [*T'ieh-han*] *Hsin-shih* (rpt., Taipei: Shih-chieh shu-chü, 1955).

33 Mote, "Confucian Eremitism in the Yüan Period," 352, n. 50.

34 *Writings Stored in a Stone Casket* was by Chang Tai. It was written to record the history of the Ming, modeled after Ssu-ma Ch'ien's *Records of the Historian*. See Chang Tai, *Shih-k'uei ts'ang-shu* (Shanghai: Chung-hua shu-chü, 1959); and Owen, *Remembrances*, 137.

35 Wen T'ien-hsiang was imprisoned for three years before being executed by the Mongols early in 1283.

36 Murray Krieger, *Visions of Extremity in Modern Literature*. Vol. 1, *The Tragic Vision* (Baltimore: Johns Hopkins Univ. Press, 1973), 3–4.

Chapter 2. The Concept of Ch'ing *and Late-Ming Images of Women*

1 Ch'ai Hu-ch'en, *I-sheng chi*, cited in Wang Ying-chih, "Ch'en Tzu-lung tz'u-hsüeh ch'u-i," in *Ming Ch'ing shih-wen yen-chiu ts'ung-k'an*, ed. Chinese Dept., Chiang-su Teachers' Normal College, 1 (March 1982), 94. The "tragic

grief at Hua-t'ing" alludes to the heroic death of the Six Dynasties poet Lu Chi (261–303) in Hua-t'ing, which was also Ch'en Tzu-lung's hometown. Sung Yü (fl. third century B.C.) was known for his depiction of erotic love in his "Kao T'ang *fu*."

2 See Lin Yutang, *Importance of Understanding* (Cleveland: World, 1960), 117–18. I owe this specific citation to Professor Patrick Hanan; see his *The Chinese Vernacular Story* (Cambridge: Harvard Univ. Press, 1981), 221.

3 Hanan, *The Chinese Vernacular Story*, 79.

4 Feng Meng-lung, *Ch'ing-shih lei-lüeh*, ed. Tso Hsüeh-ming (Ch'ang-sha: Yüeh-lu shu-she, 1984). See also Hanan's *The Chinese Vernacular Story*, 79, where he translates *Ch'ing-shih lei-lüeh* as "Anatomy of Love."

5 Hanan, *The Chinese Vernacular Story*, 97.

6 C. T. Hsia, "Time and the Human Condition in the Plays of T'ang Hsien-tsu," in De Bary, *Self and Society*, 277. For an English translation of *Mu-tan t'ing*, see Cyril Birch, trans., *The Peony Pavilion* (Bloomington: Indiana Univ. Press, 1980).

7 Translation taken from Hsia, "Time and the Human Condition," 276. Also cited with modifications by Pei-kai Cheng, in his "Reality and Imagination: Li Chih and T'ang Hsien-tsu in Search of Authenticity" (Ph.D. diss., Yale Univ., 1980), 261.

8 See Hsia, "Time and the Human Condition," and Cheng, "Reality and Imagination," 252–94.

9 Feng Meng-lung, *Hsing-shih heng-yen*, chaps. 3, 9. For the possible authorship and sources of these stories, see Patrick Hanan, *The Chinese Short Story* (Cambridge: Harvard Univ. Press, 1973), 242.

10 Richard C. Hessney, "Beyond Beauty and Talent: The Moral and Chivalric Self in *The Fortunate Union*," in *Expressions of Self in Chinese Literature*, ed. Robert E. Hegel and Richard C. Hessney (New York: Columbia Univ. Press, 1985), 239.

11 See scene 1 in *Ch'ang-sheng tien*, in *Chung-kuo shih ta ku-tien pei-chü chi* (Shanghai: Wen-i ch'u-pan-she, 1982), 613.

12 Richard Hessney discusses this problem in his "Beautiful, Talented, and Brave: Seventeenth-Century Chinese Scholar-Beauty Romances" (Ph.D. diss., Columbia Univ., 1979), 29.

13 See Oscar Wilde, "The Decay of Lying," in *The Artist as Critic: Critical Writings of Oscar Wilde*, ed. Richard Ellmann (1969; rpt. Chicago: Univ. of Chicago Press, 1982), 307.

14 Joanna F. Handlin, "Lü K'un's New Audience: The Influence of Women's Literacy on Sixteenth-Century Thought," in *Women in Chinese Society*, ed. Margery Wolf and Roxane Witke (Stanford: Stanford Univ. Press, 1975), 28. A similar suspicion of novels as reading matter for women is to be found in seventeenth- and eighteenth-century Europe: there, of course, it was religious literature that was being displaced.

15 Hanan, *The Chinese Vernacular Story*, 80–81.

16 On the evolution of the Yü-t'ang-ch'un story, see Hanan, *The Chinese Short Story*, 240–41.

17 Mao Hsiang, *Ying-mei-an i-yü*, trans. Pan Tze-yen under the title *The Reminiscences of Tung Hsiao-wan* (Shanghai: Commercial Press, 1931). Some scholars might not regard the story's conclusion as "realistic." According to Mao Hsiang, Tung Pai died of illness. There has been a controversy regarding the truth of Mao Hsiang's story—a long-popular tradition has it that Tung was simply taken away by Emperor Shun Chih of the Ch'ing to become his own imperial consort, a theory that has been proven wrong by many scholars. (See Ch'ien Chung-lien, "Wu Mei-ts'un shih pu-chien," in his *Meng-t'iao-an chuan-chu erh-chung* [Peking: Chinese Institute of Social Sciences Press, 1984], 123–33.) But according to the historian Ch'en Yin-k'o, it is entirely possible that Tung had been abducted by the Ch'ing people around 1650–51 (which was about the time Mao Hsiang claimed Tung Pai died), though she did not actually become the Ch'ing emperor's imperial consort. For some time before 1651 the Ch'ing government had indeed ransacked the entertainment quarters of the Nanking-Soochow region and "snatched away" many local courtesans, including some well-known ex-courtesans in order to establish a new music bureau for the court. For a discussion of Tung as a distinguished painter, see Marsha Weidner et al., *Views from Jade Terrace: Chinese Women Artists 1300–1912* (Indianapolis Museum of Art and New York: Rizzoli, 1988), 98–99.

18 The story of Wu-ling-ch'un was recorded in Chou Hui's *Hsü Chin-ling so-shih* (completed in 1610), *chüan* 2; rpt. in *Chin-ling so-shih*, 2 vols. (Peking: Wen-hsüeh ku-chi k'an-hsing-she, 1955), 157b–158a. It should be noted that in his inscription, Hsü Lin compares Wu-ling-ch'un to a certain Li Ko-ko, a subtle reference to the virtuous T'ang courtesan Li Wa, a fictional character created by Po Hsing-chien. Hsü Lin's particular liking for the character Li Wa may be demonstrated by the fact that one of the *ch'uan-ch'i* plays attributed to him, *Hsiu-ju chi* (The embroidered garment), was based on the T'ang *ch'uan-ch'i* tale *Li Wa chuan*. I am indebted to Wang Ay-ling for the information concerning Wu-ling-ch'un and Hsü Lin. I have also benefited from reading Lee Hui-shu's "The City Hermit Wu Wei and His Pai-miao Paintings" (manuscript, 1989).

19 Note that in scene 28 of the play, Hou Fang-yü inscribes a poem on Lan Ying's painting, "The Peach Blossom Spring." The metaphorical link between the peach blossom fan and the Peach Blossom Spring is clear.

20 Chen Shih-hsiang et. al., trans., *The Peach Blossom Fan*, by K'ung Shang-jen (Berkeley: Univ. of California Press, 1976), 203.

21 Willard J. Peterson, *Bitter Gourd: Fang I-chih and the Impetus for Intellectual Change* (New Haven: Yale Univ. Press, 1979), 143–44.

22 *Chiu-yüan* (literally "the old compound") refers to the quarter near Wu-ting Bridge where famous and artistically talented courtesans like Li Hsiang-chün

and Pien Sai lived. (When such a courtesan found a true lover for her to devote herself to, there was usually a ceremony of exchanged vows of fidelity, as was the case with Li Hsiang-chün and Hou Fang-yü in the *Peach Blossom Fan.*) *Nan-shih* (literally "South City") was, in contrast, reserved for those "lowly" prostitutes. (See Yü Huai, *Pan-ch'iao tsa-chi*, 1a.)

23 K'ung Shang-jen, *T'ao-hua shan*, rev. ed. (Peking: Jen-min wen-hsüeh ch'u-pan-she, 1980), sc. 6, p. 44.

24 For example, in Wu Ping's play "The Green Peonies" there are two matching *ts'ai-tzu chia-jen* couples. The same technique was later adopted in *P'ing-shan leng-yen* and other plays. See Hessney, "Beautiful, Talented, and Brave," 167.

25 For a brief description of Ku Mei's life and artistic accomplishment, see Weidner, *Views from Jade Terrace*, 96–98.

26 Kuan Hsien-chu proves that Yang Wen-ts'ung's correct dates were 1596–1646 rather than the commonly assumed 1597–1645. See Kuan Hsien-chu, "Yang Lung-yu sheng tsu nien k'ao," *Kuei-chou shih-ta hsüeh-pao* 50 (March 1987): 43–44.

27 For a discussion of Liu Shih's paintings and her inscriptions, see Weidner, *Views from Jade Terrace*, 99–102.

28 Yü Huai, *Pan-ch'iao tsa-chi*, trans. Howard Levy under the title *A Feast of Mist and Flowers: The Gay Quarters of Nanking at the End of the Ming* (Yokohama: Privately printed, 1966).

29 Levy, "Introduction," *A Feast of Mist and Flowers*, 9.

30 James C. Y. Watt, "The Literati Environment," in *The Chinese Scholar's Studio: Artistic Life in the Late Ming Period*, ed. Chu-tsing Li and James C. Y. Watt (New York: Asia Society Galleries, 1987), 7.

31 Ibid.

32 Ann Rosalind Jones, "City Women and Their Audiences: Louise Labé and Veronica Franco," in *Rewriting the Renaissance: The Discourses of Sexual Differences in Early Modern Europe*, ed. Margaret W. Ferguson et al. (Chicago: Univ. of Chicago Press, 1986), 299–316.

33 Jeanne Larsen, "Introduction" to her *Brocade River Poems: Selected Works of the T'ang Dynasty Courtesan Xue Tao* (Princeton: Princeton Univ. Press, 1987), xv.

34 Hessney, "Beautiful, Talented, and Brave," 36.

35 Feng Meng-lung, *Hsing-shih heng-yen*, chap. 11. For sources of the story, see Hanan, *The Chinese Short Story*, 243. Hessney also discusses this story in "Beautiful, Talented, and Brave," 177–79. The story of Su Hsiao-mei reminds us of Virginia Woolf's fictional creation of a woman poet called Judith Shakespeare, the great playwright's "wonderfully gifted sister." See discussion of Woolf's story in Sandra M. Gilbert and Susan Gubar, *The Madwoman in the Attic: The Woman Writer and the Nineteenth-Century Literary Imagination* (New Haven: Yale Univ. Press, 1979), 539–41.

36 Ho Ch'iung-yai et al., *Ch'in Shao-yu* (Chiang-su: Jen-min ch'u-pan-she, 1983).

37 See Hsü Wei, *Nü chuang-yüan [tz'u huang te feng]*, in *Ssu-sheng yüan*, ed. Chou Chung-ming (Shanghai: Ku-chi ch'u-pan-she, 1984), 62–106. There were many other Ming and Ch'ing stories on this subject, but Hsü Wei's play was perhaps most well known.

38 Ibid., 100.

39 Of course, courtesans were not the only ones to be influenced by this image of the talented woman. A considerable number of women poets came from gentry families and regularly formed poetry clubs to promote their literary interest. Their intellectual activities, however, unlike those of the courtesan-poets, who moved around more actively and were closely associated with male scholars, usually revolved around female relatives and friends. One notable gentry woman poet who combined poetic talent with domesticity was Shang Ching-lan, wife of the Ming loyalist Ch'i Piao-chia (1602–45). Ellen Widmer notes that, whereas for courtesans high achievement in poetry and art "could lead in the desirable direction of marriage with gentry men," there was a "taboo against excessive intellectual exertion" for those women who were related to these gentry men as "daughters, wives, or mothers" (Ellen Widmer, "The Epistolary World of Female Talent in Seventeenth-Century China," *Late Imperial China* 10.2 [1989]: 30).

40 I am indebted to Linda Woodbridge for this point. See her *Women and the English Renaissance: Literature and the Nature of Womankind, 1540–1620* (Urbana: Univ. of Illinois Press, 1986), 153.

41 Anne M. Birrell, "The Dusty Mirror: Courtly Portraits of Woman in Southern Dynasties Love Poetry," in Hegel and Hessney, *Expressions of Self*, 55.

42 Joanna Handlin argues that because of an increased female literacy in the late Ming, men's general attitude toward women had changed. See her "Lü K'un's New Audience," 29.

43 Of course, this does not mean there were no jealous wives who forbade their husbands to take their courtesan-lovers as concubines. For example, the tragedy of Ch'en Tzu-lung's and Liu Shih's love relationship was caused by this very problem, as will be explained later in this book.

44 Anthony C. Yu, "The Quest of Brother Amor: Buddhist Intimations in *The Story of the Stone*," *Harvard Journal of Asiatic Studies* 49.1 (1989): 70.

45 For example, she was involved in the Huang Yü-ch'i Resistance Movement in 1648 and helped the Koxinga army in the Nanking area in 1654 and 1659. For details concerning similar activities, see *LJS*, 3:827–1224.

46 K'ung Shang-jen, *T'ao-hua shan*, sc. 2, p. 16.

47 Hou Fang-yü, *Chuang-hui-t'ang chi*, Ssu-pu pei-yao ed. (Shanghai: Chung-hua shu-chü, 1936), *chüan* 5, 11b.

48 See my article, "The Idea of the Mask in Wu Wei-yeh (1609–1671)," *Harvard Journal of Asiatic Studies* 48.2 (1988): 289–320.

49 Lines 62–67 in Wu Wei-yeh's "A Song on Hearing the Taoist Priestess Pien Yü-ching Play the Zither." Translation adapted from my "The Idea of the Mask in Wu Wei-yeh," 303.

50 Wu Wei-yeh, *Wu Mei-ts'un shih-chi* [*chien-chu*], ed. Wu I-feng (1814; rpt. Hong Kong: Kuang-chih shu-chü 1975), 185.

51 See also Chu Tse-chieh's article, "Ko-wu chih shih yü ku-kuo chih ssu," *Kuei-chou she-hui k'o-hsüeh*, no. 22.1 (1984): 95–100.

52 Yü Huai, *Pan-ch'iao tsa-chi*, 1a.

53 Wang Shih-chen, *Wang Yü-yang shih-wen* [*hsüan-chu*], ed. Li Yü-fu (Chi-nan: Ch'i-lu shu-she, 1982), 69. See also Daniel Bryant's translation of poem 11, in his "Syntax and Sentiment in Old Nanking: Wang Shih-chen's 'Miscellaneous Poems on the Ch'in-huai' " (manuscript, 1986), 27.

54 Quoted in Yü Huai, *Pan-ch'iao tsa-chi*, 17a.

55 K'ung Shang-jen, *T'ao-hua shan*, 1.

Chapter 3. Ch'en Tzu-lung and the Woman Poet Liu Shih

1 In the Fogg Museum of Art at Harvard University is a portrait of Liu Shih (entitled "Portrait of Madame Ho-tung") that was believed by some to be the work of the late-Ming artist Wu Cho. See Robert J. Maeda, "The Portrait of a Woman of the Late Ming–Early Ch'ing Period: Madame Ho-tung," *Archives of Asian Art* 27 (1973–74): 46–52. Recently some art historians have doubted its authenticity. For example, James Watt argues that Wu Cho's work was a forgery, as the somewhat "vulgar" pose of the courtesan in the painting was in contradiction to the historical Liu Shih's elegant style of beauty (private communication, October 30, 1987). For a later portrait of Liu Shih, see figure 5 above.

2 James Cahill, *The Distant Mountains: Chinese Painting of the Late Ming Dynasty* (New York: Weatherhill, 1982), 63. See also *LJS*, 1:329.

3 Cahill, *Distant Mountains*, 63. See also Chu Hui-liang, *Chao Tso yen-chiu* (Taipei: National Palace Museum, 1979), 1–21.

4 See Tu Fu's "Songs on Mei-p'i," in Tu Fu, *Tu shih* [*hsiang-chu*], ed. Ch'iu Chao-ao (Peking: Chung-hua shu-chü, 1979), *chüan* 3, 1:179–82.

5 The term *Collator* (*chiao-shu*) originally referred specifically to the T'ang courtesan Hsüeh T'ao, who was recommended for the post of collator at the Imperial Court. Later the term was used to refer to all courtesans who possessed outstanding talents.

6 Atwell, "Ch'en Tzu-lung (1608–1647)," 58. See also Richard Wilhelm and Cary F. Baynes, trans. *The I Ching, or Book of Changes* (Princeton: Princeton Univ. Press, 1967), 345.

7 For the literary associations' gradual shift into the political arena, see Andrew H. Plaks, *The Four Masterworks of the Ming Novel* (Princeton: Princeton Univ. Press, 1987), 9–12.

8 See also Atwell, "From Education to Politics," 345.

9 See Woodbridge, *Women and the English Renaissance*, esp. 1–9.

10 Gilbert and Gubar, *Madwoman in the Attic*, 546.

11 See her *Women Writers and Poetic Identity* (Princeton: Princeton Univ. Press, 1980); and *Bearing the Word: Language and Female Experience in Nineteenth-Century Women's Writing* (Chicago: Univ. of Chicago Press, 1986).

12 Gilbert and Gubar, *Madwoman in the Attic*, 541. See also Richard B. Sewall, ed., *Emily Dickinson: A Collection of Critical Essays* (Englewood Cliffs: Prentice-Hall, 1963), 120.

13 Gilbert and Gubar, *Madwoman in the Attic*, 540–41. It should be noted that this does not apply to the French tradition. Both Marie de France (fl. late twelfth century) and Christine de Pizan (ca. 1364–ca. 1430) were regarded as distinguished poets in ancient France. And, of course, this does not mean that there were no women poets at all in the English-speaking world. But, unlike women who wrote fiction, the majority of those who wrote verse in England (say, in the eighteenth century) had been ignored and forgotten until modern scholars rediscovered them. (See, for example, Roger Lonsdale, *Eighteenth-Century Women Poets: An Oxford Anthology* [Oxford: Oxford Univ. Press, 1989]).

14 This device is of great antiquity in Chinese poetry. Of course, recent feminist critics would be deeply suspicious of a male poet's right (or ability) to "speak for" a woman. It is my contention that the cultural exchanges of men and women in the late Ming did much to make such substitutions believable. The history of the *tz'u* genre and especially its seventeenth-century developments show women appearing in poetry not only as metaphors but as colleagues.

15 Gilbert and Gubar, *Madwoman in the Attic*, 541.

16 Li Meng-yang was one of the Former Seven Masters who dominated the literary scene in the 1490s and 1500s. The "gentlemen of Chi-nan" refers symbolically to the Latter Seven Masters, for Li P'an-lung (1514–70), their chief spokesman, came from Chi-nan of the Shan-tung Province. These Former and Latter Masters were collectively known for their preference for the High T'ang style of poetry, but as Andrew Plaks has observed, they "often show a high degree of inconsistency in their theories, especially over the span of their entire careers, and they frequently reverse themselves on key issues" (Plaks, *The Four Masterworks of the Ming Novel*, 28).

17 Cited in A. D. Moody, *Thomas Stearns Eliot, Poet* (Cambridge: Cambridge Univ. Press, 1980), 5.

18 Gilbert and Gubar, *Madwoman in the Attic*, 563.

19 David Hawkes, "The Quest of the Goddess," in *Studies in Chinese Literary Genres*, ed. Cyril Birch, (Berkeley: Univ. of California Press, 1974), 42–68.

20 Burton Watson, trans., *Chinese Rhyme-Prose: Poems in the Fu Form from the Han and Six Dynasties* (New York: Columbia Univ. Press, 1971), 55–60.

21 Ibid., 55.

22 Ellen Moers notes the same phenomenon in women's poetry in the West. See her *Literary Women: The Great Writers* (rpt.; New York: Oxford Univ. Press, 1985), 167.

23 See Wang Po, *Wang Tzu-an chi*, ed. Chang Hsieh (rpt. Taipei: Commercial Press, 1976), *chüan* 2, p. 11, where the poet says, "I have long lost my heart to my king."

24 These refer to Chiang Yen's "Lien-hua fu" (*Fu* on lotus flowers) and Hsiao Kang's *shih* poem "Ts'ai-lien" (Picking the lotus).

25 For the Chinese text of "Ts'ai-lien *fu*," see Ch'en Tzu-lung, *Ch'en Tzu-lung wen-chi*, ed. Editorial Board of Shanghai wen-hsien ts'ung-shu (Shanghai: Hua-tung Normal Univ. Press, 1988), 1:34–39.

26 Watson, *Chinese Rhyme-Prose*, 57.

27 The convention of dropping into the river such pledges of love as rings, girdle-gems, etc. can be found as early as the "Nine Songs" of *Ch'u-tz'u*. See David Hawkes, *The Songs of the South*, 2d ed. (New York: Penguin, 1985), 106–09.

28 Watson, *Chinese Rhyme-Prose*, 60.

29 I am inspired by Shuen-fu Lin's fine distinction between the function of the preface and that of the lyric song. See his *The Transformation of the Chinese Lyrical Tradition: Chiang K'uei and Southern Sung Tz'u Poetry* (Princeton: Princeton Univ. Press, 1978), 82.

30 See Wu Wei-yeh, *Wu Mei-ts'un shih-chi* [chien-chu], ed. Wu I-feng, 201. Translation taken from Jonathan Chaves, *The Columbia Book of Later Chinese Poetry* (New York: Columbia Univ. Press, 1986), 363. For an earlier association of the theme with courtesans in *tz'u* poetry, see Marsha Wagner, *The Lotus Boat: The Origins of Chinese Tz'u Poetry in T'ang Popular Culture* (New York: Columbia Univ. Press, 1984).

31 Earl Miner also talks about a similar symbology of names in Japanese fiction. See his "The Heroine: Identity, Recurrence, Destiny," in *Ukifune: Love in the Tale of Genji*, ed. Andrew Pekarik (New York: Columbia Univ. Press, 1982), 63–81.

32 I am indebted to Barbara Johnson for this point; see her *The Critical Difference: Essays in the Contemporary Rhetoric of Reading* (Baltimore: Johns Hopkins Univ. Press, 1980), 15–16.

33 See *LJS*, 1:48.

34 Translation adapted from Pan Tze-yen, trans., *The Reminiscences of Tung Hsiao-wan*, 38.

35 Octavio Paz, *Sor Juana*, trans. Margaret Sayers Peden (Cambridge: Harvard Univ. Press, 1988), 2–3.

36 Only one or two of her early poems can be said to be imitations of the heroic style. (See *LJS*, 2:345.)

37 See *LJS*, 3:827. One may consider the lack of loyalist poetry by Liu to be a surprising lacuna, but she was certainly not the only Ming loyalist of literary gifts who did not deal with that subject in poetry. If more of Liu's works had

been transmitted to us, loyalist poems might well have been among them. But on the basis of present knowledge, Liu's case seems to show that (to echo Octavio Paz) a poet's life and work do not always explain each other.

38 My idea of the "strong poet" was inspired by Harold Bloom's *The Anxiety of Influence* (New York: Oxford Univ. Press, 1973).

39 In his preface to Sung Cheng-yü's collected poems, Ch'en Tzu-lung says, "Only when emotions are deep and durable can they be considered genuine" (*AYTK, chüan* 2, 1:124).

Chapter 4. Tz'u *Songs of Passion*

1 James J. Y. Liu, "Literary Qualities of the Lyric (*Tz'u*)," in *Studies in Chinese Literary Genres*, ed. Birch, 135.

2 Anne Birrell, *New Songs from a Jade Terrace* (London: George Allen and Unwin, 1982), 1.

3 See also Wayne Schlepp, *San-chü: Its Technique and Imagery* (Madison: Univ. of Wisconsin Press, 1970); Dale Johnson, "Ch'ü," in *IC*, 349–52.

4 For example, Yang Shen, Wang Shih-chen (1526–90), and T'ang Hsien-tsu all published their collected *tz'u*. (See Wang I, *Tz'u ch'ü shih* [1932; rpt. Taipei: Kuang-wen shu-chü, 1971], 406–19.) Wang Shih-chen and Yang Shen were also well-known critics of *tz'u* poetry (*THTP*, 1:383–93, 407–543).

5 Wang I, *Tz'u ch'ü shih*, 380.

6 Ibid., 427–29.

7 The *tz'u* was often called by some Confucian scholars the minor genre, as distinguished from the major *shih* genre. Ch'en Tzu-lung apparently did not share the view that the *tz'u* was minor.

8 See also Yeh Chia-ying, "Ts'ung wo ko-jen tui *tz'u* chih t'e-chih te i-tien hsin li-chieh t'an *ling-tz'u* chih ch'ien-neng yü Ch'en Tzu-lung *tz'u* chih ch'eng-chiu" (manuscript, 1989).

9 See Chiang P'ing-chieh et al., *Chih-chi chi*, in *Tz'u-hsüeh* 2 (1983): 241–94; 3 (1985): 249–72.

10 See, Chiang P'ing-chieh et al., "Fan-li," in *Chih-chi chi*, rpt. in *Tz'u-hsüeh* 2 (1983): 245.

11 See Shih Chih-ts'un, "Chiang P'ing-chieh chi ch'i 'Chih-chi chi,' " in *Tz'u-hsüeh* 2 (1983): 222–25.

12 A modern anthology (I po-yin, ed., *Li-tai nü shih tz'u hsüan* [Taipei: Tang-tai t'u-shu ch'u-pan-she, 1972]) brings together excellent *tz'u* poems of more than eighty women poets of the late Ming.

13 Shih I-tui says that the male literati poets in the early Sung purposely turned *tz'u* into a "feminine" genre, making it a suitable form for expressing love and other delicate sentiments formerly unavailable to the *shih* genre. See Shih I-tui, *Tz'u yü yin-yüeh kuan-hsi yen-chiu* (Peking: Chinese Institute of Social Sciences Press, 1985).

14 Ch'en Wei-sung, *Fu-jen chi*, in *Chao-tai ts'ung-shu*, vol. 74. Examples of *tz'u* by courtesans like Chang Wan-hsiang and Li Chen-li can be found in *THTP*, 3:2635, 2107–09.

15 In his *T'ing-ch'iu-sheng-kuan tz'u-hua*, Ting Shao-i points out a similar problem in Chu I-tsun's *Tzu-tsung*, an anthology that excludes works by several distinguished women poets of the Sung and Yüan. (*THTP*, 2667–72.)

16 Yeh Chia-ying, "Lun Ch'in Kuan *tz'u*," in Miao Yüeh and Yeh Chia-ying, *Ling-hsi tz'u shuo*, 240.

17 Of course, many of Liu Shih's *tz'u* songs are lost. But every one of her extant *tz'u* songs followed tune patterns adopted or invented by Ch'in Kuan.

18 A fictional account of the poet-lover Ch'in Kuan and Su Hsiao-mei appears in Feng Meng-lung, *Hsing-shih heng-yen*, chap. 11 (see the discussion in chap. 2 above). For a discussion of Ch'in Kuan's political poems, see Ho Ch'iung-yai et al., *Ch'in Shao-yu*, 63–69. See also Yeh Chia-ying, "Lun Ch'in Kuan *tz'u*," 247.

19 For Li Yü's influence on Ch'in Kuan, see Ch'in Kuan, *Huai-hai tz'u* [*chien-chu*], ed. Yang Shih-ming, 17. For Ch'in Kuan's influence on Li Ch'ing-chao, see Ho Ch'iung-yai et al., *Ch'in Shao-yu*, 62. Both Li Yü and Li Ch'ing-chao were generally admired by the Yün-chien poets. In particular, Ch'en Tzu-lung praised Li Wen's *tz'u* for having the same quality of elegant sensibility as Li Ch'ing-chao (*AYTK*, 1:281).

20 Lines 3, 4, 8, 9, 13, 17, 18, 21 are taken from James J. Y. Liu, *Major Lyricists of the Northern Sung, A.D. 960–1126* (Princeton: Princeton Univ. Press, 1974), 102.

21 See my *The Evolution of Chinese Tz'u Poetry: From Late T'ang to Northern Sung* (Princeton: Princeton Univ. Press, 1980), 117.

22 Wang Cho (d. 1160), *Pi-chi man-chih*; and Li Ch'ing-chao, "Tz'u-lun." See my *Evolution of Chinese Tz'u Poetry*, 116.

23 See Shen Ch'ien, "T'ien-tz'u tsa-shuo," in *THTP*, 1:631. The two other poets who were thought to have reached the same level of achievement were Li Yü and Li Ch'ing-chao, both models for the Yün-chien poets.

24 For the musical quality of this tune, see Yü Ts'ui-ling, "Ch'in Kuan *tz'u* hsin-lun," in *Chung-kuo ku-tien wen-hsüeh lun-ts'ung*, ed. Editorial Board of People's Literature Publishing House (Peking: Jen-min wen-hsüeh ch'u-pan-she, 1987), no. 61, p. 128.

25 Even as late as 1978, some scholars considered this poem to be the work of Liu Shih. See, for example, Chou Fa-kao, *Ch'ien Mu-chai, Liu Ju-shih i-shih, chi Liu Ju-shih yu-kuan tzu-liao* (Taipei: San-min shu-chü, 1978), 63.

26 Liu, "Literary Qualities of the Lyric (*Tz'u*)," 139.

27 I have adopted a variant reading for this line, as suggested by Ch'en Yin-k'o (*LJS*, 1:243).

28 Some critics take this to mean that the woman herself "enters the small chamber," but such a reading has been recently challenged by Wang Chün-ming

and Ch'en Chih-chai (see their *Ou-Yang Hsiu, Ch'in Kuan tz'u-hsüan* [Hong Kong: Joint Publishing, 1987], 129).

29 Ibid., 130. The *kuei-yüan* subgenre in the *shih* tradition was of course long established before the development of the *tz'u*. For the fusion of *kuei-yüan* and early *tz'u* poetics, see Hsien-ching Yang, "Aesthetic Consciousness in Sung *Yung-Wu-Tz'u (Songs on Objects)*" (Ph.D. diss., Princeton Univ., 1987), 5.

30 What the Russian Formalists said about "defamiliarization" can very well apply to the poems we are discussing. See Victor Erlich, *Russian Formalism, History-Doctrine*, 3d ed. (New Haven: Yale Univ. Press, 1981), 178.

31 A. C. Graham, trans., *Poems of the Late T'ang* (1965; rpt. New York: Penguin, 1981), 145.

32 Later Ch'ien Ch'ien-i also praised Liu for her ability to endure cold in the early morning hours (*LJS*, 2:563).

33 For this conventional image in early *tz'u*, see my *Evolution of Chinese Tz'u Poetry*, 98–99.

34 See Wen T'ing-yün's famous couplet: "Tardily she gets up, painting her crescent-shaped eyebrows / Adorning herself, doing her toilet late" (*CTWT*, 1:56). See also my *Evolution of Chinese Tz'u Poetry*, 98.

35 The alternation of inner and outer scenes is especially dramatic in the first ten poems of the song-series—e.g., poems 3, 5, 6, and 8 dwell on the former and poems 2, 4, and 7 on the latter.

36 In another context, K. C. Chang talks about animal-design vessels as an essential element in the heaven–earth communication ritual in ancient China. See K. C. Chang, *Art, Myth and Ritual: The Path to Political Authority in Ancient China* (Cambridge: Harvard Univ. Press, 1983), 63.

37 Translation taken from Graham, *Poems of the Late T'ang*, 55, with minor modifications.

38 It is possible of course that Ch'en wrote his song first and that Liu Shih wrote the "Meng chiang-nan" series only in response to Ch'en's "Wang chiang-nan" *tz'u*. But Ch'en Yin-k'o believes that Liu Shih wrote her songs first (*LJS*, 1:266).

39 The thrice-in-slumber willow alludes to a willow in the garden of Emperor Wu of Han. Legend has it that the willow tree took three naps a day. It looked like a person and was also called the "Human Willow" (*jen-liu*).

40 See my *Evolution of Chinese Tz'u Poetry*, 80.

41 I am inspired by Anthony Yü's discussion of Pao Yü's "fidelity" in the *Story of the Stone*: "He cannot, in the words of the Chinese, forget his feeling of love [*wangqing*], and his endless torment may indeed bespeak his fidelity and his being a helpless victim of familial intrigue" (see his "The Quest of Brother Amor," 25).

42 For this aspect of the romantic drama, see Hessney, "Beautiful, Talented, and Brave," 89. See also Chang Shu-hsiang, *Yüan tsa-chü chung te ai-ch'ing yü she-hui* (Taipei: Ch'ang-an ch'u-pan-she, 1980), 157; Chung-wen Shih, *The*

Golden Age of Chinese Drama: Yüan Tsa-chü (Princeton: Princeton Univ. Press, 1976), 70–78. For a brief discussion of lovesickness with regard to Chinese culture, see C. T. Hsia, *Ai-ch'ing, she-hui, hsiao-shuo* (Taipei: Ch'un-wen-hsüeh ch'u-pan-she, 1970), 227.

43 "Morning Cloud" (*Hsiao-yün*) was one of Liu Shih's nicknames.

44 Here I take the variant reading offered by Wang Ch'ang (*LJS*, 1:336).

45 This refers to the "Four Poems on the Yen Terrace" by the late-T'ang poet Li Shang-yin. See Li Shang-yin, *Li Shang-yin shih-chi* [*shu-chu*], ed. Yeh Ts'ung-ch'i (Peking: Jen-min wen-hsüeh ch'u-pan-she, 1985), 2:571–77.

46 See Yeh Ts'ung-ch'i's comments, in ibid.

47 Ibid., 2:565–66.

48 See Yeh Ts'ung-ch'i's statement in ibid., 2:577. Yeh Ts'ung-ch'i feels that Willow Branch might not be the girl's real name (2: 566).

49 For example, Yeh Chia-ying has questioned the validity of this interpretation. See her *Chia-ling t'an shih*, 175–76.

50 I am indebted to Ch'en Yin-k'o for this point. See *LJS*, 1:339.

51 Ibid.

52 T'ang Hsien-tsu, *T'ang Hsien-tsu chi*, ed. Ch'ien Nan-yang (Shanghai: Jen-min ch'u-pan-she, 1973), 3:1613–19 (hereafter cited by volume and page number in the text).

53 C. T. Hsia's comment on *Tzu-hsiao chi*, the original draft of the play. See his "Time and the Human Condition," 255.

54 Ibid., 257.

55 Ibid., 255–56.

56 Hsü Shuo-fang, "Foreword," *T'ang Hsien-tsu shih-wen chi*, ed. Hsü Shuo-fang (Shanghai: Ku-chi ch'u-pan-she, 1982), 8. Pei-kai Cheng also talks about T'ang Hsien-tsu's "painstaking effort in the employment of exquisite poetry in drama" (P'ei-kai Cheng, "Reality and Imagination," 277).

57 Wu Wei-yeh, another contemporary of Ch'en and Liu, also writes about the jade hairpin in his love poem to the courtesan Pien Sai: "I remember that wonderful autumn night we had in Heng-t'ang / Our vow of love with the jade hairpin began in a previous existence" (Wu Wei-yeh, *Wu Mei-ts'un shih-chi* [*chien-chu*], 353). For the image of the jade hairpin as a pledge of love between a married couple, see Li Po's (701–62) poem entitled "Song of a White-Haired Lady," which contains the following couplet: "The jade hairpin which I wear / Is our bond in marriage"—*Li Tai-po ch'üan-chi* (Peking: Chung-hua shu-chü, 1977), *chüan* 4, 1:246. I owe this point to Yü Ying-shih (private communication).

58 This *tz'u* can be found in Ch'in Kuan, *Huai-hai chü-shih ch'ang-tuan chü*, ed. Hsü P'ei-chün (Shanghai: Ku-chi ch'u-pan-she, 1985), 184–85.

59 The music for the "Ch'ien-ch'iu sui" tune is noted for its melancholy, mournful quality. (See Yü Ts'ui-ling, "Ch'in Kuan *tz'u* hsin-lun," 129.) For an excellent close reading of Ch'in Kuan's "Ch'ien-ch'iu sui" *tz'u*, see Yeh Chia-ying,

"Lun Ch'in Kuan *Tz'u*," in Miao Yüeh and Yeh Chia-ying, *Ling-hsi tz'u shuo*, 251–56.

60 Ch'en Tzu-lung was thought by Ch'ing scholars to have totally neglected Southern Sung poetics. But I strongly disagree with this view, a point I shall explain in chapter 6 below.

61 See the earlier discussion of the "symbology of names" in chapter 3.

62 *THTP*, 1:631; *CTLS*, 2:598.

63 See *Jen-chien tz'u-hua*, in *THTP*, 5:4245.

64 For another translation of this couplet, see Adele Austin Rickett, *Wang Kuo-wei's Jen-chien Tz'u-hua: A Study in Chinese Literary Criticism* (Hong Kong: Hong Kong Univ. Press, 1977), 41. See also Ching-i Tu, trans., *Poetic Remarks in the Human World*, by Wang Kuo-wei (Taipei: Chung-hua shu-chü, 1970), 2.

65 This line refers to a story concerning a Southern scholar, Lu K'ai, who sent a plum blossom to a good friend in Ch'ang-an, where plums were not usually grown (*T'ai-p'ing yü-lan, chüan* 19).

66 This line alludes to an ancient *yüeh-fu* song that tells the story of a woman who, while cooking carp given to her by her guest, was surprised to find a letter implanted in the stomach of one of the fish (Hsiao T'ung, ed., *Chao-ming wen-hsüan, chüan* 27).

67 Most commentators interpret these lines as referring to the idea of "receiving," rather than that of "sending," the letter. My interpretation is based on Yeh Chia-ying's comments: see her "Lun Ch'in Kuan *Tz'u*," in Miao Yüeh and Yeh Chia-ying, *Ling-hsi tz'u shuo*, 259–62.

68 The meaning of the "red mark" is ambiguous. Perhaps it refers to the lipstick stains Liu Shih intentionally left on her "farewell letter" to Ch'en. The red mark is now gone because a long time has passed. Read in this way, the last line of the poem may be paraphrased as, "If you open the letter which you gave me at our parting, you will see that your lipstick stains have disappeared."

69 This line is based on a variant reading offered by Ch'en Ying-k'o (*LJS*, 1:243).

Chapter 5. Shih *Poetry of Reflection*

1 Ancient Greek theorists also saw that a genre is conditioned by the human characters it represents. For example, Aristotle says in his *Poetics* that epic shows men greater than they are, etc.

2 For the "divine qualities" of the Southern Dynasties palace ladies in *shih* poetry, see Birrell, "The Dusty Mirror," 38. In his *The Divine Woman: Dragon Ladies and Rain Maidens* (San Francisco: North Point Press, 1980), Edward H. Schafer explains how the courtesan in Li Ho's (791–817) poetry "appears in supernatural guise" (146). Note also that, in seventeenth-century drama, courtesans are often compared to the divine woman. See, for example, scene 5 of the *Peach Blossom Fan* (Chen Shih-hsiang et al., trans.), 42.

3 The meaning of lines 3–4 is ambiguous. According to Ch'en Yin-k'o (*LJS*,

1:82), the parrot symbolizes Liu Shih here (as in Liu's own *tz'u*, "Meng Chiang-nan," no. 19). The dream of the parrot may allude to a story of Yang Kuei-fei in which Yang was compared to a parrot, tormented and killed by a ferocious bird of prey. (See also *LJS*, 1:265.)

4 The last line of the poem alludes to an old love poem ascribed to a famous courtesan, Su Hsiao-hsiao (fl. ca. late fifth century). Su Hsiao-hsiao's poem contains the lines, "Where shall we tie our love-knots? / Under the pine and cypress of the Western Grave-mound."

5 For the definition of the centrifugal and the centripetal in poetry, see Edward Stankiewicz, "Centripetal and Centrifugal Structures in Poetry," *Semiotica* 38, nos. 3–4 (1982): 217–42.

6 This line is an allusion to one of Li Shang-yin's love poems ("Untitled Poems"), which reads, "For ever hard to meet, and as hard to part / Each flower spoils in the failing East wind / Spring's silkworms wind till death their heart's threads / The wick of the candle turns to ash before its tears dry . . ." (see Graham, *Poems of the Late T'ang*, 150).

7 From *Gazetteer of Sung-chiang* (*Sung-chiang fu-chih*), as cited in *CTLS*, 1:221.

8 Hawkes, *Songs of the South*, 49.

9 For the quest-theme in ancient *sao* and *fu*, see Hawkes, "Quest of the Goddess," 42–68.

10 I am indebted to Jenijoy La Belle's *Herself Beheld: The Literature of the Looking Glass* (Ithaca: Cornell Univ. Press, 1988), 1.

11 For a discussion of the "legendary star-crossed lovers" as represented in the "Nineteen Ancient Poems" series, see Pauline Yu, *The Reading of Imagery in the Chinese Poetic Tradition* (Princeton: Princeton Univ. Press, 1987), 127.

12 For a discussion of Hsieh T'iao's poem, see my *Six Dynasties Poetry* (Princeton: Princeton Univ. Press, 1986), 131–32.

13 For a discussion of this commentary tradition, see Yu, *The Reading of Imagery*, 127.

14 "Kao T'ang *fu*" is commonly attributed to Sung Yü. See text in Hsiao T'ung, *Chao-ming wen-hsüan*, commentary by Li Shan (rpt. Taipei: Ho-lo t'u-shu ch'u-pan-she, 1975), *chüan* 19, p. 393.

15 See also line 13 of the poem, "The Evening of the Double-Seventh: In Imitation of Hsieh T'iao," cited above.

16 These are perhaps the only examples of the "prosaic *fu*" (as distinguished from the "poetic *fu*") written by Liu and Ch'en; apparently they were modeled after Chiang Yen's (444–505) "*Fu* on Parting," a *fu* known for its prosaic yet emotional qualities. For a translation and interpretation of Chiang Yen's *fu*, see Hans Frankel, *The Flowering Plum and the Palace Lady: Interpretations of Chinese Poetry* (New Haven: Yale Univ. Press, 1976), 73–81.

17 This line alludes to the opening lines of a classical poem on parting attributed by Hsiao T'ung (*Chao-ming wen-hsüan*) to Li Ling of the Han: "Holding hands, together we walk to the bridge / At dusk, where will you be, my friend?" The authorship has been questioned by modern scholars.

18 Translation adapted from my *Evolution of Chinese Tz'u Poetry*, 175.

19 Wang Chün-ming and Ch'en Chih-chai, *Ou-yang Hsiu, Ch'in Kuan tz'u-hsüan*, 108.

20 For Su Shih's enlargement of poetic vision in *tz'u*, see my *Evolution of Chinese Tz'u Poetry*, 158–206. For Su Shih's influence on Ch'in Kuan, see Yü Ts'ui-ling, "Ch'in Kuan tz'u hsin-lun," 126.

21 *LJS*, 2:353. See also my discussion of T'ao Ch'ien's "lyrical sublimation," in my *Six Dynasties Poetry*, 43–46.

Chapter 6. Loyalism as Love in Tz'u Poetry

1 See traditional commentaries cited in Hsia Ch'eng-t'ao and Chang Chang, eds., *Chin Yüan Ming Ch'ing tz'u-hsüan* (Peking: Jen-min wen-hsüeh ch'u-pan-she, 1983), 1:299–302.

2 Legend has it that when Wang-ti (king of Shu) died, his soul turned into a cuckoo, constantly weeping tears of blood because of his undying love for his country.

3 Erich Auerbach, *Scenes from the Drama of European Literature* (1959; rpt. with foreword by Paolo Valesio, Minneapolis: Univ. of Minnesota Press, 1984), 29.

4 Erich Auerbach, *Mimesis: The Representation of Reality in Western Literature*, trans. Willard R. Trask (Princeton: Princeton Univ. Press, 1953), 73.

5 See *Scenes from the Drama of European Literature*, 54, where Auerbach says that figural interpretation "differs from most of the allegorical forms known to us by the historicity both of the sign and what it signifies." Elsewhere Auerbach does qualify his argument by saying that the boundary between *figura* and *allegory* is sometimes "fluid": for example, "Tertullian uses *allegoria* almost synonymously with *figura*" (47–48). But what is certain is that "*allegoria* could not be used synonymously with *figura* in all contexts, for it did not have the same implication of 'form'" (48).

6 For the importance of "temporality" with regard to *figura*, see Auerbach, *Mimesis*, 73.

7 I am inspired by Thomas M. Greene's recent study of John Donne. See his "A Poetics of Discovery: A Reading of Donne's Elegy 19," in the *Yale Journal of Criticism* 2.2 (1989): 129–43.

8 See Daniel Bryant, *Lyric Poets of the Southern T'ang* (Vancouver: Univ. of British Columbia Press, 1982). Bryant has argued convincingly that Li Yü's captivity in the north was "much less severe than might have been expected" and that "he was summoned several times to converse with the [Sung] emperor or to attend social functions at court." But, as Bryant says, "While his life had been spared, he was reduced to circumstances that he could hardly have imagined during the years before his capture" (xxvii).

9 Daniel Bryant cautions against interpreting Li Yü's poems "as autobiographical documents," for "none of [his] lyrics can be dated precisely" (*Lyric Poets*

of the Southern T'ang, xxviii–xxix). I agree with Bryant that one's poetic style is not entirely conditioned by one's life experience, for a genre's conventional requirement plays an equally, if not more, significant role in shaping a poet's style. But it is undeniable that an author's life and work are related.

10 Translation adapted from my *Evolution of Chinese Tz'u Poetry*, 91–92.

11 See discussion in Wang Ying-chih, "Ch'en Tzu-lung tz'u-hsüeh ch'u-i," 93.

12 Hu Yün-yüan's statement can be found in *chüan* 3 of *Ch'en Chung-yü ch'üan-chi*, ed. Wang Ch'ang (1803., rpt. *CTLS*, 2:611).

13 Hu Yün-yüan is perhaps confusing poetry and biography here. Once Li Yü told one of his old acquaintances about his suffering as a man without a country: "In this place I do nothing day and night but wash my face in tears" (see Bryant, *Lyric Poets of the Southern T'ang*, xxvii). And the words, "shedding blood and burying the soul," clearly refer to Ch'en Tzu-lung's martyrdom. It is interesting to note that later Wang Kuo-wei (1877–1927) used very similar language to describe the quality of emotional intensity in Li Yü's *tz'u*: "Nietzsche said, 'Of all that is written I love only that which the writer wrote with his blood.' Li Yü's *tz'u* can truly be said to have been written with blood" (see Rickett, *Wang Kuo-wei's Jen-chien Tz'u-hua, chüan* 1, no. 18, p. 46).

14 Again, Li Yü's "love" poems should not be taken literally as autobiographical documents (see Bryant, *Lyric Poets of the Southern T'ang*, xxviii.)

15 See my *Evolution of Chinese Tz'u Poetry*, 96–105.

16 Wang Yün, "Ch'en Tzu-lung nien-p'u chüan-hsia", in *CTLS*, 2:718.

17 See Donald Holzman, "The Cold Food Festival in Early Medieval China," *Harvard Journal of Asiatic Studies* 46.1 (1986): 51–79.

18 Grace Fong, *Wu Wenying and the Art of Southern Song Ci Poetry* (Princeton: Princeton Univ. Press, 1987), 107. See also Tu Fu's poem on the Cold Food Festival, in David R. McCraw, "A New Look at the Regulated Verse of Chen Yuyi," *Chinese Literature: Essays, Articles, Reviews* 9.1, 2 (1987): 18–19.

19 Translation adapted from J. D. Frodsham, trans., *The Poems of Li Ho, 791–817* (Oxford: Oxford Univ. Press, 1970), 30, n. 1. Ch'en Tzu-lung's *tz'u* was apparently inspired by Li Ho's *shih* poem "Grave of Su Hsiao-hsiao." For a discussion of Li Ho's poem, see Frances LaFleur Mochida, "Structuring a Second Creation: Evolution of the Self in Imaginary Landscapes," in *Expressions of Self*, ed. Hegel and Hessney, 102–04.

20 The Ch'ung-chen emperor, who committed suicide at the fall of the Forbidden City in 1644, was not properly buried until long after his death. It was Dorgon (the prince-regent of the Ch'ing) who finally ordered "all of the officials and people of the capital to observe public mourning" for the Ming emperor. See Frederic Wakeman, Jr., *The Great Enterprise* (Berkeley: Univ. of California Press, 1985), 1:316.

21 Holzman, "Cold Food Festival," 74.

22 Lin Ching-hsi, *Chi-shan chi* (Peking: Chung-hua shu-chü, 1960), 103.

23 For the Chinese text of the poem, see Wang Kuo-wei, *Wang Kuo-wei shih*

tz'u [*chien-chiao*], ed. Hsiao Ai (Ch'ang-sha: Hu-nan jen-min ch'u-pan-she, 1984), 41–43. The translation cited here is adapted from Joey Bonner, *Wang Kuo-wei: An Intellectual Biography* (Cambridge: Harvard Univ. Press, 1986), 155. Wang Kuo-wei, I think, is comparing himself to Marquis Chu, a Ming loyalist who performed the sacrificial duties at the Ming tombs. (For a different interpretation, see Bonner, *Wang Kuo-wei*, 257–58, n. 118.)

24 For the incident of the desecration of Southern Sung imperial tombs, see Wan Ssu-t'ung (1638–1702), ed., *Nan-Sung Liu-ling i-shih* (rpt. Taipei: Kuang-wen shu-chü, 1968); and Huang Chao-hsien, ed., *Yüeh-fu pu-t'i yen-chiu chi chien-chu* (Hong Kong: Hokman Publications, 1975), 95–121.

25 Huang Chao-hsien, *Yüeh-fu pu-t'i yen-chiu*, 104, 112.

26 Lin Ching-hsi, *Chi-shan chi*, 103. Ellen Widmer has observed that the winter-green tree became for the Ming poets a topos of "mourning for the Ming." (See her *The Margins of Utopia: Shui-hu hou-chuan and the Literature of Ming Loyalism* [Cambridge: Council on East Asian Studies, Harvard Univ., 1987], 36.)

27 See Lin, *The Transformation of the Chinese Lyrical Tradition*, 191–93; Yeh Chia-ying, "Wang I-sun and His *Yung-wu Tz'u*," *Harvard Journal of Asiatic Studies* 40.1 (1980): 55–91; and my article, "Symbolic and Allegorical Meanings in the *Yüeh-fu pu-t'i* Poem-Series," *Harvard Journal of Asiatic Studies* 46.2 (1986): 353–85.

28 Ch'en's statement can be found in *chüan* 118 of *Li-tai shih-yü* (see THTP, 2:1260). It may be possible that Ch'en did not have access to the complete manuscript copy of *Yüeh-fu pu-t'i* (edited by Ch'en Shu-k'o and Ch'iu Yüan), as it had been kept in a private collection until Chu I-tsun rediscovered it later.

29 According to one reliable source, it was Lin Ching-hsi, not T'ang Chüeh, who completed the heroic mission of transplanting the wintergreen trees. (See Huang Chao-hsien, *Yüeh-fu pu-ti yen-chiu*, 96–97.)

30 For Chu I-tsun's preface to the collection, see ibid., 82.

31 Wan Ssu-t'ung, *Nan-Sung Liu-ling i-shih*, 16a, 36a.

32 The *yung-wu* mode, as a descriptive device in literature, was prominent in ancient *fu* and *shih* poetry. For discussions of *yung-wu fu* poetry, see Watson, *Chinese Rhyme-Prose*, 12–16; and David R. Knechtges, "Introduction," *Wen Xuan, or Selections of Refined Literature* (Princeton: Princeton Univ. Press, 1982), 1:31–32. For a study of *yung-wu shih* as a form of "verisimilitude," see chapter 4 of my *Six Dynasties Poetry*. For the development of *yung-wu tz'u* in the Southern Sung, see Lin, *The Transformation of the Chinese Lyrical Tradition*; Fong, *Wu Wenying*; and Yang, "Aesthetic Consciousness in Sung Yung-Wu-Tz'u."

33 Yang Hai-ming has observed that the Sung poets of the Hsin Ch'i-chi school were mostly from Chiang-hsi, whereas those who excelled in the elegant *yung-wu* mode largely came from the Che-chiang region, especially Hang-chow. And the contention between the Chiang-hsi School and the Che-chiang

School in *tz'u* persisted even after the Sung (see Yang Hai-ming, *T'ang Sung tz'u-shih* [Chiang-su: Ku-chi ch'u-pan-she, 1987], 541–49). It seems clear to me that, of the two schools of *tz'u*, Ch'en Tzu-lung would have preferred the Che-chiang School.

34 See Ch'en Tzu-lung's preface to *Yu-lan ts'ao* as cited in chapter 4 above. Unfortunately the somewhat categorical tone of this preface led later critics to believe Ch'en denounced all Southern Sung *tz'u*.

35 Cited in *CTLS*, 2:601.

36 C. A. S. Williams, *Outlines of Chinese Symbolism and Art Motives*, 3d rev. ed. (1941; rpt. New York: Dover Publications, 1976), 19.

37 The personification of flowers is by no means new. For a discussion of personified plum blossoms in ancient Chinese poetry, see Frankel, *Flowering Plum*, 1–6; and Maggie Bickford et al., *Bones of Jade, Soul of Ice: The Flowering Plum in Chinese Art* (New Haven: Yale Univ. Art Gallery, 1985).

38 Williams, *Outlines of Chinese Symbolism*, 428.

39 Wagner, *The Lotus Boat*, 101.

40 See, for example, poems in *CTLS*, 2:600, 604, and 605. It should be noted that in one of Ch'en's most elaborate song-sequences in the *ch'ü* form, entitled "On the Willow," Liu Shih's nickname "Morning Cloud" (*Hsiao-yün*) is used (*CTLS*, 2:620–21).

41 The subtitle of the poem, "Yang-hua," literally means "poplar blossoms," another name for "willow catkins." It may be that the poem's subtitle alludes to Liu Shih's original surname, Yang.

42 For Wang Shih-chen's "Tieh lien hua" *tz'u*, see Wang Fu-chih, *Wang Ch'uan-shan shih-wen chi* (Hong Kong: Chung-hua shu-chü, 1974), 2:592. For the "cicada poems" in *Yüeh-fu pu-t'i*, see Yeh Chia-ying, "Wang I-sun and His Yung-wu Tz'u."

43 Widmer, *Margins of Utopia*, 30.

44 Yang Feng-pao, "Hsi-hu ch'iu-liu *tz'u*," in *Ku-chin shuo-pu ts'ung-shu*, vol. 6. See Yang's own statement commenting on the allegorical function of his song-series (19a).

45 Hsiao Kang (503–51), originally prince of Chiang-nan and later Emperor Chien-wen of the Liang, once wrote a poem entitled "*Fu* on the Autumn Meditation."

46 Huan Wen (342–73), while passing by the city of Chin-ch'eng during one of his northern expeditions, compared the willow to human life and was moved to tears. See Richard B. Mather, trans. *Shih-shuo Hsin-yü: A New Account of Tales of the World*, by Liu I-ch'ing (Minneapolis: Univ. of Minnesota Press, 1976), 57.

47 See "Ts'ai Wei" (Mao no. 167) in the section of the small odes in the *Shih-ching*. Translation in Arthur Waley, trans., *The Book of Songs*, 1937; rpt. with foreword by Stephen Owen (New York: Grove Press, 1987), no. 131.

48 This alludes to the "Nine Songs" of the *Ch'u-tz'u*, which have been viewed

by many as political allegory (see Hawkes, *Songs of the South*, 95–151). Wang Shih-chen's preface and his poems with detailed annotations can be found in Takahashi Kazumi, ed., *Ō shi-shin*, in the Chūgoku shijin senshū series (Tokyo: Iwanami, 1962), 3–15.

49 For more examples of such displacement, or projection, of emotions in loyalist literature, see the discussion in chapter 2 above.

50 I am inspired by Annie Dillard's discussion of "nonallegorical symbols": "It is when these symbols break their allegorical boundaries, their commitment to reference, that they start stepping out on us" (*Living by Fiction* [New York: Harper Colophon Books, 1982], 165).

51 Translation taken from Yeh Chia-ying, "The Ch'ang-chou School of *Tz'u* Criticism," in *Chinese Approaches to Literature from Confucius to Liang Ch'i-ch'ao*, ed. Adele Austin Rickett (Princeton: Princeton Univ. Press, 1978), 179. See also Chou Chi, "Sung ssu-chia tz'u-hsüan mu-lu hsü-lun," in his *Sung ssu-chia tz'u-hsüan* [*chien-chu*], annotated by K'uang Shih-yüan (Taipei: Chuang-hua shu-chü, 1971), 2.

52 Chou Chi, *Sung ssu-chia tz'u-hsüan*, 2–3.

53 See Hsia Ch'eng-t'ao and Chang Chang, *Chin Yüan Ming Ch'ing tz'u-hsüan*, 1:302.

54 Yu-kung Kao and Tsu-lin Mei, "Ending Lines in Wang Shih-chen's 'Ch'i-chüeh': Convention and Creativity in the Ch'ing," in *Artists and Traditions*, ed. Christian F. Murck (Princeton: Princeton Univ. Press, 1976), 133–35.

55 Richard John Lynn, "Orthodoxy and Enlightenment: Wang Shih-chen's Theory of Poetry and Its Antecedents," in De Bary, *Self and Society in Ming Thought*, 252.

56 See Wang shih-chen, *Hua-ts'ao meng-shih*, as cited in Lin Mei-i, "Wan Ch'ing tz'u-lun yen-chiu" (Ph.D. Diss., National Taiwan Univ., 1979), 1: 8.

57 This no doubt was one of the reasons Wang Shih-chen concluded—in my view, mistakenly—that Ch'en Tzu-lung had completely denounced the Southern Sung *tz'u* (see *THTP*, 2:1980). For the differences between the *hsiao-ling* and the *man-tz'u* forms, see my *Evolution of Chinese Tz'u Poetry*, 110–12.

58 Cited in Wu Mei, *Tz'u-hsüeh t'ung-lun* (Shanghai: Commercial Press, 1932), 153.

59 For the allegorical interpretations of the *feng* (*Shih-ching*) and *sao* (*Li-sao*), see Yu, *The Reading of Imagery*, 44–117; see also Longxi Zhang, "The Letter or the Spirit: *The Song of Songs*, Allegoresis, and the *Book of Poetry*," *Comparative Literature* 39 (1987): 193–217.

60 See Yeh Chia-ying, "The Ch'ang-chou School of *Tz'u* Criticism"; and my "Ch'ang-chou tz'u-p'ai," in *IC*, 225–26.

61 Leo Strauss also talked about the relationship between "reading between the lines" and "writing between the lines" under similar circumstances. See his *Persecution and the Art of Writing* (1952; rpt. Univ. of Chicago Press, 1988), 24–27.

62 Yeh Chia-ying's statement concerning the relationship of love and patriotism in *tz'u* is particularly pertinent here: "So the transformation of . . . songs about love into patriotic anthems was an understandable phenomenon, and in a sense the more passionate the eroticism, the more subject the song to such interpretation. If the claim seems exaggerated, consider the treatment, in Western literature, of Solomon's *Song of Songs*." ("The Ch'ang-chou School of *Tz'u* Criticism," 186).

Chapter 7. Tragic Heroism in Shih Poetry

1 Richard B. Sewall, *The Vision of Tragedy* (New Haven, Yale Univ. Press, 1959), 5. This "tragic vision," referring to the tragic suffering of the virtuous, should be distinguished from what Aristotle called "the tragic," in which the notion of tragic flaw is considered essential to the best kind, though not the only kind, of tragedy. In his definition of the tragic vision, Sewall uses Job's suffering as an example: "There was no mortal cause for his sufferings, nothing in his past to account for these repeated . . . blows" (12).

2 Owen, *Remembrances*, 21.

3 Translation adapted from Owen, *Remembrances*, 20; Arthur Waley, trans., *The Book of Songs*, 306; and James Legge, *The Chinese Classics*, Vol. 4, *The She King* (Oxford: Clarendon, 1871), 110.

4 Owen, *Remembrances*, 21; Legge, *The She King*, 110. Pauline Yu calls such readings "tropological readings," "rooted by the commentators in specific historical contexts" (see her *The Reading of Imagery*, 69).

5 The "luxuriant park" here is a subtle reference to the "Wu Capital Rhapsody" by Tso Ssu (ca. 250–ca. 305), in which the beauty of the Wu Capital in modern Nanking is described (see Knechtges, *Wen xuan*, 1:395).

6 The Hsü Terrace, also called the Ku-su Terrace, was built by King Ho-lü of Wu (reigned 514–495 B.C.).

7 Yao-li was an assassin-retainer serving Prince Kuang of Wu (later known as King Ho-lü).

8 Hsin Pavilion was near modern Nanking. Since the Eastern Chin, it has become a symbol of loyalist sentiments (see also note 10 below).

9 K'ung Shang-jen, *T'ao-hua shan*, sc. 13, p. 87. See also Chen Shih-hsiang, *Peach Blossom Fan*, 100.

10 Liu I-ch'ing, *Shih-shuo hsin-yü* [*Chiao-chien*], ed. Yang Yung (Hong Kong: Ta-chung shu-chü, 1969), sec. 2, no. 31, p. 71. Translation taken from my *Six Dynasties Poetry*, 49, with minor modifications.

11 Sewall, *Vision of Tragedy*, 12. Aristotle also said that the best tragedy "concerns misfortunes that are undeserved." See Aristotle, *Poetics*, in Kenneth A. Telford, *Aristotle's Poetics: Translation and Analysis* (Indiana: Gateway Edition, 1961), 1453a, p. 23.

12 A. C. Bradley, *Shakespearean Tragedy* (1904; rpt. Greenwich, Connecticut: Fawcett), 33.

13 For a good discussion of heroism and how heroes were commemorated in literature and ritual, see Gregory Nagy, *The Best of the Achaeans: Concept of the Hero in Archaic Greek Poetry* (Baltimore: Johns Hopkins Univ. Press, 1981).

14 See Shih Chih-ts'un's note in *CTLS*, 2:529. For the Lake T'ai incident, see Atwell, "Ch'en Tzu-lung," 136–37.

15 See Burton Watson, trans., *Records of the Historian: Chapters from the Shih Chi of Ssu-ma Ch'ien* (New York: Columbia Univ. Press, 1969), 67.

16 See Li Kuang-ti, ed., *Chou I che-chung*, (1715; rpt. Taipei: Chen-shan-mei ch'u-pan-she, 1971), 2:1076. See also Willard Peterson, "Making Connections: 'Commentary on the Attached Verbalizations' of the *Book of Changes*," *Harvard Journal of Asiatic Studies* 42.1 (1982): 113. Richard Wilhelm translates *yu-huan* as "great care and sorrow" (see his *The I Ching*, 345), but Yü Ying-shih believes that "the consciousness of suffering" is a more correct rendering of the Chinese term "yu-huan i-shih" (private communication).

17 See Ch'en Tzu-lung, ed., *I-ching hsün-chieh*, annotated by Hsiung Ho (1247–1312), 4 *chüan* (n.p., n.d.), now in Harvard-Yenching Library.

18 Stephen Owen observes that in Chinese poems meditating on the past (*huai-ku*), the poet is often "stirred by human loss in contrast to nature's cyclical continuity" (*Remembrances*, 20).

19 Yu-kung Kao describes this lyricism as the aesthetics of "self-reflection." See his "The 'Nineteen Old Poems' and the Aesthetics of Self-Reflection" (manuscript, 1988); and his "Shih-lun Chung-kuo i-shu ching-shen" (On the spirit of Chinese art), in *Chinese Culture Quarterly* 2.2 (January 1988): 4.

20 Sleeping Dragon usually refers to Chu-ko Liang (181–234 A.D.), the wise prime minister of the Kingdom of Shu during the Age of Three Kingdoms; Leaping Horse can be identified with Kung-sun Shu, a Han general who proclaimed himself king of the Shu region. (See also Tu Fu's famous line "Sleeping Dragon and Leaping Horse have turned to dust," in his "Night in the Watch-Tower.") It should be noted also that Ch'en Tzu-lung is using Sleeping Dragon here as a subtle reference to himself—his name "Tzu-lung" means "child-dragon," and his nickname "Wo-tzu" can be literally translated as "sleeping child." But, in any case, I believe that Chu-ko Liang ("Sleeping Dragon") and other historical figures like him were of particular interest to Ch'en.

21 Wang I, the commentator of *Ch'u-tz'u*, believed that Ch'ü Yüan wrote his "Heavenly Questions" on the walls of a temple. See Hawkes, *Songs of the South*, 123.

22 For such an idealism regarding the balance of mountain and water scenes, see my *Six Dynasties Poetry*, 64–66.

23 "Wai-wu" in *Chuang Tzu* [chi-shih], ed. Kuo Ch'ing-fan (1961; rpt. in one vol., Taipei: Ho-lo t'u-shu ch'u-pan-she, 1974), 920; see also Burton Watson, trans., *The Complete Works of Chuang Tzu* (New York: Columbia Univ. Press, 1968), 294.

24 See also Wakeman, *The Great Enterprise*, 1:598.

25 See *CTS*, 4:2404. The poem was written by Tu Fu in the spring of 757 (i.e., during the An Lu-shan Rebellion), while he was being held captive in Ch'ang-an by the rebels.

26 "The man who uses jade tables" (*yü-chi jen*) usually refers to an emperor.

27 *CTLS*, 1:300.

28 Lynn A. Struve, *The Southern Ming, 1644–1662* (New Haven: Yale Univ. Press, 1984), 97.

29 For a summary of this prevalent view in modern scholarship, see K'o Ch'ing-ming, "Lun 'pei-chü ying-hsiung'," in *Ching-chieh te t'an-ch'iu*, rev. ed. (Taipei: Linking Publishing, 1984), 32–33, 92. But K'o Ch'ing-ming is a notable exception to this view.

30 Struve, *The Southern Ming*, v.

31 Both Yü-fu and Pieh-ling were ancient kings of the Shu. The allusion to Pieh-ling is especially apt and poignant here: Pieh-ling was a virtuous successor to Wang-ti of Shu, who later turned into a crying cuckoo. In this poem, Yü-fu and Pieh-ling might refer to prince of Lu and prince of T'ang, who established their fugitive courts in Che-chiang and Fu-chien, respectively. (See also Struve, *The Southern Ming*, 76–77.)

32 Hawkes, *Songs of the South*, 122–34.

33 See Wang Fu-chih, *Ch'u-tz'u t'ung-shih* (1709; rpt. Hong Kong, 1960), 54–58; see also Schneider, *A Madman of Ch'u*, 84.

34 For the Chinese text of this group of poems, see *CTLS*, 1:309–11; and Chu Tung-jun, *Ch'en Tzu-lung chi ch'i shih-tai* (Shanghai: Ku-chi ch'u-pan-she, 1984), 277–78.

35 *Yang-ch'un*, which I translate as "warm, bright sun" here, usually refers specifically to the sunny weather of spring. It can also be used to symbolize the peaceful and prosperous times in history.

36 For a story of Penumbra, see "Discussion of Making All Things Equal," in Watson, *Complete Works of Chuang Tzu*, 49. After the fall of the Ming, Ch'en changed his name in order to conceal his true identity. Thus, "I do not recognize anyone in sight" really means "I do not wish to recognize anyone in sight."

37 The term "jackals and wolves" is generally used as a symbol for wicked persons in power.

38 The image of "a white rainbow piercing the sun" is traditionally taken to be an omen of the emperor's death. It should be noted that the name Ming means literally "bright and brilliant."

39 The Golden Terrace, also called Yen Terrace, was built by an ancient king and is near modern Peking. This line refers to the fall of Peking in 1644.

40 This line alludes to the tragic death of Emperor Hsien (also called Lord Shan-yang of the Latter Han).

41 The Southern Sieve Stars belong to one of the twenty-eight constellations of the zodiac, traditionally taken to symbolize the slanderers at court (see Legge, *The Chinese Classics*, 4:347).

42 This is about the martyrdom of Ch'en's teacher Huang Tao-chou, a famous Ming loyalist who was executed near Mount Chung in Nanking. T'ung-shan stands for Huang because Huang used to study in a stone cave in T'ung-shan, Fu-chien.

43 That is, if one dies in the marketplace, one's body will be eaten by crows and hawks. But if one dies naturally and is properly buried, one's corpse will eventually be eaten by mole crickets and ants. There is very little difference between these two forms of death.

44 Huang Tao-chou served as grand secretary and secretariat of military personnel in the Lung-wu court in Fu-chien and was distinguished by his moral integrity and scholastic achievement. See Struve, *The Southern Ming*, 98; and Yeh Ying, *Huang Tao-chou chuan* (Tainan: Ta-ming yin-shua-chü, 1958), 49.

45 Melilotus is a species of fragrant orchid. This line suggests how similar the two friends are with respect to their moral quality.

46 The term "nine caldrons" is used as a metaphor for imperial power.

47 P'eng Hsien is traditionally thought to be the name of an upright minister in the ancient Shang times who drowned himself when his good advice was not taken by his king (for other possible meanings of P'eng Hsien, see Hawkes, *Songs of the South*, 84–86). The name is here used to allude to the Ming loyalist Hsia Yün-i, who drowned himself after his hometown fell to the Manchus in 1645. It is indeed a coincidence that eventually Ch'en Tzu-lung himself was to become another P'eng Hsien, as Ku Yen-wu says in his poem: "He bravely followed the example of P'eng Hsien."

48 The "flood dragon" is the symbol of the great man. When the water is dried up, there will be no opportunity for the great man to fulfill his ambition.

49 This line is an allusion to the story of Chang Liang, who came from the state of Han. Earlier, when Ch'in destroyed the state of Han, Chang Liang had "used all his family wealth to search for someone who would undertake to assassinate the King of Ch'in for him" (see Watson, *Records of the Historian*, 158).

50 This image is a metaphor for insignificant death. A heroic death is traditionally compared to the great Mount T'ai, while an ordinary death is thought to be "as light as a goose feather." More than a century later Emperor Ch'ien-lung praised Ch'en Tzu-lung's death for being "heavier than Mount T'ai"—words that seem almost a response to Ch'en's poem (see Emperor Ch'ien-lung's edict reprinted in Ch'en Tzu-lung, *Ch'en Chung-yü ch'üan-chi*, ed. Wang Ch'ang, 1a).

51 See the discussion of this poem in chapter 1 above.

52 Struve, *The Southern Ming*, 89.

53 By referring to the Yüan River in Hunan (which was near the area where the historical Ch'ü Yüan was believed to have drowned himself), the poet Ch'en Tzu-lung was no doubt comparing Hsia Yün-i to the ancient hero Ch'ü Yüan. By this poetic allusion, Ch'en was unwittingly predicting his own suicide by drowning.

54 The Yüan Chiang Pavilion has recently been repaired as part of the tomb renovation project carried out by the Shanghai Cultural Preservation Group (see
illustrations above).

55 See my "The Idea of the Mask in Wu Wei-yeh," 289–320.

56 I am borrowing Richard Sewall's words here. See his *Vision of Tragedy*, 47.

57 Ibid.

58 R. J. Dorius defines the two most important qualities of tragedy as "courage
and inevitable defeat." See his article "Tragedy," in *Princeton Encyclopedia of
Poetry and Poetics*, ed. Alex Preminger et al., enl. ed. (Princeton: Princeton
Univ. Press, 1974), 860.

59 See *CTLS*, 2:526. Juan Chi, a Six Dynasties poet, was known for crying in
public. Liang Hung was a scholar of the Eastern Han; he once concealed his
identity and escaped to the Wu to avoid political persecution. He eventually
returned home and was reunited with his wife.

60 Under Ch'ing dynasty censorship, this line was later changed to "Refusing to
submit to the shame of being a captive." See Ku Yen-wu, *Ku T'ing-lin shih-wen
chi*, ed. Hua Ch'en-chih (1959; rpt. Peking: Chung-hua shu-chü, 1983), 276. I
owe this particular point to Yü Ying-shih (private communication).

61 In *CTS*, 4:2298.

62 For example, Yü Huai (known particularly for his *Pan-ch'iao tsa-chi* on the
Ch'in-huai courtesans) also wrote a poem-series entitled "Seven Songs" to ex-
press his sorrowful feelings as a Ming loyalist. See Huang Shang, *Yin-yü chi*
(Peking: San-lien shu-tien, 1985), 40–41.

63 The Sung philosopher Chu Hsi criticized Tu Fu's *chih*, as expressed in the
poet's seventh song, as being especially "lowly." But other commentators have
come to Tu Fu's defense, saying that the poet was simply using the poem as
a means of criticizing the corrupt government at the time, which preferred
young and inexperienced officials to old and accomplished scholars (see *Tu shih*
[*hsiang-chu*], ed. Ch'iu Chao-ao, 2:700).

64 *Wen T'ien-hsing ch'üan-chi*, chüan 14, pp. 364–65.

65 This line alludes to the tragic incident in 1277 in which Sung troops led by
Wen T'ien-hsiang were defeated by the Yüan. Wen's wife and other family
members were all captured and sent north for custody.

66 The original line reads literally, "I cannot bear to part with your silk garment."

67 I am borrowing A. C. Bradley's words here (see his *Shakespearean Tragedy*,
231).

68 See *Li-tai shih-yü* in *THTP*, 2:1258. Also discussed in Miao Yüeh, "Lun Wen
T'ien-hsiang *tz'u*," in Miao Yüeh and Yeh Chia-ying, *Ling-hsi tz'u shuo*, 517.

69 While in prison awaiting execution, Wen T'ien-hsiang wrote 218 quatrains by
borrowing individual lines from Tu Fu's poems. In his preface to this group of
poems—what he called "Compiling Tu Fu's Poems"—Wen wrote, "Tu Fu was
born several hundred years before I, but his language is still pertinent for my
use. Is this not because we share the same feeling and personality?" (See *Wen
T'ien-hsiang ch'üan-chi*, chüan 16, p. 397.)

70 F. W. Mote, "The Arts and the 'Theorizing Mode' of the Civilization," in Murck, *Artists and Traditions*, 6.

71 See *AYTK*, 1:147.

72 See Wang Shih-chen, *Hsiang-tsu pi-chi* (Shanghai: Ku-chi ch'u-pan-she, 1982), *chüan* 2, p. 23.

73 For the overwhelming importance of the Kung-an School, see Ming-shui Hung, "Yüan Hung-tao and the Late Ming Literary and Intellectual Movement" (Ph.D. diss., Univ. of Wisconsin, 1974); Jonathan Chaves, "The Expression of Self in the Kung-an School: Non-Romantic Individualism," in Hegel and Hessney, *Expressions of Self*, 123–50; and Chih-p'ing Chou, *Yuan Hung-tao and the Kung-an School* (Cambridge: Cambridge Univ. Press, 1988). For Ch'en Tzu-lung's critical view of the Ching-ling School, see Wang K'ai, "Kuan-yü Chung T'an *Shih-kuei* te te-shih chi ch'i p'ing-chia," *She-hui k'o-hsüeh* (Kan-su) 4 (1986): 58. I should mention that despite his disagreement with the views of the Ching-ling School, Ch'en Tzu-lung had not failed to include works by the Ching-ling masters in his anthology of Ming poetry, the *Sheng Ming shih-hsüan*. See *chüan* 8 of *Sheng Ming shih-hsüan*, rev. and enl. ed. of Li P'an-lung's anthology.

Epilogue

1 Liu Ya-tzu, *Mo-chien-shih shih tz'u chi*, ed. Chung-kuo ko-ming po-wu-kuan (Shanghai: Jen-min ch'u-pan-she, 1985), 1:82. *Hsiang-chen* and *Yü-fan* are the titles of Ch'en Tzu-lung's and Hsia Wan-ch'un's collected works, respectively.

2 Of course, the term *loyalism* had increasingly changed its meaning toward the end of the Ch'ing dynasty—for loyalism then was far less a matter of racial opposition than of attachment to a dynasty one had served. For example, the modern scholar and poet Wang Kuo-wei considered himself a loyalist to the Ch'ing. Whether his suicide in 1927 was directly connected with his allegiance to the Ch'ing is a disputed question. For Wang as a Ch'ing loyalist, see Bonner, *Wang Kyo-Wei*, 144–56.

3 Yao P'in-wen discusses in great detail the strong impact of orthodox neo-Confucianism on women poets of that period. See Yao's "Ch'ing-tai fu-nü shih-ko te fan-jung yü li-hsüeh te kuan-hsi," in *Chiang-hsi shih-fan ta-hsüeh hsüeh-pao* 1 (1985): 53–58. Mary Backus Rankin observes that "after government power was securely reestablished in the late seventeenth century, there was some tightening of orthodox standards," although "educational opportunities for women were not cut back." See her "The Emergence of Women at the End of the Ch'ing: The Case of Ch'iu Chin," in *Women in Chinese Society*, ed. Margery Wolf and Roxane Witke (Stanford: Stanford Univ. Press, 1975), 41. Paul Ropp argues quite convincingly that the increasing pressures on Ch'ing women were provoked by "male anxiety" as a response to the spread of female literacy in late imperial China. See his "Aspiration of Literate Women in Late Imperial China" (manuscript, 1990), 42.

4 For example, the editor of *Kuo-ch'ao kuei-hsiu cheng-shih chi*, an important Ch'ing anthology of women poets, says in the preface that he has excluded from his collection all poetic works by courtesans solely on moral principles. See Yao P'in-wen, "Ch'ing-tai fu-nü shih-ko," 57.

5 For a good modern anthology that focuses on both courtesan poets and gentry women poets of this period, see I Po-yin, ed., *Li-tai nü shih tz'u hsüan*. See also Weidner, *Views from Jade Terrace*, 82–117.

6 For example, women poets such as Chin I (1770–94) and Wang Tuan (1793–1838) came from famous "literary and official families." See Chung Hui-ling, "Ch'ing-tai nü shih-jen yen-chiu" (Ph.D. Diss., National Cheng-chih Univ., 1981), 316–37, 363–89. They were known as *kuei-hsiu shih-jen* (inner-chamber women poets), as distinguished from the courtesans who once again began to be seen primarily as entertainers.

Appendix 1

1 For more details of Chinese poetic genres, see my article "Chinese Poetry, Classical," in *Princeton Encyclopedia of Poetry and Poetics*, 3d ed., rev., ed. Alex Preminger and T. V. F. Brogan (Princeton: Princeton Univ. Press, forthcoming).

Appendix 2

1 Feng-ch'eng most likely refers to Ch'en Tzu-lung's hometown, Sung-chiang (*LJS*, 1:256).

2 This line refers to Chuang Tzu's famous story about a dream experience he had: Once he dreamt he was a butterfly, "happy with himself and doing as he pleased." Upon awakening, he didn't know whether he was Chuang Tzu dreaming he had been a butterfly, or a butterfly dreaming he had been Chuang Tzu (Watson, *Complete Works of Chuang Tzu*, 49).

3 This song alludes to one of Li Shang-yin's love poems in the *shih* form: "Last night's stars, last night's winds / By the wall of the painted chamber tower, east of the hall of cassir. . . ." (See also Graham, *Poems of the Late T'ang*, 148.)

4 This line alludes to Li Ching's (916–61) line, "In the small chamber [*hsiao lou*] the song of the jade flute has become cold" (*CTWT*, 1:220). By making this allusion, Liu Shih's line is a subtle reference to the chamber in the Southern Villa.

5 The pheasant designs are part of the incense burner.

6 The "jeweled belt" might be a gift from Ch'en Tzu-lung. The black steed, a symbol of the male lover, is metaphorically connected with Ch'en here. See also the ancient *yüeh-fu* song entitled "Black and White Steeds," in Kuo Mao-ch'ien, comp., *Yüeh-fu shih-chi*, ed. Editorial Board of Chung-hua shu-chü (Peking: Chung-hua shu-chü, 1979), *chüan* 49, 3:711.

SELECT BIBLIOGRAPHY

Allen, Joseph Roe, III. "From Saint to Singing Girl: The Rewriting of the Lo-fu Narrative in Chinese Literati Poetry." *Harvard Journal of Asiatic Studies* 48.2 (1988): 321–61.

Aoki Masaru 青木正兒. *Shindai bungaku hyōron shi* 清代文學評論史. Tokyo: Iwanami, 1950.

Atwell, William S. "Ch'en Tzu-lung (1608–1647): A Scholar Official of the Late Ming Dynasty." Ph.D. diss., Princeton Univ., 1975.

———. "From Education to Politics: The Fu She." In *The Unfolding of Neo-Cofucianism*, edited by Wm. Theodore De Bary, 333–68. New York: Columbia Univ. Press, 1975.

———. "Ming Observers of Ming Decline: Some Chinese Views on the 'Seventeenth Century Crisis' in Comparative Perspective." *Journal of the Royal Asiatic Society* 2 (1988): 316–48.

Auerbach, Erich. *Mimesis: The Representation of Reality in Western Literature.* Translated by Willard R. Trask. Princeton: Princeton Univ. Press, 1953.

———. *Scenes from the Drama of European Literature.* 1959. Reprint, with foreword by Paolo Valesio. Minneapolis: Univ. of Minnesota Press, 1984.

Barnhart, Richard. *Peach Blossom Spring: Gardens and Flowers in Chinese Paintings.* New York: Metropolitan Museum of Art, 1983.

Bickford, Maggie, et al. *Bones of Jade, Soul of Ice: The Flowering Plum in Chinese Art.* New Haven: Yale Univ. Art Gallery, 1985.

Birch, Cyril, ed. *Anthology of Chinese Literature.* 2 vols. New York: Grove Press, 1965, 1972.

———, ed. *Studies in Chinese Literary Genres.* Berkeley: Univ. of California Press, 1974.

———, trans. *The Peony Pavilion*, by Tang Xianzu [T'ang Hsien-tsu]. Bloomington: Indiana Univ. Press, 1980.

Birrell, Anne, trans. *New Songs from a Jade Terrace*. London: Allen and Unwin, 1982.

———. "The Dusty Mirror: Courtly Portraits of Woman in Southern Dynasties Love Poetry." In *Expressions of Self in Chinese Literature*, edited by Robert E. Hegel and Richard C. Hessney, 33–69. New York: Columbia Univ. Press, 1985.

Bloom, Harold. *The Anxiety of Influence: A Theory of Poetry*. New York: Oxford Univ. Press, 1973.

Bonner, Joey. *Wang Kuo-wei: An Intellectual Biography*. Cambridge: Harvard Univ. Press, 1986.

Bradley, A. C. *Shakespearean Tragedy*. 1904. Reprint. Greenwich, Conn.: Fawcett, 1965.

Brown, William Andress. *Wen T'ien-hsiang: A Biographical Study of a Sung Patriot*. San Francisco: Chinese Materials Center Publications, 1986.

Bryant, Daniel. *Lyric Poets of the Southern T'ang*. Vancouver: Univ. of British Columbia Press, 1982.

———. "Syntax and Sentiment in Old Nanking: Wang Shih-chen's 'Miscellaneous Poems on the Ch'in-huai.'" Manuscript, 1984.

———. "Three Varied Centuries of Verse: A Brief Note on Ming Poetry." *Renditions* 8 (Autumn 1977): 82–91.

———. "Wang Shih-chen." In *Waiting for the Unicorn*, edited by Irving Lo and William Schultz, 127–33. Bloomington: Indiana Univ. Press, 1986.

Bush, Susan, and Christian Murch, eds. *Theories of the Arts in China*. Princeton: Princeton Univ. Press, 1983.

Cahill, James. *The Distant Mountains: Chinese Painting of the Late Ming Dynasty, 1570–1644*. New York: Weatherhill, 1982.

Carlitz, Katherine. "Gender Ideals in Ming Epitaph Literature." Paper presented at the Association for Asian Studies Annual Meeting, Boston, April 1987.

Carlyle, Thomas. *On Heroes, Hero-Worship and the Heroic in History*. Edited by Carl Niemeyer. Lincoln: Univ. of Nebraska Press, 1966.

Chang Hui-yen 張惠言. *Tz'u-hsüan [chien-chu]* 詞選[箋注]. Annotated by Chiang Liang-fu 姜亮夫. Shanghai: Pei-hsin shu-chü, 1933.

Chang, K. C. *Art, Myth and Ritual: The Path to Political Authority in Ancient China*. Cambridge: Harvard Univ. Press, 1983.

Chang, Kang-i Sun. "Ch'ang-chou tz'u-p'ai." In *IC*, 225–26.

———. "Chinese Poetry, Classical." In *Princeton Encyclopedia of Poetry and Poetics*, 3d ed., rev., edited by Alex Preminger and T. V. F. Brogan. Princeton: Princeton University Press, forthcoming.

———. "Liu Shih and the Place of Women in Seventeenth-Century Chinese Poetry." Paper presented at the East Asian Humanities Seminar, Rutgers Univ., October 1989.

———. "Liu Shih and the *Tz'u* Revival of the Late Ming." Paper delivered at conference on *Tz'u* (sponsored by ACLS), York, Maine, June 5–6, 1990.

———. *Six Dynasties Poetry*. Princeton: Princeton Univ. Press, 1986.

———. "Symbolic and Allegorical Meanings in the *Yüeh-fu pu-t'i* Poem Series." *Harvard Journal of Asiatic Studies* 46.2 (1986): 353–85.

———. *The Evolution of Chinese Tz'u Poetry: From Late T'ang to Northern Sung*. Princeton: Princeton Univ. Press, 1980.

———. "The Idea of the Mask in Wu Wei-yeh (1609–1671)." *Harvard Journal of Asiatic Studies* 48.2 (1988): 289–320.

———. "The Poet as Tragic Hero: Ch'en Tzu-lung in the Dynastic Transition." Paper presented at the Association for Asian Studies Annual Meeting, Washington, D.C., March 1989.

Chang Shao-chen 張少真. "Ch'ing-tai Che-chiang tz'u-p'ai yen-chiu" 清代浙江詞派研究. M.A. thesis, Tung-wu Univ., Taiwan, 1978.

Chang Shu-hsiang 張淑香. *Yüan tsa-chü chung te ai-ch'ing yü she-hui* 元雜劇中的愛情與社會. Taipei: Ch'ang-an ch'u-pan-she, 1980.

Chang Tai 張岱. *Shih-k'uei ts'ang-shu*, 石匱藏書. Shanghai: Chung-hua shu-chü, 1959.

———. *Lang-huan wen-chi* 瑯環文集. In *Chung-kuo wen-hsüeh chen-pen ts'ung-shu*, no. 18. Shanghai: Tsa-chih kung-ssu, 1935.

———. *T'ao-an meng-i* 陶庵夢憶. Edited by Chu Chien-mang 朱劍芒. Shanghai: Shanghai Book Store, 1982.

Chang Yen 張綖. *Shih-yü t'u-p'u* 詩餘圖譜. ca. 1594. Reprint. Peking: Jen-min wen-hsüeh ch'u-pan-she, 1982.

Chao Shan-lin 趙山林. "Ch'en Tzu-lung te *tz'u* ho *tz'u* lun" 陳子龍的詞和詞論. *Tz'u-hsüeh* 詞學 7 (1989): 184–96.

Chaves, Jonathan. "Moral Action in the Poetry of Wu Chia-chi (1618–84)." *Harvard Journal of Asiatic Studies* 46.2 (1986): 387–469.

———, trans. and ed. *The Columbia Book of Later Chinese Poetry*. New York: Columbia Univ. Press, 1986.

———. "The Expression of Self in the Kung-an School: Non-Romantic Individualism." In *Expressions of Self in Chinese Literature*, edited by Robert E. Hegel and Richard C. Hessney, 123–50. New York: Columbia University Press, 1985.

———. "The Panoply of Images: A Reconstruction of the Literary Theory of the Kung-an School." In *Theories of the Arts in China*, edited by Susan Bush and Christian Murck, 341–64. Princeton: Princeton Univ. Press, 1983.

———, trans. *Pilgrim of the Clouds: Poems and Essays by Yüan Hung-tao and His Brothers*. New York: Weatherhill, 1978.

———. "The Yellow Mountain Poems of Ch'ien Ch'ien-i (1582–1664): Poetry as *Yu-chi*." *Harvard Journal of Asiatic Studies*, 48.2 (1988): 465–92.

Ch'en Nai-ch'ien 陳乃乾, ed. *Ch'ing ming-chia tz'u* 清名家詞. 10 vols. Reprint. Shanghai: Shanghai shu-tien, 1982.

Chen, Shih-hsiang, et al., trans. *The Peach Blossom Fan*, by K'ung Shang-jen. Berkeley: Univ. of California Press, 1976.

Ch'en T'ien 陳田. *Ming-shih chi-shih* 明詩紀事. 185 chaps. Reprinted in 6 vols. Taipei: Ting-wen shu-chü, 1971.

Ch'en Tung-yüan 陳東原. *Chung-kuo fu-nü sheng-huo shih* 中國婦女生活史. Shanghai: Commercial Press, 1973.

Ch'en Tzu-lung 陳子龍. *An-ya-t'ang kao* 安雅堂稿. Reprinted in 3 vols. Taipei: Wei-wen Books and Publishing, 1977. (Abbreviated as *AYTK*.)

————. *Ch'en Chung-yü ch'üan-chi* 陳忠裕全集. Edited by Wang Ch'ang 王昶. N.p., 1803.

————. "Ch'en Tzu-lung nien-p'u" 陳子龍年譜. In *CTLS*, 2: 628–709.

————. *Ch'en Tzu-lung shih-chi* 陳子龍詩集. Edited by Shih Chih-ts'un 施蟄存 and Ma Tsu-hsi 馬祖熙. 2 vols. Shanghai: Ku-chi ch'u-pan-she, 1983. (Abbreviated as *CTLS*.)

————. *Ch'en Tzu-lung wen-chi* 陳子龍文集. 2 vols. Edited by Editorial Board of Shanghai wen-hsien ts'ung-shu 上海文献叢書編委會. Shanghai: Hua-tung Normal Univ. Press, 1988.

————. *Huang-Ming ching-shih wen-pien* 皇明經世文編. 1639. Reprint. Hong Kong, 1964.

————, ed. *I-ching hsün-chieh* 易經訓解. Annotated by Hsiung Ho 熊禾 (1247–1312). 4 *chüan*. N.p., n.d. Now in Harvard-Yenching Library.

————, ed. *Sheng Ming shih hsüan* 盛明詩選. 12 *chüan*. Revised and enlarged edition of Li P'an-lung's 李攀龍 (1514–70) anthology. N.p. Preface 1631.

———— et al. *Yün-chien san-tzu ho-kao* 雲間三子合稿. Facsimile reproduction, 1798.

Ch'en Wei-sung 陳維崧. *Fu-jen chi* 婦人集. In *Chao-tai ts'ung-shu*, vol. 74. N.p., 1833–44.

Ch'en Yin-k'o 陳寅恪. *Liu Ju-shih pieh-chuan* 柳如是別傳. 3 vols. Shanghai: Ku-chi ch'u-pan-she, 1980. (Abbreviated as *LJS*.)

Chen, Yupi. "Ch'en Tzu-lung." In *IC*, 237–38.

Cheng, Pei-kai. "Reality and Imagination: Li Chih and T'ang Hsien-tsu in Search of Authenticity." Ph.D. diss., Yale Univ., 1980.

Cheng Ssu-hsiao 鄭思肖. [*T'ieh-han*] *Hsin-shih* [鐵函] 心史. Reprint. Taipei: Shih-chieh shu-chü, 1955.

Cherniack, Susan. "Three Great Poems by Du Fu." Ph.D. diss., Yale Univ., 1989.

Chiang P'ing-chieh 蔣平階 et al. *Chih-chi chi* 支機集. Edited by Shih Chih-ts'un 施蟄存. In *Tz'u-hsüeh* 詞學 2 (1983): 241–70; 3 (1985): 249–72.

Ch'ien Chi-po 錢基博. *Ming-tai wen-hsüeh* 明代文學. Hong Kong: Commercial Press, 1964.

Ch'ien Ch'ien-i 錢謙益. *Ch'u-hsüeh chi* 初學集. In *Tsu-pen Ch'ien Tseng Mu-chai shih-chu* 足本錢曾牧齋詩注, edited by Chou Fa-kao 周法高, Vols. 1–3, pp. 1–1580. Taipei: San-min shu-chü, 1973.

————, ed. *Lieh-ch'ao shih-chi* 列朝詩集. N.p., 1652(?).

————. *Lieh-ch'ao shih-chi hsiao-chuan* 列朝詩集小傳. Reprinted in 2 vols. Shanghai: Ku-chi ch'u-pan-she, 1983.

————. *Yu-hsüeh chi* 有學集. In *Tsu-pen Ch'ien Tseng Mu-chai shih-chu* 足本錢曾牧齋詩注, edited by Chou Fa-kao 周法高, Vols. 3–5, pp. 1581–2844. Taipei: San-min shu-chü, 1973.

Ch'ien Chung-lien 錢仲聯. *Meng-t'iao-an Ch'ing-tai wen-hsüeh lun-chi* 夢苕庵清代文學論集. Chi-nan: Ch'i-lu shu-tien, 1983.

————. "Wu Mei-ts'un shih pu-chien" 吳梅村詩補箋. In *Meng-t'iao-an chuan-chu erh-chung* 夢苕盦專著二種, by Ch'ien Chung-lien, 67–245. Peking: Chinese Institute of Social Sciences Press, 1984.

Ch'in Kuan 秦觀. *Huai-hai chü-shih ch'ang-tuan chü* 淮海居士長短句. Edited by Hsü P'ei-chün 徐培均. Shanghai: Ku-chi ch'u-pan-she, 1985.

————. *Huai-hai tz'u* [*chien-chu*] 淮海詞 [箋注]. Edited and annotated by Yang Shih-ming 楊世明. Ch'eng-tu: Ssu-ch'uan jen-min ch'u-pan-she, 1984.

Ching, Julia, and Chaoying Fang, trans. and eds. *The Records of Ming Scholars*, by Huang Tsung-hsi. Honolulu: Univ. of Hawaii Press, 1987.

Cho Erh-k'an 卓爾堪, ed. *Ming i-min shih* 明遺民詩. Reprint. Shanghai: Chung-hua shu-chü, 1960.

Chou Chi 周濟. *Sung ssu-chia tz'u-hsüan* [*chien-chu*] 宋四家詞選 [箋注]. Annotated by K'uang Shih-yüan 鄺士元. Taipei: Chung-hua shu-chü, 1971.

Chou, Chih-p'ing. *Yuan hung-tao and the Kung-an School*. Cambridge: Cambridge Univ. Press, 1988.

Chou Fa-kao 周法高. *Ch'ien Mu-chai, Liu Ju-shih i-shih, chi Liu Ju-shih yu-kuan tzu-liao* 錢牧齋、柳如是佚詩，及柳如是有關資料. Taipei: San-min shu-chü, 1978.

————. *Liu Ju-shih shih k'ao* 柳如是事考. Taipei: San-min shu-chü, 1978.

Chou Hui 周暉. *Hsü Ching-ling so-shih* 續金陵瑣事, *chüan* 2. Reprinted in *Chin-ling so-shih* 金陵瑣事. 2 vols. Peking: Wen-hsüeh ku-chi k'an-hsing-she, 1955.

Chu Hui-liang 朱惠良. *Chao Tso yen-chiu* 趙左研究. Taipei: National Palace Museum, 1979.

Chu I-tsun 朱彝尊. *Ming shih tsung* 明詩綜. 1705. Reprint. Taipei: Shih-chieh shu-chü, 1962.

————, comp. *Tz'u tsung* 詞綜. Reprinted in *Wen-hsüeh ts'ung-shu* 文學叢書. Edited by Yang Chia-lo 楊家駱. Ser. 2, Vol. 6. Taipei: Commercial Press, 1965.

————. "Yüeh-fu pu-t'i hsü" 樂府補題序. In *Yüeh-fu pu-t'i yen-chiu chi chien-chu* 樂府補題研究及箋注, edited by Huang Chao-hsien 黃兆顯, 82. Hong Kong: Hokman Publications, 1975.

Chu Tse-chieh 朱則杰. "Ko-wu chih shih yü ku-kuo chih ssu—Ch'ing ch'u shih-ko ts'e-lun" 歌舞之事與故國之思—清初詩歌側論. *Kuei-chou she-hui k'o-hsüeh* 貴州社會科學22.1 (1984): 95–101.

Chu Tung-jun 朱東潤. *Ch'en Tzu-lung chi ch'i shih-tai* 陳子龍及其時代. Shanghai: Ku-chi ch'u-pan-she, 1984.

Chuang Tzu 莊子. *Chuang Tzu* [chi-shih] 莊子 [集釋]. Edited by Kuo Ch'ing-fan

郭慶藩. Peking, 1961. Reprinted in 1 vol. Taipei: Ho-lo t'u-shu ch'u-pan-she, 1974.

Chung Hui-ling 鍾慧玲. "Ch'ing-tai nü shih-jen yen-chiu" 清代女詩人研究. Ph.D. diss., National Cheng-chih Univ., 1981.

Curtius, Ernest Robert. European Literature and the Latin Middle Ages. Translated by Willard R. Trask. 1953. Reprint. Princeton: Princeton Univ. Press, 1973.

De Bary, Wm. Theodore, ed. The Unfolding of Neo-Confucianism. New York: Columbia Univ. Press, 1975.

———— et al. Self and Society in Ming Thought. New York: Columbia Univ. Press, 1970.

De Rougemont, Denis. Love in the Western World. Translated by Montgomery Belgion. 1956. Reprint. Princeton: Princeton Univ. Press, 1983.

Dennerline, Jerry. The Chia-ting Loyalists: Confucian Leadership and Social Change in Seventeenth-Century China. New Haven: Yale Univ. Press, 1981.

Dillard, Annie. Living by Fiction. New York: Harper Colophon Books, 1982.

Dorius, R. J. "Tragedy." In Princeton Encyclopedia of Poetry and Poetics, edited by Alex Preminger et al., 860–64. Englarged edition. Princeton: Princeton Univ. Press. 1974.

Egan, Ronald. The Literary Works of Ou-Yang Hsiu (1007–72). Cambridge: Cambridge Univ. Press, 1984.

Eoyang, Eugene. "Still Life in Words: The Art of Li Ch'ing-chao." Chinese Comparatist 3.1 (1989): 6–14.

Erlich, Victor. Russian Formalism, History-Doctrine. 3d ed. New Haven: Yale Univ. Press, 1981.

Feng Meng-lung 馮夢龍. Ch'ing-shih lei-lüeh 情史類略. Edited by Tsou Hsüeh-ming 鄒學明. Ch'ang-sha: Yüeh-lu shu-she, 1984.

————. Ching-shih t'ung-yen 警世通言. Hong Kong: Chung-hua shu-chü, 1958.

————. Hsing-shih heng-yen 醒世恆言. Annotated by Ku Hsüeh-chieh 顧學頡. 2 vols. Hong Kong: Chung-hua shu-chü, 1958.

————. Yü-shih ming-yen 喻世明言. 2 vols. Hong Kong: Chung-hua shu-chü, 1965.

Fisher, Tom. "Loyalist Alternatives in the Early Ch'ing." Harvard Journal of Asiatic Studies 44.1 (1984): 83–122.

Fong, Grace S. "Contextualization and Generic Codes in the Allegorical Reading of Tz'u Poetry." Paper presented at the Fifth Quadrennial International Comparative Literature Conference, Taipei, August 9–14, 1987.

————. Wu Wenying and the Art of the Southern Song Ci Poetry. Princeton: Princeton Univ. Press. 1987.

Fong, Wen C. "Images of the Mind." In Images of the Mind, by Wen C. Fong et al., 1–212. Princeton: Princeton Univ. Press, 1984.

Frankel, Hans H. The Flowering Plum and the Palace Lady: Interpretations of Chinese Poetry. New Haven: Yale Univ. Press, 1976.

Frodsham, J. D., trans. *The Poems of Li Ho, 791–817*. Oxford: Oxford Univ. Press, 1970.

Gilbert, Sandra M., and Susan Gubar. *The Madwoman in the Attic: The Woman Writer and the Nineteenth-Century Literary Imagination*. New Haven: Yale Univ. Press, 1979.

Goodrich, L. Carrington, ed. *Dictionary of Ming Biography*. 2 vols. New York: Columbia Univ. Press, 1976.

Graham, A. C., trans. *Poems of the Late T'ang*. 1965. Reprint. New York: Penguin Books, 1981.

Greene, Thomas M. "The Poetics of Discovery: A Reading of Donne's Elegy." *The Yale Journal of Criticism* 2.2 (1989): 129–43.

Hanan, Patrick. *The Chinese Short Story*. Cambridge: Harvard Univ. Press, 1973.

———. *The Chinese Vernacular Story*. Cambridge: Harvard Univ. Press, 1981.

———. *The Invention of Li Yu*. Cambridge: Harvard Univ. Press, 1988.

Handlin, Joanna F. *Action in Late Ming Thought: The Reorientation of Lü K'un and Other Scholar-Officials*. Berkeley: Univ. of California Press, 1983.

———. "Lü K'un's New Audience: The Influence of Women's Literacy on Sixteenth-Century Thought." In *Women in Chinese Society*, edited by Margery Wolf and Roxane Witke, 13–38. Stanford University Press, 1975.

Hartman, Charles. "Poetry." In *IC*, 59–74.

———. "Su Shih and Literary Persecution in the Northern Sung." Paper presented at the 41st annual meeting, Association for Asian Studies, Washington, D.C., March, 17, 1989.

Hawkes, David. "Quest of the Goddess." In *Studies in Chinese Literary Genres*, edited by Cyril Birch, 42–68. Berkeley: Univ. of California Press, 1974.

———, trans. *The Songs of the South: An Anthology of Ancient Chinese Poems by Qu Yuan and Other Poets*. 2d ed. New York: Penguin, 1985.

Hegel, Robert E. *The Novel in Seventeenth Century China*. New York: Columbia Univ. Press, 1981.

———, and Richard C. Hessney, eds. *Expressions of Self in Chinese Literature*. New York: Columbia Univ. Press, 1985.

Hessney, Richard C. "Beautiful, Talented, and Brave: Seventeenth-Century Chinese Scholar-Beauty Romances." Ph.D. diss., Columbia Univ., 1979.

———. "Beyond Beauty and Talent: The Moral and Chivalric Self in *The Fortunate Union*." In *Expressions of Self in Chinese Literature*, edited by Robert E. Hegal and Richard C. Hessney, 214–50. New York: Columbia Univ. Press, 1985.

Ho Chiung-yai 何琼崖 et al. *Ch'in Shao-yu* 秦少游. Chiang-su: Jen-min ch'u-pan-she, 1983.

Ho Kuang-chung 賀光中. *Lun Ch'ing tz'u* 論清詞. Singapore: Tung-fang hsüeh-hui, 1958.

Holzman, Donald. "The Cold Food Festival in Early Medieval China." *Harvard*

Journal of Asiatic Studies 46.1 (1986): 51–79.

Homans, Margaret. *Bearing the Word: Language and Female Experience in Nineteenth-Century Women's Writing*. Chicago: Univ. of Chicago Press, 1986.

———. *Women Writers and Poetic Identity: Dorothy Wordsworth, Emily Brontë, and Emily Dickinson*. Princeton: Princeton Univ. Press, 1980.

Hou Fang-yü 侯方域. *Chuang-hui-t'ang chi* 壯悔堂集. Ssu-pu pei-yao edition. Shanghai: Chung-hua shu-chü, 1936.

Hou, Sharon Shih-jiuan. "Women's Literature." In *IC*, 175–94.

Hsia, C. T. *Ai-ch'ing, she-hui, hsiao-shuo* 愛情、社會、小說. Taipei: Ch'un-wen-hsüeh ch'u-pan-she, 1970.

———. "Time and the Human Condition in the Plays of T'ang Hsien-tsu." In *Self and Society in Ming Thought*, by Wm. Theodore De Bary et al., 249–90. New York: Columbia Univ. Press, 1970.

Hsia Ch'eng-t'ao 夏承燾. *T'ang Sung tz'u-jen nien-p'u* 唐宋詞人年譜. Reprint. Taipei: Ming-lun ch'u-pan-she, 1970.

———, and Chang Chang 張璋, eds. *Chin Yüan Ming Ch'ing tz'u-hsüan* 金元明清詞選. 2 vols. Peking: Jen-min wen-hsüeh ch'u-pan-she, 1983.

Hsia Wan-ch'un 夏完淳. *Hsia Chieh-min kung ch'üan-chi* 夏節愍公全集. 1894 edition. Reprint. Taipei: Hua-wen shu-chü, 1970.

Hsiao Jui-feng 蕭瑞峯. "Lun Huai-hai *tz'u*" 論淮海詞. *Tz'u-hsüeh* 詞學 7 (1989): 11–25.

Hsiao T'ung 蕭統. *Chao-ming wen-hsüan* 昭明文選. Commentary by Li Shan 李善. 2 vols. Reprint. Taipei: Ho-lo t'u-shu ch'u-pan-she, 1975.

Hsieh Kuo-chen 謝國楨. *Ming Ch'ing chih chi tang-she yün-tung k'ao* 明清之際黨社運動考. Reprint. Taipei: Commercial Press, 1967.

Hsü Nai-ch'ang 徐乃昌, ed. *Hsiao-t'an-luan shih kuei-hsiu tz'u* 小檀欒室閨秀詞. N.p. 1896.

Hsü Shuo-fang 徐朔方. "Foreword." In *T'ang Hsien-tsu shih-wen chi* 湯顯祖詩文集, edited by Hsü Shuo-fang, 1–17. Shanghai: Ku-chi ch'u-pan-she, 1982.

———. *Lun T'ang Hsien-tsu chi ch'i-ta* 論湯顯祖及其他. Shanghai: Ku-chi ch'u-pan-she, 1983.

Hsü Wei 徐渭. *Nü chuang-yüan* [*tz'u huang te feng*] 女狀元 [辭凰得鳳]. In *Ssu-sheng yüan* 四聲猿, edited by Chou Chung-ming 周中明, 62–106. Shanghai: ku-chi ch'u-pan-she, 1984.

Hu Ch'iu-yüan 胡秋原. *Fu-she chi ch'i jen-wu* 復社及其人物. Taipei: Chung-hua tsa-chih-she, 1968.

Hu Wen-k'ai 胡文楷. *Li-tai fu-nü chu-tso k'ao* 歷代婦女著作考. Revised edition. Shanghai: Ku-chi ch'u-pan-she, 1985.

Hua-hsia fu-nü ming-jen tz'u-tien 華夏婦女名人詞典. Edited by Editorial Board of Hua-hsia fu-nü ming-jen tz'u-tien 華夏婦女名人詞典編委會. Peking: Hua-hsia Ch'u-pan-she, 1988.

Huang Chao-hsien 黃兆顯, ed. *Yüeh-fu pu-t'i yen-chiu chi chien-chu*

樂府補題研究及箋注. Hong Kong: Hokman Publications, 1975.

Huang Shang 黃裳. *Yin-yü chi* 銀魚集. Peking: San-lien shu-tien, 1985.

Huang Wen-yang 黃文暘. *Ch'ü hai tsung-mu t'i-yao* 曲海總目提要. 3 vols. Peking: Jen-min wen-hsüeh ch'u-pan-she, 1959.

Huber, Horst W. "The Upheaval of the Thirteenth Century in the Poetry of Wen T'ien-hsiang." Paper presented at the Association for Asian Studies Annual Meeting, Washington, D.C., March 1989.

Hucker, Charles O. *A Dictionary of Official Titles in Imperial China.* Stanford: Stanford Univ. Press, 1985.

Hummel, Arthur, ed. *Eminent Chinese of the Ch'ing Period.* 2 vols. Wahshington, D.C.: Library of Congress, 1943.

Hung, Ming-shui. "Yüan Hung-tao and the Late Ming Literary and Intellectual Movement." Ph.D. diss., Univ. of Wisconsin, 1974.

Hung Sheng 洪昇. *Ch'ang-sheng tien* 長生殿. In *Chung-kuo shih ta ku-tien pei-chü chi* 中國十大古典悲劇集. Shanghai: Wen-i ch'u-pan-she, 1982.

———. "Ssu ch'an-chüan" 四嬋娟. In *Ch'ing-jen tsa-chü erh-chi* 清人雜劇二集, edited by Cheng Chen-to 鄭振鐸. N.p., 1931.

I Po-yin 裔柏蔭, ed. *Li-tai nü shih tz'u hsüan* 歷代女詩詞選. Taipei: Tang-tai t'u-shu ch'u-pan-she, 1972.

Idema, W. L. "Poet Versus Minister and Monk: Su Shih on Stage in the Period 1250–1450." *T'oung Pao* 73 (1987): 190–216.

Johnson, Barbara. *The Critical Difference: Essays in the Contemporary Rhetoric of Reading.* Baltimore: Johns Hopkins Univ. Press, 1980.

Johnson, Dale. "Ch'ü." In *IC,* 349–52.

Jones, Ann Rosalind. "City Women and Their Audiences: Louise Labé and Veronica Franco." In *Rewriting the Renaissance: The Discourses of Sexual Difference in Early Modern Europe*, edited by Margaret W. Ferguson et al., 299–316. Chicago: Univ. of Chicago Press, 1986.

Kao, Yu-kung. "Shih-lun Chung-kuo i-shu ching-shen" 試論中國藝術精神. *Chinese Culture Quarterly* 九州學刊 2.2 (1987): 1–12; 2.3 (1988): 1–12.

———. "The Aesthetics of Regulated Verse." In *The Vitality of the Lyric Voice*, edited by Shuen-fu Lin and Stephen Owen, 332–85. Princeton: Princeton University Press, 1986.

———. "'The Nineteen Old Poems' and the Aesthetics of Self-Reflection." Manuscript, 1988.

———, and Tsu-lin Mei. "Ending Lines in Wang Shih-chen's 'ch'i-chüeh': Convention and Creativity in the Ch'ing." In *Artists and Traditions: Uses of the Past in Chinese Culture,* edited by Christian F. Murck, 131–35. Princeton: Princeton Univ. Press, 1976.

Knechtges, David R., trans. *Wen Xuan, or Selections of Refined Literature.* Vol. 1. Princeton: Princeton Univ. Press, 1982.

K'o Ch'ing-ming 柯慶明. "Lun 'pei-chü ying-hsiung'" 論悲劇英雄. In his *Ching-chieh te t'an-ch'iu* 境界的探求. Taipei: Linking Publishing, 1977.

Kolb, Elene. "When Women Finally Got the Word." *New York Times Book Review* (July 9, 1989), pp. 1, 28–29.

Kondō Mitsuo 近藤光男. *Shin shi sen* 清詩選. In Kanshi taikei series. Tokyo: Shūeisha, 1967.

Krieger, Murray. *Visions of Extremity in Modern Literature.* Vol. 1, *The Tragic Vision.* Baltimore: Johns Hopkins Univ. Press, 1973.

Ku T'ing-lung 顧廷龍. "Ch'en Tzu-lung shih-lüeh" 陳子龍事略. Inscription on the four-tablet stele at Ch'en Tzu-lung's tomb, 1988.

Ku Yen-wu 顧炎武. *Ku T'ing-lin shih-wen chi* 顧亭林詩文集. Edited by Hua Ch'en-chih 華忱之. 1959. Reprint. Peking: Chung-hua shu-chü, 1983.

Kuan Hsien-chu 關賢柱. "Yang Lung-yu sheng tsu nien k'ao" 楊龍友生卒年考. *Kuei-chou shih-ta hsüeh-pao* 貴州師大學報 50 (March 1987): 43–44.

K'ung Shang-jen 孔尚任. *T'ao-hua shan* 桃花扇. Edited by Wang Chi-ssu 王季思 et al. Revised edition. Peking: Jen-min wen-hsüeh ch'u-pan-she, 1980.

Kuo Mao-ch'ien 郭茂倩, comp. *Yüeh-fu shih-chi* 樂府詩集. Edited by Editorial Board of Chung-hua shu-chü. 4 vols. Peking: Chung-hua shu-chü, 1979.

Kuo Shao-yü 郭紹虞, ed. *Ch'ing shih-hua* 清詩話. Revised edition. 2 vols. Shanghai: Ku-chi ch'u-pan-she, 1978.

———, ed. *Ch'ing shih-hua hsü-pien* 清詩話續編. 2 vols. Shanghai: ku-chi ch'u-pan-she, 1983.

———. *Chung-kuo wen-hsüeh p'i-p'ing shih* 中國文學批評史. Revised edition. 1956. Reprint. Hong Kong: Hung-chih shu-chü, 1970.

———. "Ming-tai te wen-jen chi-t'uan" 明代的文人集團. In Kuo Shao-yu, *Chao-yü-shih ku-tien wen-hsüeh lun-chi* 照隅室古典文學論集, 1: 518–610. Shanghai: Ku-chi ch'u-pan-she, 1983.

——— and Wang Wen-sheng 王文生, eds. *Chung-kuo li-tai wen-lun hsüan* 中國歷代文論選. 4 vols. Shanghai: Ku-chi ch'u-pan-she, 1979–80.

La Belle, Jenijoy. *Herself Beheld: The Literature of the Looking Glass.* Ithaca: Cornell Univ. Press, 1988.

Larsen, Jeanne, trans. *Brocade River Poems: Selected Works of the Tang Dynasty Courtesan Xue Tao.* Princeton: Princeton Univ. Press, 1987.

Lee, Hui-shu. "The City Hermit Wu Wei and His Pai-miao Paintings." Manuscript, 1989.

Legge, James. *The Chinese Classics.* Vol. 4, *The She King.* Oxford: Clarendon, 1871.

Levy, Howard, trans. *A Feast of Mist and Flowers: The Gay Quarters of Nanking at the End of the Ming (Pan-ch'iao tsa-chi),* by Yü Huai (1616–96). Yokohama: Privately printed, 1966.

Lewis, C. S. *The Allegory of Love.* Oxford: Oxford Univ. Press, 1936.

Li Chieh 黎傑. *Ming shih* 明史. Hong Kong: Hai-ch'iao ch'u'pan-she, 1962.

Li Kuang-ti 李光地, ed. *Chou I che-chung* 周易折中. 1715. Reprinted in 2 vols. Taipei: Chen-shan-mei ch'u-pan-she, 1971.

Li Po 李白. *Li T'ai-po ch'üan-chi* 李太白全集. Commentary by Wang Ch'i 王琦.

3 vols. Peking: Chung-hua shu-chü, 1977.

Li Shang-yin 李商隱. *Li Shang-yin hsüan-chi* 李商隱選集. Edited by and commentary by Chou Chen-fu 周振甫. Shanghai: Ku-chi ch'u-pan-she, 1986.

——. *Li Shang-yin shih-chi [shu-chu]* 李商隱詩集［疏注］. Edited by and commentary by Yeh Ts'ung-ch'i 葉葱奇. 2 vols. Peking: Jen-min wen-hsüeh ch'u-pan-she, 1985.

Li Shao-yung 李少雍. "T'an Wang Shih-chen te tz'u-lun chi tz'u-tso" 談王士 禎的詞論及詞作. *Nan-ch'ung shih-yüan hsüeh pao* 南充師院學報 1 (1986): 37–44.

Lin Ching-hsi 林景熙. *Chi-shan chi* 霽山集. Peking: Chung-hua shu-chü, 1960.

Lin Hsiao-ming 林曉明. "Ch'en Tzu-lung mu hsiu-fu chün-kung" 陳子龍墓 修復竣工. *Shanghai hsin-min wan-pao* 上海新民晚報 (Dec. 14, 1988).

Lin Mei-i 林玫儀. "Wan Ch'ing tz'u-lun yen-chiu" 晚清詞論研究. 2 vols. Ph.D. diss., National Taiwan Univ., 1979.

Lin, Shuen-fu. "Intrinsic Music in the Medieval Chinese Lyric." In *The Lyrical Arts: A Humanities Symposium*, edited by Erling B. Holstmark and Judith P. Aikin. Special issue of *Journal Ars Lyrica* (1988): 29–54.

——. *The Transformation of the Chinese Lyrical Tradition: Chiang K'uei and Southern Sung Tz'u Poetry*. Princeton: Princeton Univ. Press, 1978.

——, and Stephen Owen, eds. *The Vitality of the Lyric Voice: Shih Poetry from the Late Han to the T'ang*. Princeton: Princeton Univ. Press, 1986.

Lin Ta-ch'un 林大椿, ed. *T'ang Wu-tai tz'u* 唐五代詞. 1956. Reprinted as *Ch'üan T'ang Wu-tai tz'u hui-pien* 全唐五代詞彙編. 2 vols. Taipei: Shih-chieh shu-chü, 1967. (Abbreviated as *CTWT*.)

Lin, Yutang. *Importance of Understanding*. Cleveland: World, 1960.

Liu Hsiang 劉向. *Lieh-nü chuan [chiao-chu]* 列女傳［校注］. 2 vols. Annotated by Liang Tuan 梁端 (?–1825). Ssu-pu pei-yao edition. Shanghai: Chung-hua shu-chü, 1936.

Liu, James J. Y. "Literary Qualities of the Lyric *(Tz'u)*." In *Studies in Chinese Literary Genres*, edited by Cyril Birch, 133–53. Berkeley: Univ. of California Press, 1974.

——. *Major Lyricists of the Northern Sung:* A.D. 960–1126. Princeton: Princeton Univ. Press, 1974.

——. *The Poetry of Li Shang-yin*. Chicago: Univ. of Chicago Press, 1969.

Liu, James T. C. "Yueh Fei (1130–1141) and China's Heritage of Loyalty." *Journal of Asian Studies* 3 (1972): 291–98.

Liu Shih 柳是. *Hu-shang ts'ao* 湖上草. In *Liu Ju-shih shih-chi* 柳如是詩集, pt. 2. N.p., n.d. Now in Che-chiang Library.

——, ed. *Lieh-ch'ao shih-chi kuei-chi* 列朝詩集閨集. In *Lieh-ch'ao shih-chi*, edited by Ch'ien Ch'ien-i 錢謙益. N.p., 1652(?).

——. *Liu Ju-shih ch'ih-tu* 柳如是尺牘. In *Liu Ju-shih shih-chi* 柳如是詩集, pt. 2. N.p., n.d. Now in Che-chiang Library.

——. *Wu-yin ts'ao* 戊寅草. Preface by Ch'en Tzu-lung 陳子龍. N.p., 1638.

Now in Che-chiang Library.

Liu, Wu-chi, and Irving Lo, eds. *Sunflower Splendor: Three Thousand Years of Chinese Poetry*. New York: Doubleday, 1975.

Liu Ya-tzu 柳亞子. *Mo-chien-shih shih tz'u chi* 磨劍室詩詞集. 2 vols. Shanghai: Jen-min ch'u-pan-she, 1985.

Lo, Irving, and William Schultz, eds. *Waiting for the Unicorn: Poems and Lyrics of China's Last Dynasty, 1644–1911*. Bloomington: Indiana Univ. Press, 1986.

Lonsdale, Roger. *Eighteenth-Century Women Poets: An Oxford Anthology*. Oxford: Oxford Univ. Press, 1989.

Lu Ch'in-li 逯欽立, ed. *Hsien Ch'in Han Wei Chin Nan-pei-ch'ao shih* 先秦漢魏晉南北朝詩. 3 vols. Peking: Chung-hua shu-chü, 1983.

Lynn, Richard John. "Alternate Routes to Self-Realization in Ming Theories of Poetry." In *Theories of the Arts in China*, edited by Susan Bush and Christian Murck, 317–40. Princeton: Princeton Univ. Press.

———. "Chinese Poetics." In *Princeton Encyclopedia of Poetry and Poetics*, edited by Alex Preminger and T. V. F. Brogan. Princeton: Princeton Univ. Press, forthcoming.

———. "Orthodoxy and Enlightenment: Wang Shih-chen's Theory of Poetry and Its Antecedents." In *The Unfolding of Neo-Confucianism*, edited by Wm. Theodore De Bary, 217–57. New York: Columbia Univ. Press, 1975.

———. "The Talent Learning Polarity in Chinese Poetics." *Chinese Literature: Essays, Articles, Reviews* 5.2 (1983): 157–84.

———. "Tradition and Synthesis: Wang Shih-chen as Poet and Critic." Ph.D. diss., Stanford Univ., 1970.

Ma, Y. W. "Fiction." In *IC*, 31–48.

McMahon, Keith. *Causality and Containment in Seventeenth-Century Chinese Fiction*. Monographies du T'oung Pao 15. Leiden: E. J. Brill, 1988.

McCraw, David R. "A New Look at the Regulated Verse of Chen Yuyi." *Chinese Literature: Essays, Articles, Reviews* 9.1, 2 (July 1987): 1–21.

———. *Chinese Lyricists of the Seventeenth Century*. Honolulu: Univ. of Hawaii Press. Forthcoming.

Maeda, Robert J. "The Portrait of a Woman of the Late Ming–Early Ch'ing Period: Madame Ho-tung." *Archives of Asian Art* 27 (1973–74): 46–52.

Mair, Victor H., and Maxine Belmont Weinstein. "Popular Literature." In *IC*, 75–92.

Mao Hsiang 冒襄. *Ying-mei-an i-yü* 影梅菴憶語. Reprinted in *Chung-kuo pi-chi hsiao-shuo ming-chu* 中國筆記小說名著, vol. 1, edited by Yang Chia-lo 楊家駱. Taipei: Shih-chieh shu-chü, 1959.

Mather, Richard B., trans. *Shih-shuo Hsin-yü: A New Account of Tales of the World*, by Liu I-ch'ing (403–44). Minneapolis: Univ. of Minnesota Press, 1976.

Miao, Ronald C. "Palace-Style Poetry: The Courtly Treatment of Glamor and

Love." In *Studies in Chinese Poetry and Poetics,* edited by Ronald C. Miao, 1: 1–42. San Francisco: Chinese Material Center, 1978.

Miao Yüeh 繆鉞. *Shih-tz'u san-lun* 詩詞散論. Reprint. Taipei: K'ai-ming shu-tien, 1966.

—— and Yeh Chia-ying 葉嘉瑩. *Ling-hsi tz'u shuo* 靈谿詞說. Shanghai: Ku-chi ch'u-pan-she, 1986.

Miner, Earl. "Some Issues of Literary 'Species, or Distinct Kind.'" In *Renaissance Genres: Essays on Theory, History and Interpretation*, edited by Barbara Kiefer Lewalski, 15–44. Cambridge: Harvard Univ. Press, 1986.

——. "The Heroine: Identity, Recurrence, Destiny." In *Ukifune: Love in the Tale of Genji*, edited by Andrew Pekarik, 63–81. New York: Columbia Univ. Press, 1982.

—— et al. "Nonwestern Allegory." In *Princeton Encyclopedia of Poetry and Poetics*, 3d ed., rev., edited by Alex Preminger and T. V. F. Brogan. Princeton: Princeton Univ. Press, forthcoming.

Ming i-min shu-hua yen-t'ao hui chi-lu chuan-k'an 明遺民書畫研討會紀錄專刊. Edited by Editorial Board of the Journal of the Institute of Chinese Studies. Special issue of *Chung-kuo wen-hua yen-chiu so hsüeh-pao* 中國文化研究所學報 8.2 (1976).

Mochida, Frances LaFleur. "Structuring a Second Creation: Evolution of the Self in Imaginary Landscapes." In *Expressions of Self in Chinese Literature,* edited by Robert E. Hegel and Richard C. Hessney, 70–122. New York: Columbia Univ. Press, 1985.

Moers, Ellen. *Literary Women: The Great Writers.* 1963. Reprint. New York: Oxford Univ. Press, 1985.

Moody, A. D. *Thomas Stearns Eliot, Poet.* Cambridge: Cambridge Univ. Press, 1980.

Mote, F. W. "Confucian Eremitism in the Yüan Period." In *The Confucian Persuasion*, edited by Arthur F. Wright, 202–40, 348–53. Stanford: Stanford Univ. Press, 1960.

——. "The Arts and the 'Theorizing Mode' of the Civilization." In *Artists and Traditions: Uses of the Past in Chinese Culture*, edited by Christian F. Murck, 3–8. Princeton: Princeton Univ. Press, 1976.

——. *The Poet Kao Ch'i, 1336–1374.* Princeton: Princeton Univ. Press, 1962.

——, and Denis Twitchett, eds. *The Cambridge History of China.* Vol. 7, *The Ming Dynasty, 1368–1644, Part 1.* Cambridge: Cambridge Univ. Press, 1988.

Murck, Christian F., ed. *Artists and Traditions: Uses of the Past in Chinese Culture.* Princeton: Princeton Univ. Press, 1976.

Nagy, Gregory. *The Best of the Achaeans: Concept of the Hero in Archaic Greek Poetry.* Baltimore: Johns Hopkins Univ. Press, 1981.

Nienhauser, William H., Jr. "Prose." In *IC*, 93–120.

——, ed. and comp. *The Indiana Companion to Traditional Chinese Literature.* Bloomington: Indiana Univ. Press, 1986. (Abbreviated as *IC*.)

————, et al., eds. *Liu Tsung-yüan*. New York: Twayne, 1973.

Niu, Hsiu 鈕琇 (fl. 1687–93). *Ku sheng* 觚賸. 8 chüan. In *Ku-chin shuo-pu ts'ung-shu* 古今說部叢書, 1915, vols. 27–29.

Owen, Stephen. *Mi-Lou: Poetry and the Labyrinth of Desire*. Cambridge: Harvard Univ. Press, 1989.

————. *Remembrances: The Experience of the Past in Classical Chinese Literature*. Cambridge: Harvard Univ. Press, 1986.

————. *The Great Age of Chinese Poetry: The High T'ang*. New Haven: Yale Univ. Press, 1981.

Pan Tze-yen, trans. *The Reminiscences of Tung Hsiao-wan (Ying-mei-an i-yü)*, by Mao Hsiang. Shanghai: Commercial Press, 1931.

Paz, Octavio. *Sor Juana*. Translated by Margaret Sayers Peden. Cambridge: Harvard Univ. Press, 1988.

P'eng Ting-ch'iu 彭定求 et al., eds. *Ch'üan T'ang-shih* 全唐詩. Punctuated edition in 12 vols. Peking: Chung-hua shu-chü, 1960. (Abbreviated as *CTS*.)

Peterson, Willard J. *Bitter Gourd: Fang I-Chih and the Impetus for Intellectual Change in the 1630s*. New Haven: Yale Univ. Press, 1979.

————. "Making Connections: 'Commentary on the Attached Verbalizations' of the *Book of Changes*." *Harvard Journal of Asiatic Studies* 42.1 (1982): 67–116.

————. "The Life of Ku Yen-wu, 1613–82." *Harvard Journal of Asiatic Studies* 28 (1968): 114–56; 29 (1969): 201–47.

Plaks, Andrew H. "After the Fall: *Hsing-shih yin-yün chuan* and the Seventeenth Century Chinese Novel." *Harvard Journal of Asiatic Studies* 45.2 (1985): 543–80.

————. *The Four Masterworks of the Ming Novel: Ssu ta ch'i-shu*. Princeton: Princeton Univ. Press, 1987.

Preminger, Alex, and T. V. F. Brogan, eds. *Princeton Encyclopedia of Poetry and Poetics*. 3d ed., rev. Princeton: Princeton Univ. Press, forthcoming.

Rankin, Mary Backus. "The Emergence of Women at the End of the Ch'ing: The Case of Ch'iu Chin." In *Women in Chinese Society*, edited by Margery Wolf and Roxane Witke, 39–66. Stanford: Stanford Univ. Press, 1975.

Rexroth, Kenneth, and Ling Chung, trans. *Li Ch'ing-chao: Complete Poems*. New York: New Direcions, 1979.

————, and Ling Chung, trans. *Women Poets of China*. Revised edition. New York: New Directions, 1982.

Rickett, Adele Austin. *Wang Kuo-wei's Jen-chien Tz'u-hua, A Study in Chinese Literary Criticism*. Hong Kong: Hong Kong Univ. Press, 1977.

Robertson, Maureen. "Periodization in the Arts and Patterns of Change in Traditional Chinese Literary History." In *Theories of the Arts in China*, edited by Susan Bush and Christian Murck, 3–26. Princeton: Princeton Univ. Press, 1983.

Ropp, Paul S. "Aspirations of Literate Women in Late Imperial China." Manuscript, 1990.

————. "The Seeds of Change: Reflections on the Condition of Women in the Early and Mid Ch'ing." *Signs* 2.1 (1976): 5–23.

Schafer, Edward H. *The Divine Woman: Dragon Ladies and Rain Maidens.* San Francisco: North Point Press, 1980.

Schlepp, Wayne. *San-ch'ü: Its Technique and Imagery.* Madison: Univ. of Wisconsin Press, 1970.

Schneider, Laurence A. *A Madman of Ch'u: The Chinese Myth of Loyalty and Dissent.* Berkeley: Univ. of California Press, 1980.

Scott, John. *Love and Protest: Chinese Poems from the Sixth Century B.C. to the Seventeenth Century A.D.* London: Rapp and Whiting, 1972.

Sewall, Richard B., ed. *Emily Dickinson: A Collection of Critical Essays.* Englewood Cliffs: Prentice-Hall, 1963.

————. *The Vision of Tragedy.* New Haven: Yale Univ. Press, 1959.

Shen Te-ch'ien 沈德潛, ed. *Ming-shih pieh-ts'ai chi* 明詩別裁集. Notes by Chou Chun 周準. Hong Kong: Chung-hua shu-chü, 1977.

Shih Chih-ts'un 施蟄存. "Chiang P'ing-chieh chi ch'i 'Chih chi chi'" 蔣平階及其 "支機集." *Tz'u-hsüeh* 詞學 2 (1983): 222–25.

————. "T'ang nü-shih-jen" 唐女詩人. In Shih Chih-ts'un, *T'ang-shih pai-hua* 唐詩百話, 720–29. Shanghai: Ku-chi ch'u-pan-she, 1987.

———— and Ma Tsu-hsi 馬祖熙. "Foreword." In *CTLS*, 1: 1–10.

Shih, Chung-wen. *The Golden Age of Chinese Drama: Yüan Tsa-chü.* Princeton: Princeton Univ. Press, 1976.

Shih I-tui 施議對. *Tz'u yü yin-yüeh kuan-hsi yen-chiu* 詞與音樂關係研究. Peking: Chinese Institute of Social Sciences Press, 1985.

Shih Shu-i 施淑儀. *Ch'ing-tai Kuei-ko shih-jen cheng-lüeh* 清代閨閣詩人徵略. 1922. Reprint. Shanghai: Shanghai shu-tien, 1987.

Sō Gen Min Shin meiga taikan 宋元明清名畫大觀. Edited by Nikka Kokon Kaiga Tenrankai 日華古今繪畫展覽會. Tokyo: Ōtsuka Kogeisha, 1931.

Spence, Jonathan D., and John E. Wills, Jr., eds. *From Ming to Ch'ing: Conquest, Region and Continuity in Seventeenth-Century China.* New Haven: Yale Univ. Press, 1979.

Stankiewicz, Edward. "Centripetal and Centrifugal Structures in Poetry." *Semiotica* 38, nos. 3–4 (1982): 217–42.

Strassberg, Richard E. *The World of K'ung Shang-jen: A Man of Letters in Early Ch'ing China.* New York: Columbia Univ. Press, 1983.

Strauss, Leo. *Persecution and the Art of Writing.* 1952. Reprint. Chicago: Univ. of Chicago Press, 1988.

Struve, Lynn A. "History and *The Peach Blossom Fan*." *Chinese Literature: Essays, Articles, Reviews* 2.1 (Jan. 1980): 55–72.

————. "Huang Zongxi in Context: A Reappraisal of His Major Writings." *Journal of Asian Studies* 47.3 (1988): 474–502.

————. "*The Peach Blossom Fan* as Historical Drama." *Renditions* 9 (Autumn 1977): 99–114.

————. *The Southern Ming, 1644–1662.* New Haven: Yale Univ. Press, 1984.

Takahashi Kazumi 高橋和巳, ed. Ō shi-shin 王士禛. In the Chūgoku shijin sen-shū series. Tokyo: Iwanami, 1962.

T'ang Hsien-tsu 湯顯祖, ed. T'ang Hsien-tsu chi, 湯顯祖集. Vols. 3–4. Edited by Ch'ien Nan-yang 錢南揚. Shanghai: Jen-min ch'u-pan-she, 1973.

———. T'ang Hsien-tsu shih wen chi 湯顯祖詩文集. Edited by Hsü Shuo-fang 徐朔方. Shanghai: Ku-chi ch'u-pan-she, 1982.

T'ang Kuei-chang 唐圭璋, ed. Ch'üan Sung-tz'u 全宋詞. 5 vols. Peking: Chung-hua shu-chü, 1965. (Abbreviated as CST.)

———. T'ang Sung tz'u chien-shang tz'u-tien 唐宋詞鑑賞辞典. Chiang-su: Ku-chi ch'u-pan-she, 1986.

———, ed. Tz'u-hua ts'ung-pien 詞話叢編. 5 vols. Rev. ed. Peking: Chung-hua shu-chü, 1986. (Abbreviated as THTP.)

Telford, Kenneth A. Aristotle's Poetics: Translation and Analysis. Indiana: Gateway Edition, 1961.

Todorov, Tzvetan. Symbolism and Interpretation. Trans. Catherine Porter. Ithaca: Cornell Univ. Press, 1982.

———. Theories of the Symbol. Trans. Catherine Porter. Ithaca: Cornell Univ. Press, 1982.

Tu, Ching-i, trans. Poetic Remarks in the Human World, by Wang Kuo-wei. Taipei: Chung-hua shu-chü, 1970.

Tu Fu 杜甫. Tu shih [hsiang-chu] 杜詩［詳注］. Commentary by Ch'iu Chao-ao 仇兆鰲. Peking: Chung-hua shu-chü, 1979.

Tu Teng-ch'un 杜登春. She-shih shih-mo 社事始末. In Chao-tai ts'ung-shu series (n.p., 1833–44), vol. 50.

Van Gulik, Robert H. Sex Life in Ancient China. Leiden: E. J. Brill, 1961.

Virgillo, Carmelo, and Naomi Lindstron, eds. Woman as Myth and Metaphor. Columbia: Univ. of Missouri Press, 1985.

Wagner, Marsha L. The Lotus Boat: The Origins of Chinese Tz'u Poetry in T'ang Popular Culture. New York: Columbia Univ. Press, 1984.

Wakeman, Frederic, Jr. "Romantics, Stoics, and Martyrs in Seventeenth-Century China." Journal of Asian Studies 43.4 (1984): 631–65.

———. The Fall of Imperial China. New York: Free Press, 1975.

———. The Great Enterprise: The Manchu Reconstruction of Imperial Order in Seventeenth-Century China. 2 vols. Berkeley: Univ. of California Press, 1985.

———. "The Price of Autonomy: Intellectuals in Ming and Ch'ing Politics." Daedalus 101 (Spring 1972): 35–70.

Waley, Arthur, trans. The Book of Songs. 1937. Reprint with foreword by Stephen Owen. New York: Grove Press, 1987.

Wan Shu 萬樹. [So-yin pen] Tz'u-lü ［索引本］詞律. Preface 1687. Reprint with supplements by Hsü Pen-li 徐本立. Taipei: Kuang-wen shu-chü, 1971.

Wan Ssu-t'ung 萬斯同, ed. Nan-Sung liu-ling i-shih 南宋六陵遺事. Reprint. Taipei: Kuang-wen shu-chü, 1968.

Wang, C. H. The Bell and the Drum: Shih Ching as Formulaic Poetry in an Oral

Tradition. Berkeley: Univ. of California Press, 1974.

———. *From Ritual to Allegory: Seven Essays in Early Chinese Poetry*. Hong Kong: Chinese Univ. Press, 1988.

Wang Ch'ang 王昶. *Kuo-ch'ao tz'u-tsung* 國朝詞綜. *8 chüan*. Ssu-pu pei-yao edition. Shanghai: Chung-hua shu-chü, 1936.

———. *Ming tz'u tsung* 明詞綜. 12 *chüan*. Ssu-pu pei-yao 331. Shanghai: Chung-hua shu-chü, 1936.

Wang Chün-ming 王鈞明 and Ch'en Chih-chai 陳沚齋, annotators. *Ou-yang Hsiu, Ch'in Kuan tz'u-hsüan* 歐陽修、秦觀詞選. Hong Kong: Joint Publishing, 1987.

Wang Fu-chih 王夫之. *Ch'u-tz'u t'ung-shih* 楚辞通釋. 1709. Reprint. Hong Kong, 1960.

———. *Wang Ch'uan-shan shih-wen chi* 王船山詩文集. 2 vols. Hong Kong: Chung-hua shu-chü, 1974.

Wang K'ai 王愷. "Kuan-yü Chung T'an *Shih-kuei* te te-shih chi ch'i p'ing-chia" 關於鍾、譚詩歸的得失及其評價. *She-hui k'o-hsüeh* (Kan-su) 社會科學 (甘肅) 4 (1986): 57–63.

Wang Kuo-wei 王國維. *Wang Kuo-wei shih-tz'u [chien chiao]* 王國維詩詞 [箋校]. Edited by Hsiao Ai 蕭艾. Ch'ang-sha: Hu-nan jen-min ch'u-pan-she, 1984.

Wang I 王易. *Tz'u ch'ü shih* 詞曲史. 1932. Reprint. Taipei: Kuang-wen shu-chü, 1971.

Wang Po 王勃. *Wang Tzu-an chi* 王子安集. Edited by Chang Hsieh 張燮. Reprint. Taipei: Commercial Press, 1976.

Wang Shih-chen 王士禎. *Hsiang-tsu pi-chi* 香祖筆記. Shanghai: Ku-chi ch'u-pan-she, 1982.

———. *Hua-ts'ao meng-shih* 花草蒙拾. In Chao-tai ts'ung-shu series (n.p., 1833–44), vol. 77.

———. *Wang Yü-yang shih-wen [hsüan-chu]* 王漁洋詩文 [選注]. Edited by Li Yü-fu 李毓芙. Chi-nan: Ch'i-lu shu-she, 1982.

Wang Shu-nu 王書奴. *Chung-kuo ch'ang-chi shih* 中國娼妓史. Shanghai: Sheng-huo shu-tien, 1935.

Wang Ying-chih 王英志. "Ch'en Tzu-lung tz'u-hsüeh ch'u-i" 陳子龍詞學芻議. In *Ming Ch'ing shih-wen yen-chiu ts'ung-k'an* 明清詩文研究叢刊, edited by Chinese Dept., Chiang-su Teachers' Normal College, 1 (March 1982): 85–99.

Wang Yün 王澐. "Ch'en Tzu-lung nien-p'u chüan-hsia" 陳子龍年譜卷下. In *CTLS*, 2: 710–37.

Watson, Burton, trans. *Chinese Rhyme-Prose: Poems in the Fu Form from the Han and Six Dynasties Periods*. New York: Columbia Univ. Press, 1971.

———, trans. *Records of the Historian: Chapters from the Shih Chi of Ssu-ma Ch'ien*. New York: Columbia Univ. Press, 1969.

———, trans. *The Complete Works of Chuang Tzu*. New York: Columbia Univ. Press, 1968.

Watt, James C. Y. "The Literati Environment." In *The Chinese Scholar's Studio: Artistic Life in the Late Ming Period*, Edited by Chu-tsing Li and James C. Y. Watt, 1–13. New York: Asia Society Galleries, 1987.

Weidner, Marsha, et al. *Views from Jade Terrace: Chinese Women Artists 1300–1912*. Indianapolis Museum of Art and New York: Rizzoli, 1988.

Wen Ju-hsien 聞汝賢. *Tz'u-p'ai hui-shih* 詞牌彙釋. Taipei: Privately printed, 1963.

Wen T'ien-hsiang 文天祥. *Wen T'ien-hsiang ch'üan-chi* 文天祥全集. Based on the 1560 edition of *Ch'ung-k'o wen-shan hsien-sheng ch'üan-chi* 重刻文山先生全集. Edited by Lo Hung-hsien 羅洪先. Peking: Chung-kuo shu-tien, 1985.

———. *Wen T'ien-hsiang shih-hsüan* 文天祥詩選. Edited by Huang Lan-po 黃蘭波. Peking: Jen-min ch'u-pan-she, 1979.

West, Stephen H. "Drama." In *IC*, 13–30.

Widmer, Ellen. "The Epistolary World of Female Talent in Seventeenth-Century China." *Late Imperial China* 10.2 (1989): 1–43.

———. *The Margins of Utopia: Shui-hu hou-chuan and the Literature of Ming Loyalism*. Cambridge: Council on East Asian Studies, Harvard Univ., 1987.

Wilde, Oscar. *The Artist as Critic: Critical Writings of Oscar Wilde*. Edited by Richard Ellmann. 1969. Reprint. Chicago: Univ. of Chicago Press, 1982.

Wilhelm, Richard, and Cary F. Baynes, trans. *The I Ching, or Book of Changes*. Princeton: Princeton Univ. Press, 1967.

Williams, C. A. S. *Outlines of Chinese Symbolism and Art Motives*. 3d ed. New York: Dover Publications, 1976.

Wilson, Katharina M., and Frank J. Warnke. *Women Writers of the Seventeenth Century*. Athens: Univ. of Georgia Press, 1989.

Wixted, John Timothy, trans. *Five Hundred Years of Chinese Poetry, 1150–1650: The Chin, Yuan, and Ming Dynasties (Gen Min shi gaisetsu)*, by Yoshikawa Kōjirō. "Afterword" by William S. Atwell. Princeton: Princeton Univ. Press, 1989.

Wolf, Margery, and Roxane Witke, eds. *Women in Chinese* Society. Stanford: Stanford Univ. Press, 1975.

Woodbridge, Linda. *Women and the English Renaissance: Literature and the Nature of Womankind, 1540–1620*. Urbana: Univ. of Illinois Press, 1984.

Wu Hung-i 吳宏一. *Ch'ing-tai shih-hsüeh ch'u-t'an* 清代詩學初探. Taipei: Mu-t'ung ch'u-pan-she, 1977.

——— and Yeh Ch'ing-ping 葉慶炳, eds. *Ch'ing-tai wen-hsüeh p'i-p'ing tsu-liao hui-pien* 清代文學批評資料彙編. 2 vols. Taipei: Ch'eng-wen ch'u-pan-she, 1979.

Wu Mei 吳梅. *Tz'u-hsüeh t'ung-lun* 詞學通論. Shanghai: Commercial Press, 1932.

Wu Wei-yeh 吳偉業. *Fu-she chi-shih* 復社紀事. In *T'ai-wan wen-hsien ts'ung-k'an* 台灣文献叢刊, no. 259, pp. 33–40. Taipei: Bank of Taiwan, 1968.

———. *Mei-ts'un chia ts'ang-kao* 梅村家藏稿. Facsimile reproduction of 1911 edition. 3 vols. Taipei: Student Book Store, 1975.

———. *Wu Mei-ts'un shih-chi [chien-chu]* 吳梅村詩集［箋注］. Compiled and annotated by Ch'eng Mu-heng 程穆衡 and Yang Hsüeh-hang 楊學沆. Facsimile reproduction of 1782 edition. Shanghai: Ku-chi ch'u-pan-she, 1983.

———. *Wu Mei-ts'un shih-chi [chien-chu]* 吳梅村詩集［箋注］. Edited by Wu I-feng 吳翌鳳. 1814. Reprint. Hong Kong: Kuang-chih shu-chü, 1975.

Wu, Yenna. "The Inversion of Marital Hierarchy: Shrewish Wives and Henpecked Husbands in Seventeenth-Century Chinese Literature." *Harvard Journal of Asiatic Studies* 48.2 (1988): 363–82.

Yang Feng-pao 楊鳳苞. "Hsi-hu ch'iu-liu *tz'u*" 西湖秋柳詞. In *Ku-chin shuo-pu ts'ung-shu* 古今說部叢書, 1915, vol. 6.

Yang Hai-ming 楊海明. *T'ang Sung tz'u feng-ko lun* 唐宋詞風格論. Shanghai: Institute of Social Sciences Press, 1986.

———. *T'ang Sung tz'u shih* 唐宋詞史. Chiang-su: Ku-chi ch'u-pan-she, 1987.

Yang, Hsien-ching. "Aesthetic Consciousness in Sung *Yung-Wu-Tz'u* (*Songs on Objects*)." Ph.D. diss., Princeton Univ., 1987.

Yang Li-kuei 楊麗圭. "Cheng Ssu-hsiao yen-chiu chi ch'i shih chien-chu" 鄭思肖研究及其詩箋注. M.A. thesis, Cultural Univ., Taiwan, 1977.

Yao P'in-wen 姚品文. "Ch'ing-tai fu-nü shih-ko te fan-jung yü li-hsüeh te kuan-hsi" 清代婦女詩歌的繁榮與理學的關係. *Chiang-hsi shih-fan ta-hsüeh hsüeh-pao* 江西師範大學學報, 1 (1985): 53–58.

Yeats, W. B. *Ideas of Good and Evil: Essays and Introductions*. London: Macmillan, 1961.

Yeh Chia-ying 葉嘉瑩 (Chao, Chia-ying Yeh) *Chia-ling t'an-shih* 迦陵談詩. 2 vols. Taipei: San-min shu-chü, 1970.

———. *Chia-ling t'an tz'u* 迦陵談詞. Taipei: Ch'un-wen-hsüeh ch'u-pan-she, 1970.

———. *Hsia Wan-ch'un* 夏完淳. Taipei: Yu-shih ch'u-pan-she, 1954.

———. "Wang I-sun and His *Yung-wu Tz'u*." *Harvard Journal of Asiatic Studies* 40.1 (1980): 55–91.

———. "The Ch'ang-chou School of *Tz'u* Criticism." In *Chinese Approaches to Literature from Confucius to Liang Ch'i-ch'ao*, edited by Adele Austin Rickett, 151–88. Princeton: Princeton Univ. Press, 1978.

———. "Ts'ung wo ko-jen tui *tz'u* chih t'e-chih te i-tien hsin li-chieh t'an *ling-tz'u* chih ch'ien-neng yü Ch'en Tzu-lung *tz'u* chih ch'eng-chiu" 從我個人對詞之特質的一點新理解談令詞之潛能與陳子龍詞之成就 (Manuscript 1989).

Yeh Ch'ing-ping 葉慶炳, and Shao Hung 邵紅, eds. *Ming-tai wen-hsüeh p'i-p'ing tzu-liao hui-pien* 明代文學批評資料彙編. 2 vols. Taipei: Ch'eng-wen ch'u-pan-she, 1979.

Yeh Ying 葉英. *Huang Tao-chou chuan* 黃道周傳. Tainan: Ta-ming yin-shua-chü, 1958.

Yip, Wai-lim. *Chinese Poetry: Major Modes and Genres*. Berkeley: Univ. of

California Press, 1976.

Yoshikawa Kōjirō 吉川幸次郎. *Gen Min shi gaisetsu* 元明詩概説. In the *Chūgo-ku shijin senshū* series. Tokyo: Iwanami, 1963.

Yu, Anthony C. "The Quest of Brother Amor: Buddhist Intimations in *The Story of the Stone*." *Harvard Journal of Asiatic Studies* 49.1 (1989): 55–92.

Yü Huai 余懷. *Pan-ch'iao tsa-chi* 板橋雜記. Reprinted in *Ch'in-huai hsiang-yen ts'ung-shu* 秦淮香艷叢書. Shanghai: Sao-yeh shan-fang, 1928.

Yu, Pauline. "Formal Distinctions in Chinese Literary Theory." In *Theories of the Arts in China,* edited by Susan Bush and Christian Murck, 27–53. Princeton: Princeton Univ. Press, 1983.

———. *The Reading of Imagery in the Chinese Poetic Tradition.* Princeton: Princeton Univ. Press, 1987.

Yü Sung-ch'ing 喻松青. "Ming Ch'ing shih-ch'i min-chien mi-mi tsung-chiao chung te nü-hsing" 明清時期民間秘密宗教中的女性. In *Ming Ch'ing Pai-lien chiao yen-chiu* 明清白蓮教研究, by Yü Sung-ch'ing, 295–311. Ch'eng-tu: Ssu-ch'uan jen-min ch'u-pan-she, 1987.

Yü Ts'ui-ling 于翠玲. "Ch'in Kuan *tz'u* hsin-lun" 秦觀詞新論. In *Chung-kuo ku-tien wen-hsüeh lun-ts'ung* 中國古典文學論叢, no. 6, edited by Editorial Board of People's Literature Publishing House. Peking: Jen-min wen-hsüeh ch'u-pan-she, 1987.

Yü Ying-shih 余英時. *Ch'en Yin-k'o wan-nien shih-wen shih-cheng* 陳寅恪晚年詩文釋證. Taipei: Shih-pao wen-hua ch'u-pan shih-yeh yu-hsien kung-ssu, 1984.

———. *Chung-kuo chin-shih tsung-chiao lun-li yü shang-jen ching-shen* 中國近世宗教倫理與商人精神. Taipei: Linking Publishing, 1987.

———. *Fang I-chih wan-chieh k'ao* 方以智晚節考. Rev. ed. Taipei: Asian Culture Co., 1986.

———. "Ku-tien yü chin-tien chih-chien: t'an Ch'en Yin-k'o te an-ma hsi-t'ung" 古典與今典之間：談陳寅恪的暗碼系統 *Ming Pao Monthly* (Nov. 1984): 17–20.

Yüan Chou-tsung 袁宙宗, ed. *Ai-kuo shih-tz'u hsüan* 愛國詩詞選. Taipei: Commercial Press, 1982.

Yüan-hu yen-shui san-jen 鴛湖烟水散人 (pseud.). *Nü ts'ai-tzu shu* 女才子書. 1659(?). Reprint. Shen-yang: Ch'un-feng wen-i ch'u-pan-she, 1983.

Zhang, Longxi. "The Letter or the Spirit: *The Song of Songs*, Allegoresis, and the *Book of Poetry*." *Comparative Literature* 39 (1987): 193–217.

Zink, Michael. "The Allegorical Poem as Interior Memoir." *Yale French Studies* 70 (1986): 100–26.

INDEX